PRACTICING THEOLOGY

PRACTICING THEOLOGY

Beliefs and Practices in Christian Life

Edited by

Miroslav Volf and Dorothy C. Bass

WILLIAM B. EERDMANS PUBLISHING COMPANY
GRAND RAPIDS, MICHIGAN / CAMBRIDGE, U.K.

Wm. B. Eerdmans Publishing Co.
255 Jefferson Ave. S.E., Grand Rapids, Michigan 49503 /
P.O. Box 163, Cambridge CB3 9PU U.K.
www.eerdmans.com

Printed in the United States of America

07 06 05 04 03 02   7 6 5 4 3 2 1

Library of Congress Cataloging-in-Publication Data

Practicing theology: beliefs and practices in Christian life /
edited by Miroslav Volf and Dorothy C. Bass.
p.   cm.
Includes bibliographical references.
ISBN 0-8028-4931-8 (pbk.: alk. paper)
1. Theology, Practical.   2. Christian life.
I. Volf, Miroslav.   II. Bass, Dorothy C.

BV3.P6945   2002
230 — dc21

2001051069

Acknowledgments

The development of *Practicing Theology* was supported by the Valparaiso
Project on the Education and Formation of People in Faith, a project of Lilly
Endowment Inc. based at Valparaiso University. The authors wish to thank
the Endowment and also to express their gratitude to Luke Timothy Johnson,
Bonnie J. Miller-McLemore, and Andrew F. Walls, who responded to an
earlier draft of this volume.

Contents

PRACTICING THEOLOGY, BECOMING THEOLOGIANS

PRACTICING THEOLOGY, SERVING A WAY OF LIFE

Introduction

DOROTHY C. BASS

"But what does that have to do with *real* life?"

In the final chapter of this volume, Miroslav Volf reports being asked this question by students in his theology classes. The question also appears here, at the book's beginning, because it is addressed in one way or another not only in Volf's final chapter but in every other chapter as well. "That," in the question, is theology, the study of God and God's relation to the world.[1] "*Real* life," in the questioners' likely view, is the messy realm of work, love, celebration, and suffering where human beings dwell and thus where Christian life and ministry take place.

In the experience of some students and other Christians, quotidian reality can seem remote from the doctrines, narratives, and propositions that usually occupy theologians. This is not to say that they do not encounter theological concepts. They have been baptized "in the Name of the Father and of the Son and of the Holy Spirit." They may belong to churches where ancient creeds are spoken during worship, where specific beliefs are advocated in sermons, and where people pray, work, and relate to others with the name of God on their lips and ideas about what God intends on their minds. Students also encounter these words and ideas in the critical atmosphere of the academy.

Even in the presence of all these explicit articulations of belief, how-

1. Miroslav Volf argues that "theology is an (academic) enterprise whose object of study is God and God's relation to the world and whose purpose is not simply to discover 'knowledge,' but to serve a way of life" (p. 247).

1

ever, many contemporary Christians wonder whether and how what they are supposed to believe really connects to the realities of their lives. Most express a desire to share community and to live a moral life, to be sure, and hunger for spiritual experience and understanding is widespread. However, the importance of theology, doctrine, and other elaborate articulations of belief is very often obscure.[2] Why not just go out and do good? What difference could having a critical and systematic understanding of the Trinity or of the meaning of baptism make in the daily round of life and ministry? What makes it worthwhile to do the hard work of studying theology?

What is puzzling is not so much each belief in itself — though this can also be so — but *why* and *how* beliefs matter once the theology class or the worship service is over. Are doctrines a group of stable propositions that, once learned, are then applied intact to situations of daily living? Alternatively, might beliefs themselves be a function of daily living, arising from social reality to give verbal justification to how people live anyway — whether that means persisting in the status quo or pursuing more or less radical change?

The authors of this book are theologians; most are professors of systematic theology in seminaries or divinity schools. It will come as no surprise, therefore, that we are eager to vindicate the relevance of theology. Professional pride motivates us little, if at all, however. Far more important are our convictions about Christian beliefs, the Christian life, and the purpose of disciplined reflection on God and God's relation to the world. We are convinced that Christian beliefs are already deeply implicated in the actual lives of Christian individuals, families, and communities. And we see Christian theology as a necessary dimension of these lives — helping Christian living more fully to reflect God's grace and truth. We believe that our thinking about God and our way of living should go hand in hand.

This book explicates and embodies an approach to theology that arises from these convictions. At the crux of this approach is the concept of "practices." This concept, which is used in many ways within the humanities and social sciences today, provides a way of thinking about the close relation between thinking and doing. In general use, a practice is a dense

---

2. This is a theme in recent work by sociologist of religion Robert Wuthnow. See, for example, *After Heaven: Spirituality in America Since the 1950s* (Berkeley: University of California Press, 1998).

cluster of ideas and activities that are related to a specific social goal and shared by a social group over time. In this book, we place this concept within a theological framework: Christian practices are patterns of cooperative human activity in and through which life together takes shape over time in response to and in the light of God as known in Jesus Christ. Focusing on practices invites theological reflection on the ordinary, concrete activities of actual people — and also on the knowledge of God that shapes, infuses, and arises from these activities. Focusing on practices demands attentiveness to specific people doing specific things together within a specific frame of shared meaning.

Four of the authors of this book had previously worked together on another book, *Practicing Our Faith: A Way of Life for a Searching People.*[3] *Practicing Our Faith* explores twelve Christian practices — honoring the body, hospitality, household economics, saying yes and saying no, keeping sabbath, discernment, testimony, shaping communities, forgiveness, healing, dying well, and singing our lives — as constituent elements within a way of life that is responsive to and illuminated by God's active presence for the life of the world. This earlier book situated practices within a Christian theological interpretation of God and God's relation to the world, but it offered little attention to specific Christian beliefs or to the processes of reflection by which Christian people sustain the integrity of these beliefs, whether as academic theologians or as laypeople negotiating meaning in the midst of life's complexities. To rectify this omission is one of the purposes of *Practicing Theology.*

This book's focus on practices is also a response to contemporary currents within the academic field of theology. As modernity gives way to postmodernity, the enduring question of the grounds for Christian believing has taken on fresh urgency. "What grounds what?" Miroslav Volf asks in the final chapter. As he notes, contemporary academic and popular culture tends to subordinate beliefs to practices "to the point of completely functionalizing beliefs."[4] At the same time, other academic and popular

---

3. Ed. Dorothy C. Bass (San Francisco: Jossey-Bass, 1997). *Practicing Our Faith* was written by a team that included Amy Plantinga Pauw and L. Gregory Jones, who along with Dykstra and Bass are also contributors to the present volume, as well as M. Shawn Copeland, Thomas Hoyt Jr., John Koenig, Sharon Daloz Parks, Stephanie Paulsell, Ana Maria Pineda, Larry Rasmussen, Frank Rogers Jr., and Don E. Saliers.

4. Page 258 in this volume.

voices, claiming the mantle of tradition, resist this approach by insisting that the influence goes only in the other direction, from beliefs to practices, with practices being mere enactments of beliefs. The essays in this book offer a more complex response. At stake in this complexity is the vitality of a living tradition capable of being fully engaged with history and culture without becoming their captive.

Most of the authors of *Practicing Theology* were already doing theological work employing the concept of practices, and we gathered in part because we were interested in sharing, testing, and extending this work.[5] As academic theologians, we also welcomed the opportunity to address a problem that is at the heart of contemporary theological concern. Our focus on practices has led us beyond these initial intentions, however, into a process of reflection on the vital messiness and adaptive interplay of practices as they have been embodied in Christian communities across time and in our own communities today. In the process, the rough textures of our own lives entered our conversation more fully than they usually do at theological conferences. At our first meeting, for example, each of us told the others about our own life and the practices that have shaped it. Later, when we decided to focus one of our sessions on a single Christian practice — hospitality to strangers — some of us began to volunteer in ministries serving homeless people (Gilbert Bond's chapter is a direct result of this experience) while others began to remember how encountering this practice had shaped them profoundly in the past (as recounted, for example, in

---

5. For example, Dorothy C. Bass, *Receiving the Day: Christian Practices for Opening the Gift of Time* (San Francisco: Jossey-Bass, 2000); Nancy Bedford, "Tres hipótesis de trabajo en busca de una teología. Vías para la renovación de la teología latinoamericana," en *Cuadernos de Teología* 43 (1999): 41-51; Sarah Coakley, *Powers and Submissions: Spirituality, Philosophy and Gender* (Oxford: Blackwell, 2002); Craig Dykstra, *Growing in the Life of Faith: Education and Christian Practices* (Louisville: Geneva Press, 1999); Reinhard Hütter, *Suffering Divine Things: Theology as Church Practice*, trans. Doug Stott (Grand Rapids: Eerdmans, 2000); L. Gregory Jones, *Embodying Forgiveness: A Theological Analysis* (Grand Rapids: Eerdmans, 1995); Serene Jones, *Feminist Theory and Christian Theology: Cartographies of Grace* (Minneapolis: Fortress, 2000); Amy Plantinga Pauw, "Dying Well," in *Practicing Our Faith*, ed. Dorothy C. Bass (San Francisco: Jossey-Bass, 1997); Christine D. Pohl, *Making Room: Recovering Hospitality as Christian Tradition* (Grand Rapids: Eerdmans, 1999); Kathryn Tanner, *Theories of Culture: A New Agenda for Theology* (Minneapolis: Fortress, 1997); and Miroslav Volf, *Exclusion and Embrace: A Theological Exploration of Identity, Otherness, and Reconciliation* (Nashville: Abingdon, 1996).

Miroslav Volf's chapter). Several chapters are closely tied to the authors' reflections on the practices embodied in their own communities of faith (including those written by Serene Jones, Tammy Williams, Nancy Bedford, and L. Gregory Jones), and all attend closely to the Christian life *as lived*. We hope that this book will encourage readers to reflect in a similar down-to-earth manner on beliefs and practices in their own contexts.

Writing this book together confirmed anew the conviction each of us had already reached in previous years of theological study and Christian living: theology is a communal enterprise. Each of us (we the authors and you the reader) belongs over time to a number of theological communities — congregations, seminaries, friendship circles, social movements, professional societies, and more. In today's mobile and changing world, some Christians have only a tenuous experience of community; many others may belong to several communities at once; and most find belonging to be episodic, as were the gatherings of this group of authors. Within this context, those who lead theological communities need to find ways of learning with and from people of varied views and histories, while also preventing theological reflection from becoming overly abstract or distant from the messy realm where human beings dwell and where Christian life and ministry take place.

This group of authors, which includes theologians from several ecclesiastical and intellectual traditions, reiterates the makeup of the theological communities from which we come — seminaries, divinity schools, academic societies, denominations, and even congregations. Partly because of such diversity, some differences regarding the term "practices" are evident in the several chapters of this book. Various Christian traditions inform the several essays, explicitly and deliberately making manifest the distinctive character and relative status of beliefs and practices in each. This feature of the book both displays the multiplicity of Christian beliefs and practices and encourages readers to be articulate about the significance of distinctive voices within the larger tradition.

Intellectual orientations also differ, with some authors drawing heavily on the moral philosophy of Alasdair MacIntyre and others relying more on the work of social theorists such as Pierre Bourdieu.[6] These dif-

---

6. Among the essays here, the one by Craig Dykstra and Dorothy C. Bass shows greatest indebtedness to Alasdair MacIntyre's concept of "social practices" as set forth in MacIntyre, *After Virtue,* 2d ed. (Notre Dame: University of Notre Dame Press, 1984),

ferences matter: MacIntyre's virtue ethics emphasizes that practices pursue the good in a coherent, traditioned way, while social scientists influenced by Marxist thought stress the constant negotiations over power that give particular shape to practices in specific social situations. When differences such as these appear in the chapters, the authors flag them for readers and explain their own approaches. We are convinced that our differences have enriched and strengthened our individual chapters and the book as a whole.

Most significant, however, is the fact that the convergence among the several understandings of practices represented here is more formative of and evident in these chapters than are any differences among us. Several key components of practices are important to every author. First, as meaningful clusters of human activity (including the activity of thinking) that require and engender knowledge on the part of practitioners, *practices resist the separation of thinking from acting,* and thus of Christian doctrine from Christian life. Second, *practices are social, belonging to groups of people across generations* — a feature that undergirds the communal quality of the Christian life. Third, *practices are rooted in the past but are also constantly adapting to changing circumstances,* including new cultural settings. Fourth, *practices articulate wisdom that is in the keeping of practitioners who do not think of themselves as theologians.* Through negotiations of meaning at dinner tables and in congregations, hospitals, businesses, schools, and countless other places, ordinary believers seek to discern the contours of faithfulness. So long as social change continually destabilizes both beliefs and practices, and so long as habituation and institutionalization tug to keep them in stasis, Christian living involves the whole community in ongoing theological work. Academic theologians have much to learn from this work and the wisdom *in situ* that it engenders.

Through this book, the authors of *Practicing Theology* hope to invite you the reader to ask questions like the ones we address here within your own classroom, congregation, or study group. This will require you to be attentive to the practices of your community — the mundane, ordinary clusters of beliefs and actions that may disclose, upon reflection, God's re-

---

pp. 187-88. Kathryn Tanner's essay is most attuned to the social scientific conversation about practices, as in Pierre Bourdieu, *Outline of a Theory of Practice,* trans. Richard Nice (Cambridge: Cambridge University Press, 1977). However, both of these essays also depart at many points from these two general schools of influence.

demptive activity within your own setting. This is what happened when a committee member in Serene Jones's church in New Haven noticed that the committee's "vision" made her feel exhausted by everything that needed doing rather than inspired to live more fully in Christ, initiating a rich exploration of both the form and the freedom of this community's life together.[7] This is what happened when the members of Gilbert Bond's church in Chicago realized that they had allowed the federal government to co-opt their communion table, thereby alienating them from their economically impoverished neighbors; when they invited these neighbors to a love feast in the church basement, beliefs and practices grew more vital and authentic in that place.[8] This is what happened when Miroslav Volf remembered his parents' insistence on welcoming to the family table the uncouth stranger who had just joined them at the Lord's table.[9] To reflect theologically on practices is a demanding intellectual agenda, but it will not leave anyone asking "what does this have to do with real life?"

The first and last chapters of this book set forth the overarching themes that are pursued throughout all the chapters. In "A Theological Understanding of Christian Practices," Craig Dykstra and Dorothy C. Bass explore the way of life that Christian people enter at baptism. To think of this life as made up of a coherent set of Christian practices, they argue, can help Christian people more fully to understand their shared life of response to God's active presence in Christ and to embody God's grace and love to others amid the complexities of contemporary life. This chapter focuses on practices and how they are integrally related to God and Christians' knowledge of God.

The book's concluding chapter emphasizes the other side of the same concern. In "Theology for a Way of Life," Miroslav Volf considers Christian beliefs and the character of Christian theology in terms of their relation to Christian practices. Volf argues that practices are not external to Christian beliefs and doctrine, but integral to them. This chapter provides a model of theological reflection on practices and the Christian life and the normative role of Christian beliefs within such reflection. Volf concludes that theology, whose object of study is God and God's relation to the world, ought to be pursued chiefly in the service of a Christian way of life.

7. Page 52.
8. Page 147.
9. Pages 248-49.

Joining Dykstra and Bass's chapter in the section on "Practicing Theology — Embracing a Way of Life" is a chapter by Amy Plantinga Pauw, which attends to the gaps that arise in Christian life, where "right" belief and "right" practices do not always go hand in hand; Pauw uses the ministry of the prophet Jonah as an intriguing example of this problem. The other chapters are grouped into two sections. The first major cluster of essays, "Practicing Theology, Engaging in Ministry," offers a series of cases that show how and why theological reflection on practices is a crucial aspect of ministry. Serene Jones examines the tension between excellent practice and the freedom of God's grace, drawing on her own congregation's experience of this tension. Sarah Coakley offers an account of ascetical and mystical practices, historically and in the life of a contemporary parish priest, noting how participation in practices makes available a distinctive sort of theological knowledge. Tammy Williams retrieves and evaluates three different theologies of healing that she finds embedded in the healing practices of African American Christian congregations. Christine Pohl explores how a specific practice — hospitality to strangers — both shapes communities whose lives are organized around this practice and necessarily draws them into relationship with other communities and other practices. Gilbert Bond also focuses on the practice of hospitality, looking at how two different congregations negotiate the discrepancies between hospitality's liturgical expression and its embodiment in outreach programs for poor and homeless persons. Nancy Bedford tells how her Baptist congregation in Buenos Aires adopted the practice of discernment as a way of making "little moves against destructiveness" within a context of constrained political and economic horizons; her essay suggests a promising opening for theology in Latin America.

The second cluster of essays, "Practicing Theology, Becoming Theologians," offers more programmatic proposals for the discipline of theology and the education of theologians, including those who will serve the church as pastors. L. Gregory Jones argues that Christian formation for ministry necessarily involves church, academy, and the settings of public life; he concludes by proposing ways in which theological schools can strengthen relations among these three arenas. Reinhard Hütter challenges the supposition that being hospitable and being truthful are irreconcilable virtues, arguing from the Trinitarian character of God that authentic Christian practices of hospitality and truth-telling are inseparable. Kathryn Tanner argues that constant real-life negotiations about the specific moves of particular practices necessarily involve all Christians in theological reflection (much of it implicit and uncritical); she stresses that attention to the cultures, religions, and social forces influencing these negotiations is a crucial aspect of contemporary theological education.

In a time when academic theology often neglects the actual practices of Christian communities, the authors of *Practicing Theology* hope to demonstrate that practices can be a generative focus for rigorous theological reflection. We offer this book as an invitation to perceive both the theological quality of everyday practices and the practical importance of theology and doctrine for Christian living.

PRACTICING THEOLOGY,
EMBRACING A WAY OF LIFE

A Theological Understanding
of Christian Practices

CRAIG DYKSTRA AND DOROTHY C. BASS

Midway through *Tender Mercies,* a 1984 film featuring an Oscar-winning performance by Robert Duvall, something happens that is rarely the stuff of movies. In a modest service in an unremarkable church in a small Texas town, a boy and a man are baptized in the name of the Father and of the Son and of the Holy Spirit. Entering into Christian life that Sunday morning are Mac Sledge, a once-successful country singer whose recent marriage to Rosa Lee has reversed a tailspin brought about by alcohol and thwarted ambitions, and Sonny, Rosa Lee's ten-year-old. As the minister lowers first Sonny and then Mac back into the water, Rosa Lee watches from her seat in the choir. Riding home afterwards in their pickup truck, Sonny asks a question. "Do you feel different, Mac?" Mac looks unsure at first. "Not yet," he replies. But laughter wells up in him as he speaks, gentle laughter that soon embraces all three. Something has happened that is beyond mere feeling.

In the water, under the threefold name, Mac and Sonny have been given new life as children of God. And this new life is already finding expression in a family marked by self-giving love. Hardships and temptations will not simply disappear; troubles remaining from Mac's former marriage will soon visit his new home, and it will be a while before Sonny can come to terms with his father's death. Even so, this is a story of gift upon gift. Though burdened by difficult emotions and the strain of eking out a living from the country gas station she owns, Rosa Lee consistently notices God's

13

grace. "Every night, when I thank God for all his blessings and his tender mercies to me, you and Sonny are at the top of the list," she tells Mac when he is disheartened.

In Rosa Lee and Sonny, and like Rosa Lee and Sonny thanks to his presence in their lives, Mac has received a gift, a tender mercy. The grace that opened him to receive this gift was God's prior gift of a new, true self. Mac — a has-been who lay drunk on the floor in the movie's opening scene — would have found the account of salvation given in the letter to the Ephesians an apt description of his new condition: "It is God's gift, not a reward for work done. There is nothing for anyone to boast of. For we are God's handiwork, created in Christ Jesus to devote ourselves to the good deeds for which God has designed us" (Eph. 2:9-10). With new life, Mac is learning, comes a new way of life: caring for Sonny, weeding Rosa Lee's garden, and casting his lot with a struggling young band in Texas rather than racing back to Nashville when given the chance. Mac's good deeds are humble ones, and his faith is humble, too: the last words he speaks in the film show that he is still far from serenity. In spite of his agonized questioning, however, it is evident as he plays catch with Sonny in the film's closing scene that he has been "made new in mind and spirit, [having] put on the new nature of God's creating" (Eph. 4:23-24). Mac has been and is still being restored — from bondage to freedom, from isolation to community, from despair to hope. He has even been restored to music, Saturday night country music, though in a different way than before. Coming to faith he enters a new way of life, one that is truly life-giving.

Romero is another, quite different movie about the Christian way of life. This film biography of the martyred bishop of El Salvador tells the story of how a new way of life characterized by freedom, community, and hope emerged among the poor in Latin America. At the film's beginning, the behavior of the church hierarchy is guided by a centuries-old habit of special favor for the rich and mighty of the land. In the barrios and countryside, however, priests, nuns, and other grassroots leaders have begun to share a theology of liberation with the oppressed and marginalized. As Bishop Romero's eyes are opened to injustice, he gradually joins their efforts and comes to understand and participate in Christ's solidarity with the poor and the suffering. One implication, he realizes, is that Catholics of all classes and ethnic groups, belonging as they do to "one Lord, one faith, one baptism" (Eph. 4:5), should bring their children, together, to a common font of water for the liturgy that incorporates them into the one

Body of Christ, the church. This decision is presented as a key point of rupture between Romero and the social and economic elite, which is represented in the film by a wealthy young woman who is Romero's own goddaughter. She has planned a lavish private baptism for her baby, and she is appalled that anyone expects her to stand side by side with peasants and allow water that has touched their children to touch hers.

That elites were permitted to rely for centuries on privileged treatment at the baptismal font suggests that the baptismal rite itself does not automatically bestow either new life such as that experienced by Sonny and Mac or solidarity such as that which emerged in El Salvador as faithful people struggled against injustice during that country's long civil wars. Indeed, the best-known cinematic depiction of a baptism shows just how thoroughly this rite can be abused. In *The Godfather*, the scene in which the infant godson of Don Michael Corleone is baptized is intercut with scenes of several murders, which the Don has ordered for that same hour. Viewing this abuse of baptism makes Christians recoil, however, aware that this basic act of initiation into the Christian community means to give life, not death — indeed, abundant life, life that is joined to the life and love of Christ.

In this essay, we set forth a way of thinking about how a way of life that is deeply responsive to God's grace takes actual shape among human beings. To be sure, many of us feel that we already know such a way when we see it: Salvadorans struggling for justice, yes; the Mafia, no. This essay proposes, however, that learning to think more systematically and theologically about the shape and character of such a way of life may be helpful as we seek to discern its contours in new situations, to enjoy and give thanks for it, and to share it with others.

In a sense, what we offer here is a specific way of engaging in a dynamic that exists within the Christian life itself. Because the circumstances in which human beings live are always concrete, conflicted, and in flux, those who seek to live faithfully must necessarily wonder where and how to discern the specific shape that a way of life abundant might take in a given time and place. What moves do people make as they encounter one another in the context of God's grace? What words do they say, what gestures do they perform, what relationships do they enter? These questions may be asked consciously, or they may be implicit in the day-to-day decisions of a community, but they are surely somewhere in play, for the contours of a life-giving way of life are usually not readily apparent. Moreover,

15

these questions are theological. Addressing them is one of the most urgent tasks confronting theologians, whose vocation it is to reflect not only on God but also, in the light of God, on human life and all creation.[1]

Reflection of this sort takes on special urgency in a time and place where far more attention is given to *life-styles of abundance* than to *ways of life abundant.* Thus we offer this essay because we hope to contribute to building up ways of life that are abundant not in things but in love, justice, and mercy. Today rapid social change and intense spiritual restlessness evoke fierce yearning in many people, in our own neighborhoods and around the world. Some observers see this yearning as a quest for meaning, others as a longing for spiritual consciousness or experience. Important as these quests are, we think that they arise from a deeper longing, a longing for a life that adds up to something that is in a deep sense good for oneself, for other people, and for all creation. As Christians, the two of us affirm that such a way of life — right down to the specific words, gestures, and situations of which it is woven — finds its fullest integrity, coherence, and fittingness insofar as it embodies a grateful human response to God's presence and promises.

Awareness of the possibility of a way of life shaped by a positive response to God pervades the Bible and Christian history — as do examples of the human tendency to fall short of God's invitation to such a life, from the Garden of Eden to the churches of ancient Asia Minor to the inequities that divide contemporary Christians. Without neglecting the sin that is part of Christian history, it is vital that those who seek to walk in such a way today learn to recognize the lived wisdom of Christian people over time and across cultures as a constructive resource. The earliest accounts of Christian origins depict groups of people doing things together in the light of and in response to God. Jesus gathered disciples, with whom he healed and taught, ate and sang, and prayed and died, while immersed in Jewish communal life and walking Roman roads. In later years, as these disciples and those who came after them gathered into communities to celebrate the presence of the risen Christ, their communities too were im-

---

1. The New Testament epistles characteristically address this concern. Ellen T. Charry has identified the centrality of this concern to key theologians in Christian history and urged it upon the attention of contemporary theologians in *By the Renewing of Your Minds: The Pastoral Function of Christian Doctrine* (New York: Oxford University Press, 1997).

mersed in the ordinary stuff of specific times and places. The Acts of the Apostles and the letters of Paul give us glimpses of people breaking bread together in memory of Jesus, sharing their possessions with those in need, singing, healing, and testifying together — men and women, slaves and citizens, Jews and Greeks, makers of tents and dyers of cloth. Over the centuries, ways of living that shared this deepest source and purpose would take shape in the quite different daily experiences of the Egyptian desert, European cities, Salvadoran villages, American small towns, suburbs, and cities, and countless other places. In all these places, specific human beings have sought to live in ways that responded to the mercy and freedom of God as it is made known in Jesus Christ. They have done things that other people also do, simply because these things are part of being human — they have cared for the sick, buried the dead, brought up children, made decisions. But they have done them somehow differently because of their knowledge of God in Christ.

When we reflect on this heritage as theologians concerned about building up ways of life abundant in our own time, we must ask not only whether it provides resources that seem helpful, but also whether what we find there is true, as far as we can discern, to the purposes of God. In a sense, each community of Christians in every generation is already engaged, implicitly or explicitly, in just such discernment. Inheriting much but also drawn into relationship with God in Christ in the present moment, they care for the sick, bury the dead, bring up children, tell stories, and make decisions, sometimes pausing in midstream to ask whether the forms these activities take in their own time and place are faithful to God's purposes. Theologians take up these questions in a more deliberate and ordered manner. But to describe this entire way of life is a daunting task, particularly when done in a way that is responsive to the purposeful presence of the Triune God who has created and is bringing redemption to everything that is. The task is rightly and necessarily large, potentially attentive to the entire universe. Yet it would fail if it lost sight of the One who understood the value of a single lost coin to a housewife and of one lost sheep to a shepherd.

The effort to offer a theological description of a way of life abundant, then, is complicated by *the problem of the too big and the too small*. The problem of the too big is that the task is all-encompassing; reflecting at this level would be too grand to be of much direct use by itself, conceptually or strategically. The problem of the too small is the opposite. In theological reflection, and also in the actual work of living as Christians and trying to guide others in doing so as well, it often seems that we do a little of this and a little of that and a little of something else; too often it becomes difficult to keep in view the larger wholes to which these smaller pieces belong. The connections get lost, and when that happens we lose any sense of the overall significance and import of particular activities, ideas, doctrines, biblical texts and narratives, and beliefs.[2]

Rather than speak of a Christian way of life as a whole, therefore, we shall speak of the "Christian practices" that together constitute a way of life abundant. By "Christian practices" we mean *things Christian people do together over time to address fundamental human needs in response to and in the light of God's active presence for the life of the world.*[3] Thinking of a way of life as made up of a constitutive set of practices breaks a way of life down into parts that are small enough to be amenable to analysis, both in relation to contemporary concerns and as historic, culture-spanning forms of Christian faith and life. At the same time, practices are not too small: each Christian practice is large enough to permit us to draw together the shards and pieces of particular understandings, beliefs, events, behaviors, actions, relationships, inquiries, and skills into sets that are capacious and cohesive enough to show how they might guide one into a way of life.

We advocate a concept of practices that allows us to draw together under a single rubric ideas and activities of many kinds, and the fact that this move gives us a concept of manageable size is only one reason for doing so. Even more important is the fact that such a concept enables us to recog-

---

2. Craig Dykstra considered "the problem of the too big and the too small" from the perspective of the Christian educator in *Growing in the Life of Faith: Education and Christian Practices* (Louisville: Geneva Press, 1999), pp. 66-67.

3. This is the definition of Christian practices that provides the basis of *Practicing Our Faith: A Way of Life for a Searching People,* ed. Dorothy C. Bass (Jossey-Bass Publishers, 1997); it is explicated in the book's first chapter, which we coauthored. In retrospect, we think that the definition of practices quoted here would be strengthened by the addition of the words "in Jesus Christ" at the end, which would clarify the character and content of the active divine presence that is so central to our understanding of practices. The authors of *Practicing Theology* were first convened for the purpose of reflecting on how the concept of practices that informs *Practicing Our Faith* might contribute to and be challenged by the work of systematic theologians. As will be seen later in this essay and in other essays in the present volume, some of them conceptualize "practice" differently than we have done.

nize the practical and theological kinship of certain beliefs, virtues, and skills with certain behaviors, relationships, and symbols, because all of them contribute to building up a recognizable, and finally coherent, Christian practice.

In the book *Practicing Our Faith,* which the two of us wrote with eleven colleagues, we identified a list of twelve practices that meet this definition: honoring the body, hospitality, household economics, saying yes and saying no, keeping sabbath, discernment, testimony, shaping communities, forgiveness, healing, dying well, and singing our lives to God. We did not claim that these twelve practices are the only things Christians do together over time that could be identified as practices. We did, however, intentionally limit the list, wishing to focus concern for a way of life on a number that was small enough to be comprehensible but sufficient in scope to address fundamental human needs. We also excluded those shared activities whose primary use is in liturgy, arguing that each of the practices we treated has both liturgical expressions and expressions in other settings.[4]

Take, for example, the practice of hospitality to strangers. As we understand this practice, the action that occurs when the staff members of a homeless shelter provide a homeless man with a bed is only one movement within it; it is not in itself a practice. The practice of hospitality, as we understand it, also encompasses, among other things, the biblical stories that have shaped the way in which the hosts perceive their guests; the specific habits, virtues, knowledge, and other capacities of mind and spirit that the hosts bring to the situation, many of which could have been developed only within the context of the practice itself; the liturgical words and gestures that make manifest in crystallized form the hospitality of God to humankind and our obligations to one another; and the domestic hosting that prepares family members to break bread with strangers in less familiar surroundings as well.

Over the centuries and still today, countless Christians have actually engaged in this practice. Often they have done so without a high degree of theological articulation — a lack that does nothing to exclude them from

---

4. *Practicing Our Faith* was written by a team that included Amy Plantinga Pauw and L. Gregory Jones, who are also contributors to the present volume, as well as M. Shawn Copeland, Thomas Hoyt Jr., John Koenig, Sharon Daloz Parks, Stephanie Paulsell, Ana Maria Pineda, Larry Rasmussen, Frank Rogers Jr., and Don E. Saliers.

being numbered among practitioners. But the theological scholar who carefully researches the history of the Christian practice of hospitality, assesses the ethical tensions in which it involves practitioners, and analyzes the strengths and limitations of the current state of the practice has also done something that is an indispensable aspect of this Christian practice: she has provided hosts and guests with an opportunity to reflect critically and constructively on the practice itself and thus to understand more fully what it is they are actually doing.[5] Within a social and intellectual context in which connections are often severed or obscured — connections between thinking and doing, domesticity and public life, liturgy and social justice — the capacity of this concept of practices to show how such apparently different things do indeed belong together seems to us to be of great value.

The two of us are aware, however, that others — including some of the other contributors to this book — use the term "practices" in different ways. Drawing on the social sciences, many contemporary scholars refer to much smaller bits of action by this term; in this use, a "practice" can be almost any socially meaningful action, such as keeping records for the homeless shelter, or welcoming visitors to a worship service, or sharing a family meal. Kathryn Tanner's chapter reflects this approach, which emphasizes the improvisational character of practices and the way in which practices involve non-elites in the production of meaning.[6] An older, more specific use of the term applies it to the ascetical and spiritual disciplines and exercises by which people deliberately seek to become more attuned to the sacred, the focus of the chapter by Sarah Coakley.[7] A third understanding of practices arises from moral philosophy, especially the work of Alasdair MacIntyre; this use grounds a concept of virtue in what MacIntyre calls "social practices," complex social activities that pursue certain goods internal to the practices themselves. Our own understanding of

5. See Christine D. Pohl, *Making Room: Recovering Hospitality as a Christian Tradition* (Grand Rapids: Eerdmans, 1999).

6. See the chapter by Kathryn Tanner; Pierre Bourdieu, *Outline of a Theory of Practice,* trans. Richard Nice (Cambridge: Cambridge University Press, 1977); and Tanner, *Theories of Culture: A New Agenda for Theology* (Minneapolis: Fortress Press, 1997).

7. An example is Margaret Miles, *Practicing Christianity: Critical Perspectives for an Embodied Spirituality* (New York: Crossroad Publishing Co., 1988). Authors in this school of thought tend to use "practice," "discipline," and "exercise" almost interchangeably.

practices reflects the influence of MacIntyre more fully than the other essays in this book, while also differing in crucial ways from MacIntyre.[8] All three basic approaches agree, however, on this volume's key claim that beliefs and practices can and should be understood in relation to one another: they all reject the separation of thought and action, seeing in a practice a form of cooperative and meaningful human endeavor in which the two are inextricably entwined.

The distinctive understanding of *Christian practices* set forth in this essay focuses on practices as the constituent elements in a way of life that becomes incarnate when human beings live in the light of and in response to God's gift of life abundant. Thus, when we refer to Christian practices, we have something normative and theological in mind. Each element in our approach presumes that Christian practices are set in a world created and sustained by a just and merciful God, who is now in the midst of reconciling this world through Christ. Christian practices address needs that are basic to human existence as such, and they do so in ways that reflect God's purposes for humankind. When they participate in such practices, Christian people are taking part in God's work of creation and new creation and thereby growing into a deeper knowledge of God and of creation. This is something that is necessarily done with other people, across generations and cultures. And it is something that is always done imperfectly, and sometimes even in such a distorted manner that practices become evil. We hope that the definition that follows will clarify our distinctive way of using this term. Even more, we hope that it will suggest some of the characteristic features of the way of life abundant whose edification is our central concern.

---

8. Our own reflection on practices began with, and is still deeply indebted to, Alasdair MacIntyre's concept of "social practices" in *After Virtue*, 2d ed. (Notre Dame: University of Notre Dame Press, 1984), pp. 187-88. Each of us relied on MacIntyre in our earlier work on practices; see Craig Dykstra, "Reconceiving Practice," in *Virtues and Practices in the Christian Tradition: Christian Ethics after MacIntyre*, ed. Nancey Murphy, Brad J. Kallenberg, and Mark Thiessen Nation (Harrisburg, Pa.: Trinity Press International, 1997), and Dorothy C. Bass, "Congregations and the Bearing of Traditions," in *American Congregations*, vol. 2, ed. James P. Wind and James W. Lewis (Chicago: University of Chicago Press, 1994). Our present understanding of practices differs from MacIntyre's account in *After Virtue* in that ours is now theological and thus normed not only internally but also through the responsive relationship of Christian practices to God.

Christian practices address fundamental human needs and conditions. Christian practices, theologically understood, are directed to humanity's most basic needs, needs that arise out of the very character of human existence. They address conditions fundamental to being human — such as embodiment, temporality, relationship, the use of language, and mortality — and they do so through concrete human acts joined inextricably to substantive convictions about how things really are.

A fundamental human condition is that we all have bodies; the Christian practice we call "honoring the body" insists in myriad ways that human bodies be honored — not violated, not ridiculed, not murdered — because they are made in the image of God. A fundamental human condition is that we are all mortal; the Christian practice we call "dying well" takes shape as Christians help one another to know that they are upheld by the One who is the source of life itself and that their lives have mattered, profoundly and appropriately, to themselves and to others, ultimately because they have mattered to God. A fundamental human condition is our vulnerability to the unknown and thus potentially threatening stranger; the Christian practice of hospitality involves practitioners in presuming the stranger to be guest and neighbor, rather than enemy, by acknowledging the stranger's own vulnerability and enfolding the stranger in care.

A practice is a practice in our meaning of the term only if it is a sustained, cooperative pattern of human activity that is big enough, rich enough, and complex enough to address some fundamental feature of human existence. Christian practices also have a normative dimension that is thoroughly theological in character. That is, our descriptions of Christian practices contain within them normative understandings of what God wills for us and for the whole creation and of what God expects of us in response to God's call to be faithful. Christian practices are thus congruent with the necessities of human existence as such, as seen from a Christian perspective on the character of human flourishing.

Normatively and theologically understood, therefore, Christian practices are the human activities in and through which people cooperate with God in addressing the needs of one another and creation. As parents honor the body of a teen-aged daughter, she begins to understand her God-given strength and beauty. When mourners surround the bereaved with song and prayer, the bereaved become able to thank God for the life of their beloved. When an overstressed worker takes one day every week to worship, feast, and play, he is renewed in relation to God, other people, and

22

the work that he does on the other days of the week. Because these people have done certain things together in the light of and in response to God's active presence, they have in a sense shared in the practices of God, who has also honored the human body, embraced death, and rested, calling creation good. And the other practices are like this, providing concrete help for human flourishing that is informed by basic Christian beliefs about who human beings really are and what God is doing in the world.

The wisdom about fundamental human needs that is embedded in historic Christian practices can be a profound resource for contemporary people who seek to sustain a measure of freedom within the prevailing economic culture, where "needs" for specific, often branded, material products seem to multiply as global markets expand. Being able to tell the difference between fundamental human needs and manufactured ones can mean the difference between lives that are grasping and lives that are in a deep sense free. For most North Americans, for example, this would mean the difference between being driven by market-induced desires and being free to share possessions and keep sabbath. In a situation in which the cultural celebration of what Miroslav Volf has called "product-needs" subjectively overwhelms attention to "the fundamental non-product-needs [that] are objectively rooted in the nature of human beings as creatures made in the image of God," Christian practices embody the freedom that is rightly ours.[9]

Theological reflection plays an essential role in sustaining the capacity of Christian practices to embody such freedom. As Martin Luther learned during his years as a monk, ardent engagement in practices can become a form of self-securing, an effort to win one's own salvation apart from God. His reading of Paul's epistles led him to a revised account of the

---

9. See Miroslav Volf, *Work in the Spirit: Toward a Theology of Work* (New York: Oxford University Press, 1991), pp. 152-154. Volf identifies five "non-product-needs" that are fundamental to people's humanity and argues that "product-needs" should not be indulged to the detriment of these. The five are the needs for communion with God; solidarity with nature; tending to the well-being of one another; the development of moral capacities and practical and intellectual skills; and the new creation, the kingdom of freedom. Margaret Miles's treatment of Christian asceticism in *Fullness of Life: Historical Foundations for a New Asceticism* (Philadelphia: Westminster Press, 1981) also makes a relevant argument; i.e., that ascetical practices have historically been the means by which many Christians have sought freedom from cultural mandates and from whatever within themselves would restrict their communion with God.

Christian life as a response to God's grace.[10] Alternately, a self-satisfied grasp of God's grace can seem to make participation in Christian practices unimportant — a view criticized by virtually every theologian.[11] Sin can urge us toward either mistake; indeed, it is difficult to think of a time in which we humans are more likely to deceive ourselves and others than when we are distinguishing between our desires and our needs. Thus helping one another to understand what God-shaped fundamental human needs and conditions actually are and what a God-shaped faithful response to them actually consists of a crucial theological task. Any such reflection will encounter the quandary with which Calvin began the *Institutes:* "Nearly all the wisdom we possess, that is to say, true and sound wisdom, consists of two parts: the knowledge of God and of ourselves. But, while joined by many bonds, which one precedes and brings forth the other is not easy to discern."[12] A full understanding of a set of Christian practices includes both a profound knowledge of humankind in its most fundamental and orienting needs and capacities, including its capacity to sin, and a profound knowledge of God's purposes for all creation. In other words, both theological anthropology and theological assessment of what God is doing in the world are relevant to a theological account of practices, and to the community's ability to engage in authentically Christian practices.

Christian practices thus involve a profound awareness, a deep knowing: they are activities imbued with the knowledge of God and creation. Indeed, we believe that it is precisely by participating in Christian practices that we truly come to know God and the world, including ourselves.

When we participate over a long period of time in addressing fundamental human needs in the light of and in response to God's active presence in the life of the world, we grow into a double-sided knowledge of God and ourselves. This knowledge is not first and always articulate and ordered; many worthy practitioners would be unable to offer a coherent

10. Martin Luther, "The Freedom of a Christian," in *Martin Luther: Selected Works,* ed. John Dillenberger (Garden City, NY: Anchor Books, 1961), pp. 52-85.

11. Virtually all Christian theologians commend engagement in acts of faith, hope, and love that fall within our notion of practices. Specifying this aspect of the Christian life is an important part of the theological task — one, indeed, to which Luther himself turns in the final sections of "The Freedom of a Christian."

12. John Calvin, *Institutes of the Christian Religion,* ed. John T. McNeill, trans. Ford Lewis Battles (Philadelphia: Westminster Press, 1960), I.1.1, p. 35.

theology. Rather, this knowledge has first to do with knowing that the world and oneself belong to God, who is present and active in certain ways. To grow in this kind of knowledge is also to grow in trust, generosity, and freedom as a practitioner. Christine Pohl's account of the Christian practice of hospitality depicts generations of hosts who have come to know God in this way.[13]

Christian practices also open possibilities for knowledge that is theological in other ways. First, insofar as a Christian practice is truly attuned to the human condition in a given time and place and to the intentions of God, participating in it increases one's knowledge of humanity and all creation. Entering the Christian practice of healing, for example, develops in practitioners certain skills, habits, virtues, and capacities of mind and spirit; one learns the properties of certain foods and remedies, the effects of different kinds of touch, and the locations of organs and bones. The content of each practice challenges, lures, and sometimes drags its practitioners into new ways of being and knowing that are commensurate with that practice — and thus, if it is rightly attuned, commensurate with the well-being of creation. Living within such a practice gives men and women certain capacities that enable them to read the world differently — even, we would argue, more truly.

Second, insofar as a Christian practice is truly attuned to the active presence of God for the life of the world, participating in it increases our knowledge of the Triune God. For example, Christians who keep holy a weekly day of rest and worship acquire through the Christian practice of sabbath-keeping an embodied knowledge that the world does not depend on our own capacity for ceaseless work and that its life is not under our control. Observing sabbath on the Lord's Day, Christian practitioners come to know in their bones that creation is God's gift, that God does not intend that anyone should work without respite, and that God has conquered death in the resurrection of Christ. And this knowledge is not only embodied; the words of liturgies, the songs of people gathered for worship, and the difficult decisions that must be made about the actual characteristics of a "holy" day are an intrinsic part of this practice. Across the centuries, certain Christians who are highly conversant with the history, texts, and liturgical forms of the tradition (and often of the Jewish tradition as well, especially in this case) have led reforms in the shape of sabbath-keeping, urging

---

13. Pohl, *Making Room*.

stricter or more relaxed observance. They have also written hymns, prayers, and books that they hoped would deepen the capacity of the larger community to know this practice and, through it, to know God more fully. Thanks to their creative work, which may serve the community for centuries without attribution, practitioners who are not in any academic sense "theologians" may draw from the rich language and the embodied experience of sabbath a knowledge of realities toward which more formal theologies point, and which they seek to explicate: grace, justice, and salvation.[14]

Christian practices are social and historical. They are activities people engage in together over time. Practices, as understood here, are patterned activities carried on by whole communities of people, not just in one particular location, but across nations and generations. Since each individual human being is mortal, only corporate, social action can be extended over long periods of time and across a wide variety of social and cultural circumstances. An individual person may engage in a certain practice in solitude for a while, of course, but even then the practice has been learned from, and exists in continuity with, other people who have done it in the past and who do it around the world today. When a practice is vital and authentic, however, it is also necessarily concrete and particular, taking appropriate shape in a distinctive time and place in the form of a cluster of apparently small gestures, words, images, and objects. Therefore specific forms are flexible enough to take on the contours of many societies and cultures. Each practice can, and indeed must, be crafted in varied ways and forms, some of them not yet imagined. Practices allow for — indeed, they thrive on — such improvisation and negotiation.

So far, these claims that practices are social and historical contain nothing that is especially theological or Christian. A *theological* account of our understanding of Christian practices, however, could be founded on God's decision to work in and through human communities living in particular times and places. The biblical stories of Israel and of the church suggest that these trans-generational human communities are intrinsic to

14. The relation of what is here called "the Christian sabbath" to the Sabbath of Judaism is treated further in Dorothy C. Bass, *Receiving the Day: Christian Practices for Opening the Gift of Time* (San Francisco: Jossey-Bass Publishers, 2000). At issue in this essay is how a practice such as keeping sabbath bears theological content, which can become articulate in theological terms. Jewish reflection on the Sabbath provides an excellent example within Jewish theology; e.g., Abraham Joshua Heschel, *The Sabbath* (New York: Farrar, Straus, and Giroux, 1952).

God's way of being in and for the world. Subsequently, Christians have also linked the specific congregations in which they gather to other Christian congregations across generations and cultures and to the unifying power of the Holy Spirit by affirming their belief in "the holy catholic church." Indeed, we would argue that the practices of all Christian congregations are intricately linked to one another as well as to the practices of communities long ago. Historians trace these links, but on occasion those involved in a Christian practice also experience them, sensing the unity of their singing or testimony or forgiveness with the practices of their spiritual forebears. At the same time, Christian practices are always oriented toward the future as well; just as communities in the past and present have appropriated and altered for their own contexts the specific moves and signs that embody hospitality or forgiveness or healing, so also will future practitioners devise improvisations that we cannot yet imagine.

Christian practices share in the mysterious dynamic of fall and redemption, sin and grace. For Christians, any theological discussion of human beings and our activities must also take account of the problem of sin and evil. Both individual human failings and unjust social structures set countless obstacles in the way of practices that are good for all people. Moreover, in history and in the present day, practitioners who bear the name of Christ have participated in shared activities that are distorted, damaging, and manifestly not embodied responses to the active presence of God for the life of the world. Egregious examples leap to mind, but the quieter damage that can be wrought in the course of everyday life also evokes this problem, as people who bear the name of Christ fail to practice forgiveness, or discernment, or hospitality. Indeed, any given practice — including any practice that is historically Christian — can become so distorted that its pursuit and outcome are evil rather than good. Therefore, much of the thinking we need to do about practices is critical thinking, thinking that discloses how destructively the basic activities of human life are often organized — globally, in American society, in our churches, and in our homes.

The normative and theological concept of Christian practices that we propose situates Christian practices themselves within the mystery of fall *and* redemption, of sin *and* grace, that informs Christian reflection on the problem of evil. Within the history of any given practice, there have been points at which the social forms of the practice became unjust — for example, by becoming allied with national hostilities or rigid class boundaries. Christine Pohl's fine history of the Christian practice of hospitality to strangers describes the gradual removal of hospitality from homes to institutions and the impact of the church's shift from marginal to established status — changes that combined to destroy the personal and egalitarian qualities of early Christian hospitality. In some times and places, hostility to certain strangers has gone and continues to go virtually unchallenged among Christians. Yet Pohl's account also tells how a theologically normed practice of hospitality has been retrieved by Christians called to be hosts to refugees and the poor in more recent times, including our own. Even so, Pohl argues, the possibility that hosts and guests will abuse or demean one another continues to be an intrinsic danger within this practice. That the danger is sometimes not avoided provides evidence of the continuing power of human sin within Christian practices.[15]

Even practices that are in modest disrepair can provide the space within which selves made new by God can respond to God's grace by extending it to others. On the other hand, even apparently sound practices can become abodes of bondage rather than freedom for practitioners who forget that it is God's activity rather than their own that is healing the world. The theological shape of Christian practices, as we understand them, substantively addresses the human tendency to grasp more control than is rightly ours — a grasping that can be harmful even when it seems to be for a good purpose. While the point of most human practices is the achievement of some form of mastery over a specific kind of conflict or chaos, Christian practitioners do not *master* death in the practice of dying well, or enmity in the practice of forgiveness, or sound in the practice of singing our lives to God. Instead, in trying to engage in such practices faithfully and well, they seek to enter more fully into the receptivity and responsiveness, to others and to God, that characterize Christ and all who share in the new creation.

Engagement in Christian practices, indeed, provides situations in which practitioners can live into the promises made at their baptism. Freed of the impossible task of mastering death, they can live in the shadow of death in a way that does not paralyze but rather grants freedom, freedom to offer hospitality or forgiveness or healing to those who need it, and to sing their lives to God, even when death's shadow looms large and immediate. Even when this kind of freedom is not perfectly realized, to

15. Christine Pohl, *Making Room.*

know it is to see the world and all who dwell therein as belonging to a gracious God.

A critical theological awareness of the Christian practices that constitute a way of life abundant presses practitioners to see things whole at several levels. This is crucial to the criticism, retrieval, and strengthening of practices, for when the concern of practitioners does not reach beyond the self or the cares of a self-absorbed community, Christian practices lose touch with the larger realities within which they are normatively embedded. One of these realities is the historic and global church. Even the most parochial examples of Christian practice exist in relation to and indeed are part of a movement that spans centuries and cultures, and this movement has always provided resources for mutual criticism and renewal, resources that are especially accessible and pertinent in the contemporary context of globalization. In addition, as constituent elements of a way of life abundant, the various Christian practices are deeply integrated with one another: when practicing hospitality, one is drawn into forgiving those once considered alien, and into perceiving one's own forgiveness as well; in keeping sabbath, one honors the body, reorders the economics of the household, and grows in capacity to participate in the practice of saying yes and saying no. Other connections emerge as well: we begin to understand that the family table, the table provided for the destitute, the table of holy communion, and the eschatological table where all people will feast in the fullness of God are not isolated from one another, but are part of a coherent whole constituted by the encompassing, unifying reality of God's active presence for the life of the world.

A way of life abundant keeps connections such as these strong. Its pieces add up to something that is good because it is responsive to the grace that is at the heart of everything. Thinking about this way of life in terms of the practices that constitute it discloses some of its characteristics, each of which we have already encountered as the characteristics of Christian practices themselves. This way of life addresses fundamental human conditions and needs. It involves its adherents in God's activities in the world. It arises from and imparts a profound knowledge of God and creation. It is lived together with others, and in continuity across many years. It catches up those who live it in the mysterious, dynamic process by which God is bringing a new creation into being.

This is the way of life abundant that Mac Sledge begins to glimpse in *Tender Mercies* when he decides that he wants to be baptized. It is a way he has not so much found as been found by, mainly through Rosa Lee, who as she offers him her trust and her love also offers him her faith in Christ. His needs have been transfigured: this man who once "needed" alcohol and fame now needs only love and music and a modest living. He knows the limits of his knowledge of God — "Why?" he cries in anguish after his daughter dies in a car crash — but he also knows that the only appropriate responses to his new life are gratitude to God and kindness to the people around him. He is caught up in the new creation that is coming into being right there in that small town in Texas.

This is also the way of life that began to shape the vision of the people of El Salvador as they brought their children to Archbishop Romero for baptism. The shadow of death would not paralyze them, they promised and were promised, even when it burst into their villages in the form of government-sponsored death squads. Resisting the powers of death, they would embrace the Christian practices of discernment, testimony, shaping communities, and dying well. They had long known the suffering of poverty and marginalization, and they were preparing to add the suffering of resistance to these more familiar forms. Their suffering would take on a different character, however, when joined to one another's suffering and the suffering of the great company of those united in and through the passion of the One who suffered, died, was buried, and rose again.

Baptism is the rite that marks entry into such a way of life. It involves the pouring of actual water on a unique human body, as a specific individual is honored and received in his or her embodied integrity. At the same time, it incorporates the baptized person into a social and historical Body that spans centuries and cultures. And it incorporates that person into the very mystery of Christ. "Do you not know that all of us who have been baptized into Christ Jesus were baptized into his death?" writes Paul to the Romans (6:3-4). "Therefore we have been buried with him by baptism into death, so that, just as Christ was raised from the dead by the glory of the Father, so we too might walk in newness of life." When it is detached from a way of life abundant, as in the Corleone baptism, the pouring of water accomplishes nothing. We cannot be sure what becomes of the little godson, but it is clear that the godfather himself has only a life-style of abundance, not a way of life abundant, however impressive the riches and might he secures for himself.

At its heart, baptism is not so much a distinct practice as it is the liturgical summation of all the Christian practices. In this rite, the grace to

30

which the Christian life is a response is fully and finally presented, visibly, tangibly, and in words. Here all the practices are present in crystalline form — forgiveness and healing, singing and testimony, sabbath-keeping and community shaping, and all the others. Unlike each particular practice, baptism does not address a specific need; instead, it ritually sketches the contours of a whole new life, within which all human needs can be perceived in a different way. Under water, we cannot secure our own lives, but we can know, in a knowing beyond words, that God's creativity overcame the darkness that covered the face of the deep at earth's beginning, and that water flowed from Jesus' side on the cross, and that the new creation to which we now belong anticipates a city where the river of the water of life nourishes the roots of the tree whose leaves are for the healing of the nations. When a new Christian rises from the baptismal water, human needs are not just met; they are transformed. Even the need not to die no longer overpowers all other needs, and the true freedom of a life formed in love, justice, mercy, and hope is no longer too frightening to embrace. "In baptism," said St. Francis, "we have already died the only death that matters."

Part of the work of Christian theologians in every age is to reflect on the shape and character of the way of life Christians enter when we rise from the watery death of baptism. How should the new selves we have been given walk in newness of life? Exploring this question involves us both in contemplating the deepest foundations of Christian faith and in figuring out the shape our living should take amidst the immediate concerns of each day.

The letter to the Ephesians may be read as an articulation of this kind of reflection on a way of life, written for the sake of guiding people more fully into it.[16] The letter begins with a vision of the situation of the faithful that is cosmic in scope: they are "blessed in Christ with every spiritual blessing in the heavenly places" and "chosen in Christ before the foundation of the world" (1:3-4). In a sense, the letter's author is telling his readers who they really, most fully, most truly are. As the letter nears its end,

---

16. David F. Ford, *Self and Salvation: Being Transformed* (Cambridge: Cambridge University Press, 1999), offers such an interpretation of Ephesians, which Ford calls "a testimony to the quality of transformed life in a worshiping community. Its horizon for human flourishing is unsurpassably vast. . . . Within that, its special focus is on what it means to have a particular social identity in relation to God and other people" (pp. 107-8).

however, the author describes the specific moves and gestures that would result from bearing this identity in the face-to-face social arrangements of a first-century city in Asia Minor, urging men and women of high estate and low to "be subject to one another out of reverence for Christ" (5:21).

The way of life set forth in Ephesians is not without suffering; the letter's author writes of imprisonment (3:1, 4:1) and of the need of the faithful to withstand "all the flaming arrows of the evil one" (6:16). Nor is it without division; the reconciliation of Gentile and Jew is the letter's urgent theme. But it is, in the midst of all this, a way of life that is whole, because it is in the keeping of the Triune God who was and is and shall be, and because it is responsive to and reflective of the character of that God:

> With this in mind, then, I kneel in prayer to the Father, from whom every family in heaven and on earth takes its name, that out of the treasures of his glory he may grant you strength and power through his Spirit in your inner being, that through faith Christ may dwell in your hearts in love. With deep roots and firm foundations, may you be strong to grasp, with all God's people, what is the breadth and length and height and depth of the love of Christ, and to know it, though it is beyond knowledge. So may you attain to fullness of being, the fullness of God himself (Eph. 3:14-19, NEB).

Attending to the Gaps
between Beliefs and Practices

AMY PLANTINGA PAUW

There is a temptation to turn to exemplary cases when talking about the relationship between religious beliefs and practices. We are naturally drawn to the unflinching radicalness of Dorothy Day, to the humble courage of the Christians in Le Chambon, France.[1] In these instances, the connection between beliefs and practices seems so clear and vibrant that observers of all religious persuasions are filled with admiration and wonder. We all have our own saints of the faith, people whose religious lives display a seemingly effortless integrity. Despite their idiosyncrasies and failings, these "friends of God and prophets" give us glimpses of the depths of the gospel and nourish our hopes for God's promised future.

But there is also something to be said for looking at efforts by less exemplary believers to bridge the troublesome gaps that keep reappearing in various ways between their beliefs and practices. Their struggles reveal the continual slippage and compromise that occur between these two central aspects of the religious life. Certain beliefs and practices are so

---

1. Dorothy Day, *The Long Loneliness; The Autobiography of Dorothy Day,* illustrated by Fritz Eichenberg (New York: Harper & Row, 1952). Philip Haillie, *Lest Innocent Blood Be Shed: The Story of the Village of Le Chambon and How Goodness Happened There* (New York: Harper & Row, 1979); also the documentary film *Weapons of the Spirit,* Pierre Sauvage Productions and Friends of Le Chambon, Inc. (New York: Palisades Institute, 1986).

33

constitutive of this way of life that it would be utterly disfigured if they were altogether lacking. Yet it is a key Christian belief that no form of earthly religious life entirely escapes disfigurement. In their palpable imperfections, less exemplary believers point us away from notions of heroism and mastery in religious practice;[2] they draw our gaze instead toward the gracious God who works in and through them. Any excellence in their religious lives is less a matter of dogmatic precision or moral virtuosity than a readiness to repent and a keen awareness of their dependence on God. They point us towards the importance of a theology of grace in understanding practices.[3]

In exemplary cases of discipleship, the coherence of belief and practice is so impressive that it masks the extent to which beliefs and practices underdetermine each other. By contrast, the ordinary struggles of religious people lay bare the ligaments that hold beliefs and practices together. Their struggles reveal how easily these connections become strained and broken when admirable belief fails to nurture admirable practice, or when vibrant practice fails to stimulate vibrant belief. The recurring gaps between beliefs and practices reveal that these two components do not by themselves comprise the religious life, and point us to the significance of the affective dimension of faith. Desires and dispositions play a key role in connecting beliefs and practices.

Religious practices are "an ongoing, shared activity of a community of people."[4] The excellence of particular saintly practitioners can obscure this communal dimension as well; their virtuosity can seem to be primarily a matter of individual gift or initiative.[5] The question of how communal beliefs shape communal practice is a deeply ecclesiological one. It cannot be answered apart from critical discernment about the institutional forms of religious life and their structures of authority and accountability. In this essay I will be assuming what Miroslav Volf has termed a "polycentric" understanding of Christian community, in which religious beliefs and practices emerge and are nurtured within "a communion of interdependent

2. Indeed, the self-perception of "saints" is usually antithetical to these notions as well.

3. Serene Jones and Sarah Coakley's essays explore complementary theologies of grace in relation to practices.

4. Craig Dykstra, *Growing in the Life of Faith: Education and Christian Practices* (Louisville: Westminster/John Knox Press, 1999), p. 48.

5. Though again, this is rarely the saints' internal perception of their lives.

subjects."[6] The beliefs and practices of the laity are at the heart of this understanding of the church. Ecclesiologies that presuppose more asymmetry between ordained and lay Christians will understand the linkage between beliefs and practices differently. But in all ecclesial forms, struggles persist over gaps between beliefs and practices.

To emphasize the centrality of grace, the importance of the affective dimension in linking beliefs and practices, and the communal context of practice, this essay will explore the contours of religious struggles, rather than religious triumphs. The biblical figure of Jonah[7] will orient this exploration, because the scriptural narrative vividly depicts his struggles with the gaps between his religious beliefs and practices. Jonah represents neither exemplary discipleship nor brazen disobedience. He proclaims the God of Israel to be merciful and abounding in steadfast love, yet he struggles to reflect this love and mercy in his practices. His admirable beliefs fail to shape admirable practice. Why is this such a common predicament for people of faith, and what does it tell us about the relationship between beliefs and practices?

Practices and the Question of Truth

I understand God's practices in the world to constitute the normative moment for the Christian life. Christian beliefs and practices are mutually implicated ways of knowing and responding to "God's active presence for the life of the world."[8] The logic of the Christian life is shaped by the shifting interactions between constellations of beliefs and practices. My understanding of the interdependence between beliefs and practices is informed by a critically realist epistemology, in which religious beliefs are beliefs about God, human beings, and the rest of creation. Beliefs presuppose the human possibility of some critical purchase on truth: for example, Jonah's

6. Miroslav Volf, *After Our Likeness: The Church as the Image of the Trinity* (Grand Rapids: Eerdmans, 1998), p. 224.

7. I am assuming that the historical "Jonah son of Amittai" was a prophet to Jeroboam II (2 Kings 14:25) and not a post-exilic figure. Yet the post-exilic story of Jonah, despite its lack of historicity, retains a prophetic function: calling the people of Israel to repentance and reminding them of God's wide mercy to all the peoples of the earth.

8. Dorothy C. Bass, ed., *Practicing Our Faith: A Way of Life for a Searching People* (San Francisco: Jossey-Bass Publishers, 1997), p. 5.

belief in God's indiscriminate mercy involves a truth claim about divine reality. At the same time, this epistemology affirms that all human beliefs are culturally and materially situated and inseparable from practice. Beliefs about God are not pure truths grasped by a Cartesian ego and then "applied" to the messy, ambiguous realm of practice. Religious beliefs are interwoven with a larger set of other beliefs and embedded in particular ways of life. They are couched in the language, conceptuality, and history of a particular people and reflect personal and communal experience and desires. Religious beliefs shape and are shaped by religious practices.

One example of this shaping is the way a community's beliefs become more credible to them as they engage in practices congruent with those beliefs. As Craig Dykstra asserts, by sustained engagement in Christian practices "a community comes to such an immediate experience of the grace and mercy and power of God that the 'nasty suspicion' that . . . theology is really about nothing more than human subjectivity simply loses its power."[9] Belief in God's indiscriminate mercy is rendered more credible by religious practices of mercy. This is even the case for people standing outside the religious community. The startling congruence between the Chambonnais' mercy to strangers and their belief in a merciful God rendered their belief more plausible for non-Christians as well.

Yet no one who has read church history can conclude the truth of Christian belief from the moral superiority of Christian practice. Belief in God's indiscriminate mercy is more credible when accompanied by Christian practices of mercy, but this belief is still true even if Christian communities frequently fail to instantiate it in their practice;[10] in fact, a firm belief in God's prevenient mercy keeps their struggles to practice mercy from succumbing to hypocrisy or despair. The distinction between credibility and truth indicates that the relationship between beliefs and practices is not strictly symmetrical. Christian practice is a response, always inadequate, to merciful divine presence; it does not establish the truth of this presence. Christian practices shape beliefs and may render them more (or less) credible. But they do not in themselves render Christian beliefs true.

Practices shape religious beliefs, but religious beliefs also shape practices. As Kathryn Tanner notes, "religious beliefs are a form of culture, in-

9. Dykstra, *Growing in the Life of Faith*, p. 53.

10. Nor does the genuine mercy to strangers exhibited by non-Christians in itself render their beliefs true.

extricably implicated in the material practices of daily social living on the part of those who hold them." They are an indispensable dimension of coherent human agency: "In the concrete circumstances in which beliefs are lived, . . . actions, attitudes, and interests are likely to be as much infiltrated and informed by the beliefs one holds as beliefs are to be influenced by actions, attitudes, and interests."[11]

This tensive relationship between beliefs and practices means that beliefs influence but are not reducible to certain actions, attitudes, and interests. Belief in God's indiscriminate mercy, for example, is not reducible to "an assertion of psychological fact in metaphorical language," for example, a believer's resolve to adopt a posture of praise toward God and love toward her fellow human beings.[12] Clearly there are strong connections between religious beliefs and resolve about religious practice. Yet, as the case of Jonah demonstrates, belief in divine mercy frequently coexists in religious life with the failure of resolve to be merciful, revealing that this "psychological fact" is not the truth content of this belief. Nor is the believer's assertion of God's mercy simply a self-justifying gesture that masks her own quest for power. The history of Christian thought is littered with examples of self-justifying appeals to religious beliefs. Yet in their role of helping us make sense of the world, beliefs often put up a certain resistance to our current desires and practices, and may at times interrogate or even temporarily disband them. Despite their insights into the political and psychological functions of belief, these reductive approaches correlate beliefs and practices more directly than religious experience warrants, and thus have a hard time accounting for persistent gaps between belief and practice.

The Case of Jonah

Jonah's beliefs and practices exhibit the kind of gaps that religious believers find all too familiar: he holds admirable beliefs, but struggles mightily with how to live them out. Precisely because he is not an exemplary figure,

11. Kathryn Tanner, *The Politics of God: Christian Theologies and Social Justice* (Minneapolis: Fortress Press, 1992), p. 9.
12. R. B. Braithwaite, *An Empiricist's View of the Nature of Religious Belief* (New York: Cambridge University Press, 1955), p. 7.

Jonah's inclusion in the books of the prophets has served as an ongoing source of encouragement to generations of believers who know the same struggles in integrating belief and practice.[13] Jonah's religious beliefs are evident throughout the story. On the ship going to Tarshish, he declares that the God he worships is "the Lord, the God of heaven, who made the sea and the dry land" (Jonah 1:9). From the belly of the great fish he proclaims that "Deliverance belongs to the Lord!" (2:9). In his bitter disappointment over the success of his Nineveh mission, he cries out, "I know that you are a gracious God and merciful, slow to anger and abounding in steadfast love, and ready to relent from punishing" (4:2). Jonah is depicted as having admirable beliefs; his basic orienting convictions regarding divine grace and human dependence on the creative and redemptive agency of God find continuing affirmation among both Jews and Christians. Yet in obvious ways, Jonah's beliefs fail to shape his practice. God summons Jonah to the practice of testimony: proclaiming the truth by word and deed for the edification of all. Jonah's hearers are the Ninevites, long-time enemies of Israel. Their wickedness has come up before God, and Jonah is called to cry out against them. Yet his beliefs about God's grace and mercy do not fund a vibrant practice of testimony — his beliefs and practice lack integrity.

In its focus on the tumultuous career of the title figure, the book of Jonah gives little direct indication of the ongoing, communal nature of practices. We will have occasion later to return to this central feature of religious practices, but for the moment, we will abstract Jonah's practice from its communal setting in order to get better purchase on its deficiencies. In their introduction to *Practicing Our Faith*, Craig Dykstra and Dorothy Bass note that practices are done "together over time in response to and in the light of God's active presence for the life of the world."[14] Jonah is still practicing his faith: he does not simply refuse to testify to his enemies about God's judgment and mercy. The disjunction between his belief in divine graciousness and his practice of testimony is far from complete. Yet

---

13. This is especially clear in the prominence of the story of Jonah in the Jewish liturgy for Yom Kippur, the Day of Atonement. Reading the entire book of Jonah draws the community's attention to the gracious willingness of God to hear their cries for repentance and to use their inadequate expressions of obedience as a conduit for divine presence in the world.

14. Bass, *Practicing Our Faith*, p. 5.

neither is Jonah's practice of testimony done in the full light of God's gracious presence for the life of the world; it would be fairer to say that his testimony is done *in spite of* his belief in God's active, merciful presence. His compliance with God's call to go to Nineveh is reluctant and grudging, because he does not want the community of Nineveh to experience the truth of his belief.

Jonah's testimony to the Ninevites is true, and it brings astoundingly good results. The other prophets in Scripture go to dramatic lengths to get their message across — digging up moldy ropes, holding up baskets of rotten figs, marrying questionable persons — with little result. The anti-prophet Jonah walks only a third of the way across the huge city, shouting "Forty days more, and Nineveh shall be overthrown," and meets with stunning success. The whole city repents — even the livestock. But Jonah's practice of testimony is not excellent, even though he speaks the truth about God's threat of judgment on Nineveh's sin, and Nineveh is edified. True belief and good results are not sufficient conditions for excellent practice. The war between Jonah's beliefs and practices disfigures his actions: he resists any positive connection between his beliefs in God's mercy and compassion and his practice of testimony.

Jonah's beliefs are not inert; they appear to help him make sense of his world in a way that is distinguishable from the (lack of) guidance they give him in his practices. Jonah's belief that God is gracious and merciful involves making a truth claim about a reality outside of himself, namely God. (How he came to hold this belief, and how to decide whether his belief is true are matters we cannot pursue.) It is not simply a metaphor for his own posture of love toward his fellow human beings, as is clear from his overt reluctance to adopt such a posture. If his belief in God's grace and mercy is true, it is true despite his faulty practice. Nor is Jonah's belief that God is merciful and gracious a self-justifying gesture, since it clearly *destabilizes* his own refusal to go to Nineveh. God's concluding rhetorical question to Jonah, "And should I not be concerned about Nineveh, that great city . . . ?," lingers in the air after the book is finished. Jonah's belief in a merciful and gracious God demands an affirmative answer to the question. His religious worldview interrogates his practice of testimony.

On the other hand, Jonah's convictions about God also reinforce and guide his religious practices. For example, since he believes that God answers those that call in distress, he calls out to God from the heart of the seas, and then thanks God for sending the big fish to deliver him. Without this belief about God, Jonah's practice of petitionary prayer is hard to explain. Beliefs are what make practices intentional as opposed to random or reflexive actions. Certain basic beliefs seem prerequisite for practices to form part of a coherent way of life. For example, the author of Hebrews affirms that, "whoever would approach God must believe that he exists and that he rewards those who seek him" (11:6). Even where beliefs in fact fail to reinforce and guide practice, it is often clear how they could do so. Jonah's belief that God is merciful and gracious could have guided a practice of testimony that was vigorous and sincere; given his religious convictions, we could imagine Jonah longing for the repentance of the Ninevites, energetically and creatively proclaiming his message, and rejoicing in God's forgiveness to them.

Instead, Jonah's belief in God's indiscriminate grace and mercy fuels his prophetic disobedience. Upon hearing that God had relented from punishing Nineveh, Jonah wails, "O Lord! Is not this what I said while I was still in my own country? That is why I fled to Tarshish at the beginning" (4:2). Jonah's exemplary theological beliefs shape his willingness, even eagerness, to die. He knows that he cannot finally elude the Maker of the sea and dry land. He knows that God's favor to him, as evidenced by the plant, is not something he can possess or manipulate. He knows that he cannot dissuade God from being gracious to his enemy, the Ninevites. Given all these beliefs, he angrily chooses death as his best option. Though it is possible to overemphasize the determinative power of first-order convictions in the life of faith, they clearly have a role in guiding and warranting practice, whether good or bad.

Community and Critique

The inconsistency of the relation between belief and practice in the story of Jonah raises the issue of communal context: How long and how wide is a practice? Taking communal context into account opens the way for a more sympathetic reading of individual struggles to connect beliefs and practices. If a practice is an intrinsically communal activity, then individual failure in practice may be an aberration and not an indication of systemic corruption. A community that proclaimed and nurtured belief in God's graciousness to all might shape a vibrant communal practice of testimony even if some of its individual members failed to participate in it.

The community's practice may eventually have a reforming influence on recalcitrant individuals, and their willingness to stay in that community may mark an openness to this reformation. If a practice is by definition something done over time, then a particular failure, either individual or communal, may be seen as a temporary setback, not part of an inevitable moral trajectory. A community that failed to embody God's mercy to its enemies during wartime might later repent and seek reconciliation. If both religious belief and practice are intrinsically long-term communal endeavors, gaps between them during certain times or in particular instances do not necessarily call into question the viability of a practice or the strength of a belief. Of course, wide gaps between communal belief and practice can also indicate the moral degeneration of a community. In either case, these gaps call for persistent critical analysis of the relations and misrelations between beliefs and practices, both by those within the community of faith and by those outside it.

The role beliefs play in both challenging and reinforcing our religious practices indicates the importance of ongoing theological reflection, even of relatively stable, long-term beliefs. As David Cunningham notes, "without occasional attempts to devote some sustained thought to the meaning and significance of a particular Christian belief, the practices that embody that belief can become hollow, insignificant, and ultimately unpersuasive — even to those who undertake such practices with diligence and love."[15] Sometimes this reflection is called forth by what Kathryn Tanner in her essay calls the "hitches and glitches in the smooth flow of practice." This kind of theological reflection is often best done by those immersed in the religious practices themselves, whether formally trained or not. There is a distinctive knowledge of a religious tradition that is best constructed within the framework of its ongoing practices. Engagement in these practices, with other people, over time, can give rise to new knowledge and new capacities for perception that are not accessible to phenomenal, descriptive approaches to a religious tradition. Standing sympathetically within the circle of a religious community's self-understanding and figuring out how to move ahead is an appropriate intramural exercise.

15. David S. Cunningham, *These Three Are One: The Practice of Trinitarian Theology* (Malden, MA: Blackwell Publishers, 1998), p. viii. The essays by Kathryn Tanner, Miroslav Volf, and L. Gregory Jones in this present volume examine the work of theology in reflections on beliefs and practices.

Yet theological reflection is also needed precisely when, in Charles Taylor's words, there is "a perfectly stable relation of mutual reinforcement" between beliefs and practices — when the belief reinscribes the practice even as the experience of the practice constantly regenerates the belief.[16] And here the critical scrutiny of those perched on the margins or outside of the religious community may be valuable. The tremendous power of communal and long-term religious beliefs and practices is easily corrupted. A good fit between beliefs and practices is not necessarily an indicator of their truth or goodness, nor is a close fit between beliefs and practices that results from "on the ground" theologizing necessarily more trustworthy than the result of more abstracted theological reflection. The case of the theology of apartheid in South Africa is a disturbing example. White South African Christians originally confronted a gap between their belief that Christians of all races were welcome at one Lord's table and their preference for the practice of separate communion celebrations for whites and blacks; they developed the theology of apartheid to bridge this gap. This theology shaped and reinforced the practice of separate communion by inculcating the belief that this was not a provisional arrangement created on account of the Afrikaners' "weakness," but was in fact God's eternal will for the church. In this case, the original gap between beliefs and practice was a sign of spiritual health.

Even in less extreme cases, a tight fit between beliefs and practices may indicate a spiritual logjam, not admirable religious integrity. Practices can be so strong that they can dominate the conceptual space, leaving no room for critical reflection on beliefs. The influence of the practice of infant baptism on sacramental beliefs and the influence of the practice of marriage on beliefs about human relationships are possible examples. Likewise, beliefs can be so strong that they exert enormous pressure against attempts to develop alternate practices — consider the effect of supersessionist beliefs on Christian-Jewish relations or of traditional eschatological beliefs on Christian evangelism. What seems like consistency may instead be a coerced or unreflective uniformity. While right belief and right practice should fit hand in glove, the tenuous human hold on truth and goodness suggests that the desirable connection between beliefs and practices is one of flexible integrity, not unbending rigidity. Living by

---

16. Charles Taylor, *Sources of the Self: The Making of the Modern Identity* (Cambridge: Harvard University Press, 1989), p. 205.

grace requires an openness to the correction and deepening of both our beliefs and practices.

A religious community's best insight into the possibilities and deformities of its beliefs and practices often comes from the outside.[17] Critical theological reflection is required in order to unmask perennial human tendencies to triumphalism and self-deception, and those within the circle of communal self-understanding may not be sufficiently alert to these tendencies in their midst. While theological reflection is an important intramural activity, it should also be a widely shared task to which the contributions of various disciplines and worldviews are invited.

While critical scrutiny is required both within the community and from the outside, the charge of hypocrisy that might come from such scrutiny should not be leveled too quickly at individuals who affirm communal beliefs while failing to participate in communal practice. God's grace towards believers is instantiated in community; the length and breadth of a practice can carry them as individual practitioners over the inevitable rough spots and dry stretches in their faith, when their beliefs and practices become disconnected. For example, L. Gregory Jones points out that believers can lean on the communal practice of forgiveness by asking others to forgive the enemies they find themselves incapable of forgiving.[18] The communal character of practice can nourish the beliefs of individuals even when they find themselves incapable of participating in the practice directly. They may find their belief in the power and reality of God's forgiveness strengthened by the practice of others, even as they continue to fail miserably in practicing forgiveness themselves. Likewise, their belief in the power of forgiveness can shape the practice of a community, even when their own practice falters. My beliefs shape more than my individual practice alone.

---

17. In this regard, I appreciate Merold Westphal's advice to Christians to read Freud, Marx, and Nietzsche for Lent. That is, to read them not in a defensive, polemical posture, but with a vulnerability and receptivity that allows them to cast light on pretensions and failings of the Christian tradition. See Westphal, *Suspicion and Faith: The Religious Uses of Modern Atheism* (Grand Rapids: Eerdmans, 1993).

18. L. Gregory Jones, *Embodying Forgiveness: A Theological Analysis* (Grand Rapids: Eerdmans, 1995).

Practices of the Heart

At other times, deep and vibrant communal connections between belief and practice can nudge believing individuals toward at least an external correlation between the two. Gabriel Marcel has helpfully distinguished constancy from fidelity in the religious life.[19] When my practices exemplify fidelity, my whole self, including my beliefs, is present in them; there is a vital connection between my deepest sense of the world and how I conduct myself in it. When I am merely constant, my practices exhibit a bare conformity to my beliefs, but I am not "present" in them in the same way. Marcel clearly sees fidelity as morally superior to constancy. Yet constancy and fidelity are not merely opposed; it is possible for constancy to be a part of fidelity, a way of struggling to be present until we are capable once again of a vital connection between our convictions and our practices. Constancy is not exclusively a sign of moral weakness; as Margaret Farley points out, constancy can even represent moral strength — a determination to affirm our links to a practicing community, to practice our faith whether we "feel" present or not. In this case, she notes, "we *are* present in our actions — not just conforming to an ideal of ourselves, or avoiding a sense of guilt, or pretending we are not indifferent."[20] A nursing mother may believe that her baby is a child of God and that she has been given a unique role in demonstrating God's unfailing love to him. But when she is awakened for the fifth time during the night by her baby's hungry cries, her practice of hospitality may exemplify only constancy, not fidelity. Her beliefs have not changed, and her practice is consistent with her beliefs; yet she does not experience full integrity between her beliefs and practices. Nevertheless, her constancy can be considered a sign of moral strength. It reaffirms her maternal relationship, reinforces her religious beliefs about her child, and keeps open the way for future fidelity. Her constancy recognizes the claims that her beliefs make on her, even if she cannot muster the "presence" required for excellent practice.

Perhaps even Jonah's dismal practice of testimony can be seen as an example of constancy. He does not, after all, simply reject God's demand to

19. Gabriel Marcel, *Creative Fidelity,* trans. Robert Rosenthal (New York: Noonday Press, 1964).

20. Margaret A. Farley, *Personal Commitments: Beginning, Keeping, Changing* (New York: Harper & Row, 1986), p. 46.

go to Nineveh; even after his dramatic detour, he does go to Nineveh, and he does testify truthfully. To be sure, his practice exhibits "a kind of inert conformity to the letter of the law."[21] It is hard to tell whether Jonah's constancy in obeying God's command may open the way to fidelity, or whether this constancy has become utterly separated from fidelity, fueling only his resentment and despair. God's question to Jonah at the end of the story leaves the door open. The relationship between beliefs and practices is shifting and dynamic; previous patterns of connecting the two influence, but do not determine, their future interactions.

There is a long Socratic tradition of explaining failures of practice in terms of intellectual deficiency or ignorance. This tradition posits a rather straight line between beliefs and practices, and thus holds out great hope for remedying bad practice. If a person truly sees what is right, she will have what is required for doing the right. Perhaps Jonah's belief in God's indiscriminate mercy is not held strongly enough. Perhaps Jonah holds contrary beliefs that disable his practice of testimony — for example, a belief that the Ninevites are so evil that they have forfeited their share of divine mercy. If Jonah's epistemic house were in order, according to the Socratic view, good practice would follow.

There is no doubt that weakly held or inconsistent beliefs are a barrier to good practice. Though the epistemic capital of a religious community can carry its doubting or theologically disinclined members along for a considerable time, the long-term viability of a community demands efforts at consistency between belief and practice. Yet the Socratic diagnosis of Jonah's religious condition appears to miss the mark. God's commands and questions to Jonah consistently address his attitudes and emotions, not the strength or correctness of his belief. "Is it right for you to be angry?" God asks Jonah twice. "Should I not be concerned about Nineveh?" God's questions imply that the problem with Jonah's practice cannot be solved merely on the level of beliefs.

The problem is not that Jonah fails to believe the right things; he fails to *desire* the right things. As the Augustinian tradition insists, the link between belief and practice is forged by human desire and attitude. Both our cognitive and practical efforts arise out of our loves. Right beliefs are by themselves insufficient in shaping good practice. As Kathryn Tanner points out, "Motivated action banks on an appropriate attitude, a positive

---

21. Farley, *Personal Commitments*, p. 46.

45

evaluative stance, toward an action or its end."[22] This appropriate attitude is what Jonah lacks. His practice is deplorable because he resents the truth of his beliefs. He arguably has true insight into God's nature, but his beliefs are not productive of appropriate attitudes towards God and neighbor. Jonah's spiritual shortcomings are primarily affective, not epistemic.

Of course, beliefs and desires should not be too sharply distinguished. Robert C. Roberts helpfully describes the affective dimension of Christian faith as "a way of seeing." Religious attitudes and emotions are not simply spontaneous reflexes, events that "occur" in consciousness outside the boundaries of human freedom and responsibility. Rather, they are conscious construals of particular situations that provide a link between relatively stable religious beliefs and appropriate practice. The exemplary hospitality of Dorothy Day and the Christians at Le Chambon, for example, is rooted in their capacity to see the needy strangers at their door not as an offensive or dangerous intrusion, but as Christ in their midst. Growing in faith requires the patient cultivation of this capacity for alternative construal.

Roberts's description implies that persons can acquire some degree of cognitive control over their affective responses. In other words, beliefs can shape desires. To succeed in dispelling a negative attitude "I must somehow get myself to cease to see the situation in one set of terms."[23] Reflecting on my long-term beliefs can help; so can acting in contradiction to my original construal of the situation. Through both these means, a nursing mother can attempt to "reframe" her attitude toward her baby's cries, so that she no longer sees them as an unwarranted intrusion on her sleep. But as Roberts notes, "Sometimes that initial construal just seems so right, and so heavily superior to every alternative construal, that no amount of dissonant behavior will change the original construal."[24] Jonah's negative construal of the Ninevites appears impervious to the influence of either his practice of testimony or his beliefs in God's mercy. Ultimately his affective posture may shift his beliefs about divine mercy and his own practice. If beliefs can shape desires, the opposite is also true: desires can shape beliefs, as well as practices.

The story of Jonah echoes the experience of many believers. Religious

22. Tanner, *Politics of God*, p. 13.
23. Robert C. Roberts, *Spirituality and Human Emotion* (Grand Rapids: Eerdmans, 1982), p. 22.
24. Roberts, *Spirituality and Human Emotion*, p. 23.

attitudes and emotions exert enormous resistance against our best efforts at integrity between beliefs and practices. As Margaret Farley asserts, "I do not have anything like total power in respect to my love. I experience myself as fragmented and conflicted, conditioned as well as self-determining, 'swept away' as well as 'self-possessed.'"[25] While we know, at least to some degree, the good practice to which our beliefs about God's love and mercy lead us, we turn away from it. While we know, at least to some degree, the attitudes and emotions consonant with our beliefs, we fail to embody them. Like Jonah, we find ourselves resentful and peevish when we know we should be full of gratitude for God's mercy to us, and full of joy in God's mercy to others. As Charles Williams has described this predicament, human beings now know "good as antagonism."[26]

The ability of religious beliefs to shape practice is hampered by the split believers experience between the desire for righteousness and the willingness to live in unrighteousness. A paradoxical aspect of our predicament is that our second-order affections are typically less antagonistic toward the good than our first-order affections are. As an anonymous Christian confesses,

> O my God I do not love Thee,
> O my God I do not want to love Thee,
> But O my God I do want to want to love Thee.[27]

The disorder of our first-level affections indicates that stronger beliefs and increased moral striving will not remedy the gap between beliefs and practices. Greater human effort, both cognitive and moral, will not resolve the basic antagonism to the good that infects human knowing and doing. The strength of second-order affections promises not so much a solution to the gap between beliefs and practices as a reorientation of them both toward the grace of God and the gifts of a worshiping community.

---

25. Farley, *Personal Commitments*, p. 33.

26. Charles Williams, *He Came Down from Heaven* (London: Faber and Faber, 1950), pp. 21-22. "The contradiction in the nature of man is thus completely established. He knows good, and he knows good as evil" (p. 22).

27. This prayer is frequently but, I believe, mistakenly ascribed to Teresa of Avila. Alvin Plantinga notes the obverse of this same insight: "I often want to do what is wrong; wanting to want to do what is wrong is much less frequent." *Warranted Christian Belief* (New York: Oxford University Press, 2000), p. 211.

A remarkable aspect of the exemplary lives of the saints is how little they are marked by conscious striving for moral mastery or divine approval. Like the puzzled sheep in Jesus' parable in Matthew 25, they have not been preoccupied with impressing the Lord by their good works. Instead the integrity between their beliefs and practices, though inevitably flawed, seems to be grounded in a deep receptivity to God's mysterious presence. In a similar vein, Margaret Farley has advocated a "relaxation of heart," in which we relinquish the straining for perfection that undermines our ability to love. Relaxation of heart encourages the fearlessness to question unexamined beliefs and the melting of our "icy and forbidden reaches" by the warmth of new insight. Relaxation of heart infuses our practices with patient endurance and a trustful "letting go" of our desire for mastery.[28]

Excellence in belief involves the critical self-knowledge that we are often antagonistic towards the good and prone to self-deception. Excellence in practice involves confessing our inability to practice our faith in a consistent way. When belief shapes practice in an excellent way, we celebrate God's grace, not human effort. For us as people of faith who "want to want to love God," the communal settings of proclamation, sacraments, and confession frame our hopes for closing the gap between beliefs and practices. In those settings, we can reaffirm the truth about our dependence on the richness of God's grace. Freed by God's assurance of forgiveness, we can dare to probe the corruptions in our beliefs and practices, and our failures to connect them. Filled with thanksgiving and gratitude, we can pray for a creative and fruitful integrity between our beliefs and practices.

28. Farley, *Personal Commitments*, p. 59.

PRACTICING THEOLOGY, ENGAGING IN MINISTRY

Graced Practices:
Excellence and Freedom
in the Christian Life

SERENE JONES

This past year, I was asked to be a part of the newly designated "Millennial Committee" in my local United Church of Christ congregation. The congregation is located in downtown New Haven and has spent the last decade trying to decide what it means to be a small church in a poor but thriving inner-city environment. The purpose of the Millennial Committee was to design a "structure" for the church we hoped to become — a structure that would faithfully embody our vision of what a Christian community, in this context, should be and do.

In good congregational style, the committee began by talking to everyone. We spent the first three months listening to people's ideas about the church and the next three months envisioning positive responses to both our perceived problems and our hopes. We talked about many things: reinvigorating the children's program, upgrading our stewardship campaign, developing a neighborhood mentoring program, and starting a younger women's spirituality group. We also talked about involving more people on our standing committees, getting members to commit to a weekly, one-day practice of honoring sabbath (not shopping, working, etc.), making the community more aware of our "Open and Affirming" position toward gays and lesbians, and doing parts of the Sunday service in Spanish. Our list of activities was long and ambitious; in fact, looking at it, one could not help but feel that a church capable of doing all these things

51

must be thriving, full of energy, and enlivened by the Spirit. Our recommendations looked good on paper, and we were certain that they would look good in practice as well. With ideas like this, we felt, our church had a wonderful future to look forward to.

When we moved into the third stage of meetings, however, it became clear that our plans were not as good as they had initially seemed. As we began developing strategies for implementing all these ideas, people's faces looked increasingly strained, attendance began to drop, and ideas flowed less freely. At the end of a painfully unproductive meeting, the convener asked a senior member of the committee what she thought about the emerging plans. Lois had sat quietly through the last two meetings, and when everyone now turned to her, she looked a bit surprised by the question. "I'm sorry," she began, "I don't mean to be negative, but when I look at this list I feel . . . so tired."

In the silence that followed, there was a palpable shift in the energy of the room. Several people heaved sighs of recognition and an air of honesty settled upon us. A young woman who works in the city planner's office and has a three-year-old son spoke first. "You know Lois, I am really tired, too. I want to faithfully serve God through the work of this church, but I can't imagine how I am going to do all these things either." She was smiling but had tears in her eyes. Following her, one by one, the rest of the members shared their sense of being overwhelmed and worn out not just by their church commitments, but by the stresses of their daily lives; and they confessed feeling guilty about their lack of enthusiasm for our future plans and projects.

"Is this what it means to be church?" one of the church's newer members finally asked, "believing you should do all these things and then feeling worn out and guilty because you can't? Is this the Good News we celebrate?" While everyone knew that the answer to his question wasn't yes, no one knew quite what to say. It was clear that our collective exhaustion, now that it had been voiced, had precipitated a kind of crisis in our process, and it needed to be addressed. (It was a crisis not unlike the one described by Kathryn Tanner in her discussion of the relation between the breakdown of convention in a community and its corresponding need for explicit theological reflection).[1] The question hung in the air: what were we going to do?

1. See Kathryn Tanner's chapter in this volume. For a fuller discussion of this point, see Kathryn Tanner, *Theories of Culture: A New Agenda for Theology,* Guides to Theological Inquiry (Minneapolis: Fortress Press, 1998).

Fortunately, when we reached this point, the committee did not just forge ahead with its already established agenda and ignore the problem. Instead, we paused, put our committee reports aside, and had a long discussion about how best to proceed. Out of this discussion came the collective decision that what we needed to do was to put our ambitious list of projects on hold for a while and spend some time getting our bearings straight with respect to the "Good News" that drew us together in the first place. We needed time to do what is traditionally referred to as the ongoing work of "catechesis," the work of reflecting on and learning anew what it means for us to be "a people of faith" and how our most basic Christian beliefs about God relate to the various things we do together as a church. We knew that this discernment process would not be easy. We also knew that without this reflection, our plans for church might remain merely paper ideals. As we embarked upon a reflective practice that people of faith have followed for centuries, the practice of theologically exploring the beliefs and practices that constitute our faith, we knew that our future depended upon it.

In the weeks and months that followed, the committee slowly came back to life; members began to smile again and new ideas began to flow as the group meditated upon the substance of our faith and the theological texture of our practices. At the heart of our reflections was an ongoing discussion of a word we frequently used but needed to stop and ponder more carefully: the word "grace." We asked: What does it mean to say that we are saved by "grace" through faith? What are the "grace-filled" benefits of faith that we receive as people who confess the saving power of Christ? And how do these benefits relate to the practical patterns of living that structure our daily lives together? In the language of Christian doctrine, we were asking about the soteriological significance of our practices (a term we never actually used). What is the relation between our salvation and the concrete way we structure our lives? Because we were exploring this question in the context of a church committee, we discussed grace and salvation not only as they pertain to the patterns of living that marked our individual and family lives; we asked as well about the relation between grace and our concrete church practices. The topic of ecclesiology (although we didn't call it that) thus entered our conversations again and again.

Many things were said about the relation between salvation and practices in these discussions. While I cannot trace them all here, I want to highlight two themes that we returned to often, themes that profoundly shifted the way we understood our committee's call to restructure our church's life and the exhaustion that everyone felt in the wake of this call. The two themes to which I refer are justification and sanctification, two terms that traditionally describe what grace accomplishes in the community of faith. (Unlike "soteriology" and "ecclesiology," we actually became used to using these two terms.) It should not be surprising that justification and sanctification played such an important role in our discussions; as a United Church of Christ congregation, our community had been deeply shaped, at the level of both belief and practice, by these two common themes of the Reformed tradition. Although some in our church were more aware than others of the determinative role of the Reformed tradition in our self-understanding, the committee as a whole discovered in its renewed engagement with justification and sanctification that these concepts define — at least at an ideal level — our most basic disposition toward all we do.

The rest of this essay is devoted to the insights about practices, theology, and church life that emerged in our church's discussions. Our pastor and two lay leaders led these discussions; our study involved reading scriptures as well as other traditional Christian texts and contemporary theology. Although the committee was well aware of my position as a professor of systematic theology, I did not "lead" them through this process; instead I enjoyed being an active, though not privileged, member of the discussions. I mention my role here because I do not believe that churches need to have resident seminary professors if they are to have the kinds of discussions we did. An educated pastor, an intellectually energetic community of conversation partners, and access to good resources are all that is needed.

Having said this, I should also say that in contrast to my laid-back role on the committee, in this paper I am clearly wearing the hat of the systematic theologian as I take the committee's insights and use them as the occasion for more explicitly reflecting on the historical and doctrinal roots of the theological themes our discussions raised. More specifically, in these pages I expand upon our committee's conversation by exploring further the themes of justification and sanctification as they relate, in different ways, to both ecclesial and personal understanding of Christian practices. In the first section I introduce these two concepts by describing briefly the broader theological story within which they are located. In this story, I argue, one finds the narrative core of Reformed faith informing a two-sided account of the operation of grace in Christian lives. I then explore different ways in which this twofold understanding of grace informs Christian practices. The doctrine of sanctification provides the convictional ground for understanding the importance of "the excellence of practices"; as sanctified believers, we are empowered to perform, in disciplined beauty, the reality of grace in our midst. Justification complements this understanding of forming grace by stressing "the freedom of practices"; when grace justifies, it sets us free to practice freely and with joy. While all Christian practices must be simultaneously marked by both views of grace, certain practices lean more toward formational "excellence" while others lean more toward "freedom." Maintaining the dynamic interplay between these two is crucial for a healthy community of faith.

The Theological Story of Faith: A Reformed Version

Before I begin explicating the broad theological framework that holds the Reformed tradition's understanding of justification and sanctification, let me begin with a methodological comment about how we approached the task of theological reflection in our Millennial Committee. There are a number of different angles from which a church committee like ours could have chosen to enter into conversation about the character of our faith and its relation to practices. If we had come out of a highly liturgical tradition, we might have begun by reflecting on the theology of our worship, exploring its liturgical logic and the motions of living it suggests. In such a context, reflections on the Eucharist or disciplined prayer might have been appropriate places to start (as in Sarah Coakley's powerful contribution to this volume).[2] Had we been from the Anabaptist tradition, we most likely would have begun not with liturgy but with the ongoing communal practices that mark our daily lives together, choosing to focus on the mundane but richly textured patterns of our living and remaining duly suspicious of unduly doctrinal discussions of faith (as in Gilbert Bond's exciting essay on hospitality, an essay reflecting his own roots in the Church of the Brethren).[3]

Given our committee's roots in the Reformed tradition, it should not be surprising that we chose neither of these routes. We began instead by

2. See Sarah Coakley's chapter in this volume.
3. See Gilbert Bond's chapter in this volume.

turning to what our tradition refers to as "the Word." As a historically Word-centered, confessional community, we began by trying to identify the set of core beliefs that formed the explicitly cognitive content of our faith. To discern this core, we asked ourselves the question: What is the Good News that we come to hear proclaimed each week from the pulpit? Asking this question made it clear that the cognitive content we sought to explicate is a deeply engaged, self-involving, and trusting form of knowledge — the knowledge of faith. By asking it this way, we also demonstrated that our practices include more than just our obvious forms of patterned bodily actions. Asking about faith in the manner that we did meant engaging in a distinctly Reformed "habit of thought." Turning to the Word, we collectively enacted the distinctive pattern of theological thought-practice typical of our tradition.

To explicate this Word, we found it necessary to first tell the broad story of the "Word event" — the event of Jesus Christ coming to dwell in our midst, the story of God with us. It is a story told to us each week in scripture, the hymns, and the sermon, all of which enable us to see how this story remains the ongoing story of our lives. As such, it is a story that not only reaches back through time but also stretches forward into the present and through it to a future for which we wait with hopeful expectation. It is the story of God's gracious relating to creation — the story of grace.

Let me tell the story as it is confessed in the statement of faith we read. The story begins at creation. In the beginning, God creates out of pure love a world that is radically different from God; and in and through this loving act of creation, God determines to love this world freely and unendingly. God does not only choose to love this creation, however; God actively seeks responsive relationship with the human creatures that inhabit this world, that they might know the depth of God's love for them and, in knowing, experience the joy of life abundant in God. God thus calls this world into covenant relationship with the promise: I will be your God; you will be my people.

From the beginning, this call to covenant relationship is marked by two features. First, the love of God for creation is a gift; it originates in God's divine, loving freedom and hence cannot be earned by those to whom it comes. This grace simply is. It comes to us freely as the very condition of our existence. Second, this freely given love is not formless; it has a pattern, a structure, a rhythm to it. It suggests a way of life that we find embodied in the Law and in the incarnate reality of Jesus Christ. Grace thus comes to us as a free gift, which forms and empowers us. This forming grace constitutes the conditions of the covenant: the Law of love. As a covenant people, we are called to accept this grace and to be formed by its reality. To be the church is to be the people who witness to this truth.

This is not the end of the story, however. In the mystery of our freedom, the world that is loved by God and called into covenant relation with God decides to reject that love and to deny that call to relationship. In so doing, the world, for unfathomable reasons, falls into sin. In sin, we live against the love of God that marks our deepest reality. In the midst of this sin, God nonetheless continues to be who God has been eternally, the One who loves us freely. Thus, despite our sin, God continues to seek relationship with us for our own sake, that we might flourish and take joy in this abundant love. The history of Israel and the church bears witness to this continued drama of divine seeking and the struggle of people to respond, sometimes with success, but often with failure.

In the life, death, and resurrection of Jesus Christ, we meet this gracious love face to face, as it were. In Jesus Christ, the incarnate God proclaims to the world that grace indeed takes fleshly form and that it remains a gift so powerfully free that not even the sins of the world can constrain or vanquish it. In him, the entire history of God with us happens. He is both the *freeing* gift and the *form* of grace, a gift with which we continue to struggle, sometimes accepting but often failing to receive that which we already have. In this One, the Word of God is proclaimed: in all our sin and finitude, we remain profoundly and unrelentingly loved by a God who continually forgives us, calls us to life anew, and promises us life abundant, now and in the time of things to come.

Justification and Sanctification: The Twofold Character of Grace

As our committee reflected on what it means for us, as individuals and as a community, to understand our lives as unfolding in the context of this drama of divine grace, we continually returned to the question: How are we concretely "saved by grace" and what does this say about the shape of our daily patterns of living, our collective and individual practices? Although the terms "justification" and "sanctification" were not frequently used by the committee as it struggled to answer this question, we found ourselves again and again thinking about the grace that saves us in two ways, each of which corresponds to one of the Reformed doctrines that go by these names. These doctrines are implied directly by the story of divine grace told above. According to this story, God forgives and frees us by a grace that we cannot merit; we are justified and hence saved by an act of divine love that comes to us as pure gift. Similarly, the grace that frees us is also sanctifying grace, which forms in us a pattern of living that reflects the structure of that freeing love. As two parts of the unified reality of God's love for us, justification and sanctification thus describe the twofold character of the grace that saves. It *frees us* and *forms us*.

In the Reformed tradition, a great deal of doctrinal energy has been spent over the years elaborating the twofold character of this justifying and sanctifying grace. At the heart of many of these discussions is the question: How are justification and sanctification both different from and yet intimately related to one another as parts of an indissoluble whole? As he struggled with this question, John Calvin argued that the two are not related sequentially, as if justification came first and sanctification followed as a secondary moment. He insisted instead that they occur always together as two dimensions of a singular grace. As he states it:

> [T]he sum of the gospel is held to consist in repentance and forgiveness of sins. Any discussion of faith, therefore, that omitted these two topics would be barren and mutilated and well-nigh useless. Now, both repentance [sanctification] and forgiveness of sins [justification] — that is, newness of life and free reconciliation — are conferred on us by Christ, and both are attained by us through faith. As a consequence, reason and order of teaching demand that I begin to discuss both. . . .[4]

He then describes the character of each of these "benefits of faith," as he calls them, using metaphors that suggest that justification and sanctification are simply two ways of imaging — dramatizing, describing — the reality of a unified saving grace. These different images of grace were very helpful to the committee as it struggled with the double challenge of being a church both freed and formed by this grace.

4. John Calvin, *Institutes of the Christian Religion,* ed. John T. McNeill, trans. Ford Lewis Battles (Philadelphia: Westminster Press, 1960), III.3.1, p. 592.

Sanctification: Forming Grace

Calvin begins his discussion of the Christian life by describing what happens when, in faith, a believer is sanctified by grace. The simplest images he uses to describe what happens in this event of grace are "newness of life" and "holiness" — the person is "remade" in Christ. The term "sanctification" itself draws on these images; it translates from the Latin *sanctificatio*, "to be made holy or saint-like [*sanctus*]." As Calvin explains it, this newness of life occurs when one comes to know, in Christ, "the right way" to live.[5] When this happens, Calvin claims that the believer undergoes a process of "mortification and vivification."[6] In Christ, one comes to know God's will for one's life, a will embodied in the Law and in the way of life shown by Jesus Christ. Here the Law refers not only to the Ten Commandments but more broadly to those rules of living that make for "shalom," the flourishing of God's creation. When we grasp this "will," the old person within us dies and a new person is born, a person whose life decisively turns away from sin and toward God and, in so doing, seeks to do God's will. In the language of the broader story of faith told above, sanctification occurs when our eyes are opened to the grace-filled covenant God has made with creation and we seek to live according to its order, the Law. In other words, we seek to live in a Christ-like fashion. According to Calvin, both the *form* of that living (its basic pattern) and the *power to enact* it are gifts of the Spirit.

Another image Calvin uses to depict this dynamic is "regeneration." Like a plant that receives the water, soil, air, and light it needs to grow, when we come to know God's will for our lives, we grow in it and are substantively and materially formed by it, changed and shaped by it. In other words, in faith, God's grace — the form of the holy life — becomes the very stuff of who we are, the water, soil, air, and light of our life. What this image suggests so vividly is the concrete forming power of grace. To know Christ is to live a certain way, to be disciplined into certain patterns of living, to become a person disposed toward certain kinds of actions and thoughts. Although Calvin never uses the explicit language of practices to capture the character of this new material reality, his description comes close to an understanding of practices put forth in this volume. As Doro-

5. Calvin, *Institutes,* III.3.1, p. 593.
6. Calvin, *Institutes,* III.3.5, p. 597.

thy Bass and Craig Dykstra define practices, they are "things that Christian people do together over time in response to and in the light of God's active presence for the life of the world."[7] To translate this into the language of sanctification, practices are the things that Christians do as their lives are conformed to patterns of living that embody God's will, patterns embedded in the Law and manifest in the life of Christ, patterns of holiness — *sanctus*.

Building on Calvin's description, I have found two other images helpful in conceptualizing the way in which sanctifying grace moves in the Christian life, both drawing on more contemporary accounts of how selves are formed and identities constructed. The first is the image of performance. According to the work of theorists such as J. L. Austin and Judith Butler, human beings become certain types of persons by learning to perform the often unconscious but socially constructed scripts of personhood embedded in the language and cultures in which they live.[8] These scripts are not only performed by us; they also have the constitutive power to perform us. When this image is rethought in theological terms, it offers clues about how persons are formed by the sanctifying power of grace. When one is sanctified, one performs and is performed by the script of divine love that comes to us in Jesus Christ, a script mediated to us ecclesially. It is the script of Christian identity, and its patterns of movement and thought are the patterns that comprise the essence of our Christian practices. This script, it is important to note, is not just something that Christians learn to enact. Rather, as the very context within which we become who we are, it is the script of our most fundamental selves. As such, when we perform and are performed by grace, our lives take on the form that we are.

The second image is taken from the work of the French feminist theorist Luce Irigaray, who uses "adornment" to metaphorically describe the activity by which we put on the clothes, behaviors, beliefs, and other elements that define who we are. According to Irigaray, when we adorn ourselves (or when we are adorned by external elements, such as language or culture), we put on the material shapes, forms, textures, colors, and pat-

---

7. Dorothy C. Bass et al., *Practicing Our Faith: A Guide for Conversation, Learning and Growth* (San Francisco: Jossey-Bass, 1999), p. 5.

8. Judith Butler, *Gender Trouble: Feminism and the Subversion of Identity* (New York: Routledge, 1990); J. L. Austin, *How to Do Things with Words*, ed. J. O. Urmson and Marina Sbisía (Cambridge, MA: Harvard University Press, 1978).

terns — the clothes, or even better, the skin — that present to the world who we are in relation to it. This skin, she argues, is not just a superficial covering, as might be suggested by the image of ornamental clothing; rather, the adorning material that sheathes us is the very materiality of who we are. To use Irigaray's term, it is the "envelope that holds us in our becoming."[9] It is the container of our existence. These adorning materials determine not only how others perceive us, but also how we perceive and embody our understanding of our own deepest identity in relation to others. It strikes me that sanctifying grace might well be described in a similar fashion — that is, as a grace that "adorns us." When a person of faith "puts on Christ" (as Paul often reminds us in his epistles), that person wears forms of behavior, beliefs, actions, attitudes, and specific practices that conform that person to Christ. Such a person puts on the law of love, and this gift of grace adorns the self, giving specificity, edge, skinned determinativeness to the self in Christ. When one is sanctified, one is regenerated, formed anew — adorned in the grace of God's redeeming love.

What all these images of sanctification share is their emphasis on the shaping, determinative work of grace in Christian lives. They all point to the fact that "grace matters" — grace renews us in very material, specific, concrete ways. When Calvin developed this concept of sanctifying grace, he rightly saw that implicit in the notion of "forming" grace is the concept of *excellence*. He saw this sanctifying process of conforming to Christ as one in which there is real growth and change; it is a process in which one can slowly get better at following the Law, at performing love, at being adorned with garments appropriate to Christian living. In fact, Calvin argued, one of the central tasks of the Christian life is to increasingly excel at following the Law. While one must always remember that perfection belongs to God alone and that the power to perform is a gift, not an inherent capacity, he insisted that we are called to try to constantly improve our capacity to live according to God's will for our lives. This means that in the Christian life, we go through stages of development in which, we hope, we are constantly improving in our ability to embody God's will for our lives. This perpetual striving for excellence is complex because one needs to make constant judgments about the appropriateness of given performances or adornments to particular contexts, a point well made in both

---

9. Luce Irigaray, *An Ethics of Sexual Difference*, trans. Carolyn Burke and Gillian C. Gill (Ithaca: Cornell Univ. Press, 1993), pp. 72-83, 116-32.

Amy Plantinga Pauw's essay on Jonah and Kathryn Tanner's analysis of the complexity of practices.[10] But even in the midst of making such judgments, one is driven by the faith-filled desire to embrace with ever increasing conviction and skill "the way of life abundant."

Although our church group never actually used images of performance, regeneration, or adornment to describe what we were doing, I believe that at the heart of the Millennial Committee's work were lively convictions about the importance of sanctification in the Christian life. When the committee was given the task of restructuring the life of our church, what were we being called to do if not to give what we believed to be graced form and structure to our corporate practices? As we struggled to determine what it means to be a small church in inner-city New Haven, what were we doing if not trying to make judgments about the appropriateness of our practices to our context? As we constructed lists of projects that we felt were important to our mission, what were we doing if not struggling for a kind of ecclesial excellence? And as we debated and hammered out the patterns of corporate behavior we sought to embrace, what were we doing if not trying to decide how our collective lives might be adorned by grace in the public square we occupy? Mentoring students, gathering women together for prayer, embracing gays and lesbians, learning to read scripture in Spanish, what are these if not patterns of collective, institutionalized action that we believe conform our community to Christ — the form of holiness, the shape of grace?

Anyone familiar with the rigors of Reformed understanding of the Christian life can see in these actions the convictional force that this notion of sanctification exerts on the lives of persons and institutions shaped in this tradition. And the seriousness with which our community took up this task is to be celebrated; the sanctifying work of the Spirit was bearing fruit in our midst. Looking at our committee, one can also see, however, the reason why this understanding of sanctification needs to be immediately complemented by an appreciation for the justifying power of grace. This high calling, this struggle for excellence, this commitment to concretely "mattering" grace in specific forms of Christian living can become an overwhelming burden to people if they forget that God's love for them does not *depend upon* the excellence of their practices. It can become overwhelming if they begin to think that through the excellence of their lives, they are somehow

10. See Amy Plantinga Pauw's and Kathryn Tanner's chapters in this volume.

improving their chances of being saved by God, somehow earning their salvation. When this happens, not only have they begun to misunderstand the character of sanctification, they have completely overlooked the power of sanctification's complement, the doctrine of justification.

A version of this is what happened in our committee. In good congregational form, we had placed so much emphasis on our call to live perfect lives and to be a perfect, loving church in our community that we had begun to be exhausted rather than enlivened by the enterprise. As the young woman on the committee put it, we wanted to be good Christians and do all the things we put on our list, but we realized that we couldn't; since we were finite and broken creatures living in a world profoundly broken by sin, the task was simply too large and our energies too meager. In this context, we needed to have our appreciation for the forming power of grace complemented by the freeing power of grace. We needed to be reminded that we are saved not by works but by grace alone: we needed to hear afresh the Good News embedded in the doctrine of justification in order that we might truly grasp the character of our sanctification.

Justification: Freeing Grace

Having laid out the central features of the regeneration that occurs when one "puts on Christ," Calvin immediately turns to a description of God's justification of the sinner. Referring to the doctrine of justification as "the main hinge upon which religion turns," he defines it "simply as the acceptance with which God receives us into [God's] favor as righteous [persons]. . . . it consists of the remission of sins and the imputation of Christ's righteousness."[11] Elaborating upon this definition, he demonstrates that unlike the imagery of sanctification, which highlights the ways God's grace materially shapes us, justification describes what happens to us when God makes the decision to forgive us and to love us — a decision that makes us righteous before God. In this context, Calvin emphasizes God's fundamental disposition toward God's creatures, a disposition of unconditional acceptance and unceasing forgiveness. Recall the story of grace outlined earlier as a summary of my church's confession. In this narrative, God's justification of God's creatures occurs in God's original decision to create

11. Calvin, *Institutes,* III.11.1, p. 726; and III.11.2, p. 727.

an other whom God determines to love and to whom God promises life abundant. What this story captures well is the radically gratuitous character of that love. The creature does nothing to merit it; God's love simply comes to and defines the creature because God has decided it will.

As with sanctification, theologians in the Reformed tradition have devoted enormous amounts of energy over the years to exploring the implications embedded in this claim that God justifies us freely. Although it is impossible to lay out here the intricacies of their discussions, let me highlight several features of the doctrine that are important to understanding Christian practices. At the heart of the doctrine of justification is the claim that because God decides to love us freely, there is nothing we can do to earn that justification. This means that no degree of excellence in Christian practices has the power to win for us the saving love of God; it can neither be won as if it were a prize nor claimed as if it were a right. That love is a gift, pure and simple, and comes to us quite apart from our own merit. The doctrine of justification reminds us that we do not, in any way, save ourselves. We are saved by grace alone.

Comprehending the full force of the radically unmerited quality of this love is a difficult task for believers, particularly because we live in a world that consistently assesses our worth based on calculated evaluations of what we do and who we are. The power of the doctrine of justification comes in its announcement of God's forthright rejection of such evaluations with respect to God's love for us. God loves us simply because God has decided to do so, not because of who we or others think we are or because of what we do. When one comprehends the force of this unconditional love, one is empowered to develop a certain detachment from worldly evaluations of the self. One begins to see that what one does and who one becomes in the messy unfolding of our daily lives are not finally determinative of who we are in the eyes of God. Ultimately and finally, God has chosen us as beloved, and our salvation rests in that decision and not in the penultimate decisions that constitute the texture of our day-by-day existence. When one realizes that the ultimate truth about one's life rests in this divine decision, one is enabled to develop a more critical posture toward one's socially construed identity and one's constantly enacted practices. Another way of making this point is to say that when we comprehend the power of God's decision for us, the hold of worldly claims upon us is ruptured. Justification breaks that hold by reminding us of the prior hold that grace has upon us.

When we discussed this understanding of justifying grace in our Millennial Committee, we focused on four ramifications it has for our church's understanding of the activities and structures that composed our exhausting list. First, the doctrine of justification relativizes the importance of the numerous programs and projects that appeared on our list. Insofar as we knew ourselves to be justified by grace alone, we had to acknowledge that the practices we sought to perform have dramatically relativized soteriological significance. We began to see more clearly that our church is called to constantly confess that it has been saved by virtue of God's gracious decision to love the church and not because we have done anything to earn, in collective actions or our shared confession, this love. This means admitting that the church's own practices do not save the church, and through them, the church does not save the world — an important reminder to a community of faith like ours which has often estimated its justice-seeking function in the broader community to be of salvific proportions. Further, the doctrine of justification reminded us that the practices of the Christian life not only earn us nothing with respect to grace, but they can also be the occasion of our own inability to know grace if we take them too seriously. For this reason, when we reflected theologically on our practices, we tried to avoid falling into an idolatrous state of mind wherein the things on our list become rarefied commodities that must be preserved and defended at all costs. The doctrine of justification, we found, allows this critical detachment. It releases the church from what can become a "bondage of practices."

The committee found that with this critical, relativized posture toward practices comes a second feature of justification — the positive freedom it affords with respect to the activities of the church. When one comes to know that there is nothing one can do to earn God's love, that one's actions are not constantly evaluated by a divine judge who may at any point punish our failures at excellence with a divine withdrawal of salvation, one is freed to engage life with greater vigor. In classical Reformed terms, one is freed to practice boldly. When the burden of perfection is lifted from the shoulders of the Christian life, the motions of Christian living are allowed to be more expansive and risky in scope. This means that we, as a church, have been given divine permission to creatively imagine what we might be and do as a community of faith in an inner-city context.

It is important to note, however, that this freedom to practice boldly was not interpreted by the committee as permission to simply do anything it pleased, or even more importantly, not to do anything at all (our own version of antinomianism). We saw that according to the doctrine of justification, the works that constitute the Christian life — the graced performances that we do, the adornments of faith that we wear — do not cease to matter entirely. Rather, their importance is resituated; they are understood as joyous, celebratory gestures and not as meritorious, salvation-earning duties. When one accepts the fact that one does not have to earn the love of God, one cannot help but turn and offer praise and thanksgiving to the God who has bestowed this love. Further, in praising God, one desires to please God, not so that God might bestow more grace but rather that one might delight the God who has given this gift of life abundant. Similarly, one cannot help but spontaneously proclaim to the world the glory of this love; one desires to witness to others concerning this love that has embraced the totality of one's existence. Most importantly, in this posture of thanksgiving, joy, delight, and witness, one cannot help but seek to conform one's life to the will of the One who so loves. To use the classical language of Reformed thought, one's life unfolds in patterns of action that "bear the fruits of justification." It is at this point that one begins to see, theologically, how the doctrine of sanctification is folded deeply into the logic of grace's justifying power. This is the third feature of justification's relation to practices. When one comes to know the *freedom* that grace affords, one cannot help but take up a posture of thanksgiving that allows the *form* that grace offers to take hold.

It is not hard to see how this understanding of the sanctified fruits of justification directly related to the work of our committee. When we began truly to grasp the depth of God's love for the world and the freedom that is given to us in that love, we not only felt the burden of our list lifted from our shoulders, we simultaneously came to see our list as a joyous response to the love that so freed us. We came to see our plans for the future of the church as plans that bore witness to the gracious embrace with which God holds us. As such, our plans shifted from being a list of ways we might save the world to a list of the ways we were witnessing to and celebrating the reality that God saves the world. Our relativized practices were subsequently reinvigorated by the very grace that rendered them unnecessary. As one member put it, "When we begin to see that what we do as a church doesn't matter ultimately, we are freed to see how very much our practices do matter." They are the adornments we wear to the celebratory party of faith — the party that glories in our unending life abundant in God.

This brings me to a fourth and final dimension of justification's relation to Christian practices. As just stated, our committee came to see anew that a freed church is a church that is always performing not to earn salvation but joyously to tell the world about the depth of divine love that marks it. This means concretely, for us, that when the church engages in practices that seek to witness to the world of God's grace, it is free to reflect realistically on the practical effectiveness and contextual appropriateness of its witness. It is free to make pragmatic judgments about whether its witness is doing what it is supposed to do: praising God and telling others about the Good News. This means that if we want to determine whether this witness is effective or fitting, we need to look at the ways in which our audience receives the witness. How do the people for whom these practices are performed interpret our witness? How do they read our practices? The justified, witnessing church does not privately own its evaluative criteria; its worldly audience has a real evaluative claim on it — be it an audience of friends or strangers. The way in which the world makes sense of our practices thus matters enormously but, it must be remembered, not ultimately. In this sense, practices in the justified church are soteriologically expendable; hence, in their function as witness, practices are freed to be pragmatically crafted according to the discursive effects they yield.

This point had important implications for how our Millennial Committee evaluated our list of projects. In considering the character of the celebratory witness that we felt compelled, in joy, to offer the world, we needed to reflect upon the character of the broader community in which we witness. What is the culture of the city in which our practices are performed as witness? If it is the grace of God to which we witness, how might the patterned motions of our living reflect this in a manner that others can recognize? Here, the committee found it important to acknowledge the degree to which our practices do not exist in isolation from other cultural frames of reference and patterns of living, and that they subsequently negotiate complex and constantly shifting relations of power. For this reason, one and the same practice can witness to dramatically different realities depending upon the power relations and cultural codes that mark the context of its performance. We saw, therefore, that as a witnessing community of faith, we needed to make careful pragmatic decisions about the character of our church's performance in the broader community. This means, for instance, that even though we may have considered a mentoring program to be a practice wherein hospitality, honoring the body, and stewardship all coincide, we need to be aware that if those being mentored perceive it differently — as imperialistic or demeaning — it must be critically re-evaluated.[12]

The Interrelated Nature of Sanctification and Justification and Its Significance for Practices

Thus far in this discussion of sanctification and justification I have focused primarily on the differences between these two manifestations of grace in the Christian life and how they affect our understanding of the many practices that constitute that life. In spite of those differences, however, I should mention again that Calvin insisted that the two are part of an *indissoluble* whole. Recall that for Calvin, these two descriptions of grace should ideally be spoken simultaneously; neither should precede or follow the other in order of importance or stature, lest believers fail to grasp the two-fold character of the grace that holds them. When sanctification is given priority over justification, we lean toward Pelagian "works righteousness" — the exhausted committee syndrome; when justification is given priority over sanctification, we lean toward antinomian carelessness — the "anything goes" syndrome. When both exist in simultaneous fullness, we lean in neither direction but stand upright, supported equally by both as the benefits of life abundant in Christ embrace us.

As the committee struggled with the interconnected character of these two descriptions of grace, we were most interested in the question: How do the interconnections between justification and sanctification influence our understanding of Christian practices? Or, as we engage in the many practices involved in our committee's list of projects — practices of welcoming strangers, honoring the body, discerning the Spirit, forgiveness, healing, and keeping sabbath — how do our basic convictions about grace's justifying and sanctifying power affect these practices themselves? While there are no doubt a number of different ways we could have approached such questions, the group focused on how the doctrines of sanctification and justification gave us *a distinctive orientation toward all our practices.* We affirmed that in every practice, *both these views of grace should ideally mark our basic disposition toward what we are doing.* To-

12. See Nancy Bedford's chapter on discernment in this volume.

gether they should serve to dispose us to practice our faith in a manner that both seeks excellence and celebrates freedom.

To grasp the complexity of this distinctive disposition toward practices as a whole, let us look briefly at the intricate way sanctification and justification are bound together in faith, how each serves to situate the other. First, as noted earlier, it is clear from the doctrine of justification that Christian practices must never be understood as "saving practices." Thus justification relativizes the drive toward excellence trumpeted by sanctification. The unmerited-gift nature of grace thus constrains all claims about perfected forms of Christian living. Justification can thus be said to precede sanctification, or to be the ground out of which it grows. Second, central to justification's understanding of grace is the realization that the works that sanctification honors are not to be simply dismissed as unnecessary. Rather, when one recognizes the power of God's justifying love, one cannot help but celebrate that reality by forming one's life in the image of the One who has so freely loved. Hence, knowledge of our justification leads to a celebratory posture that manifests itself in practices that conform to the will of God. In this regard, justification requires sanctification as the substance of justifying grace's promise.

If these first two comments about the interconnections between justification and sanctification make the former seem to precede the latter, a third aspect of this relation presents a different picture. If the concept of sanctification describes the process whereby grace transforms the life of the believer in material, substantive ways, then it also describes the process whereby one comes to know oneself as justified. To grasp this point, recall my description of sanctification as a process whereby a person is formed (through the practices of the church) into a distinctive mode of being. One may see sanctification as a process in which one learns to perform (and to be performed by) an identity script that has as its central feature the claim that "God's love comes to us as a free gift." When stated this way, it becomes clear that the ecclesial formation of sanctification has as its most central feature the identity claim "you are justified." The same point can be made using the image of adornment. In this scenario, sanctification is the process whereby we "put on Christ's forgiveness and mercy" as the skin, the envelope, the containing form within which the specificity of our existence is determined; this specificity is marked profoundly by God's justifying love for us. In other words, when one "puts on Christ" (when one is sanctified), one is adorned in the freedom that Christ gives us (the reality of justification). In this context, sanctification is thus seen not only to follow justification but also to precede it as the condition in which the reality of justification takes hold in one's life. Again, the interconnections between the two forms of grace come vividly into view.

Adorned in freedom: this strikes me as a wonderful description of the basic posture Christians are called to take toward the practices that constitute the substance of their living. It describes well the fundamental disposition we must take toward all we do; it captures the dynamic set of beliefs about grace that ground the many ways we practice that grace in our daily lives. I suggested this image in one of my few "teaching" interventions into our committee's conversations, and the others seemed to find it helpful not only because it grasped the interconnected complexity of the issues they had been struggling with, but also because it expressed something of the aesthetic quality of our enterprise. To see the church as a community adorned in freedom was to see it — in quite visual ways — as a community that embodies a very particular kind of beauty, a beauty in which form exists to serve openness and openness is worn as the contour of form. To see the church in this manner is to imagine it as a community in which there is both constant striving for excellence of form and continued realization that excellence of grace cannot be earned, only received as a gift. In this sense, the church is a community of the beautiful in which the patterns of Christian living — the many practices we do and are — both matter not and matter enormously.

Excellence and Freedom in Practice

Up to this point, my comments about the interconnections between justification and sanctification have consisted of rather grand statements about what it means for the church to understand its practices in a manner that emphasizes both excellence and freedom. When the committee pondered these matters, however, they were concerned with the details beyond the grand statements. Let me conclude this discussion of the double character of grace by suggesting two different ways in which justification and sanctification help us think about specific practices.

First, as I mentioned above, this disposition of both seeking excellence and celebrating freedom is a disposition that in its double character should ideally be applied to every practice. Every practice we engage in should be done with an attitude of both strenuous seriousness and relaxed joy. To see how this applies concretely, let us look at several of the activities on our committee's list. Take our plan to develop a women's spirituality group that might speak to the lives of some of the women who had recently joined the community. Implicit in our conception of this project were a number of practices described in *Practicing Our Faith*. We wanted to help these overworked, stressed-out women find a place to rest and be nurtured in our community — practices of sabbath; we wanted a place that felt safe from the oppressive dynamics that often accompany being women in today's world — practices of honoring the body; we wanted a context where those who had felt marginalized by practices of the church might feel welcomed and cared for — practices of hospitality; we wanted a group where women might receive from others nourishing advice on how to manage faithfully the complexities of their lives — practices of discernment and of saying yes and saying no; and the list went on.

When one of the pastors began describing how she might run such a group, it was clear from the outset that this was not something that would happen easily; it would take careful planning and attention to detail. For the working women in the church to attend, it would have to meet on a weekday night; for mothers to come, we would need childcare. For the space we met in to facilitate a sense of comfort and safety, we would need a room that is relatively private; and within that space, we would need a small altar with candles to invoke the prayerful, worshiping character of our gathering. The pastor had to decide how to start each meeting: with prayer or with a loosely constructed "check-in" time? And she needed help thinking about what her tasks as leader might include: Would she lead each session with a meditation or would we change leaders every week, or would we perhaps decide that the meetings should be formally structured as "unstructured"? Again, the list of issues she had to attend to went on and on, as did a number of other significant decisions she felt the women needed to make about the purpose of such a group.

I list the various things the pastor had to think about because I believe they embody, in the instance of this one project, the dynamics of grace emphasized in the doctrine of sanctification. What she was doing was attending carefully to the form of our meeting, its material shape and texture. She was attending to the clothes that this meeting would need to wear if it were to be appropriately adorned for the task at hand. She was trying to figure out a whole set of material dynamics that she believed were necessary for this group to be faithful in its performance of Christian living.

71

Further, she was attending to these things because, in the practical wisdom she had gained from years of working with women in the church, she knew that certain patterns of action would be more or less effective in transforming the lives of the women who came. We could thus see in the care she brought to this enterprise that striving for "excellence of practice" was central to her work and the future of the group.

Yet at the same time that she described all the challenges that attended creating and sustaining such a group, she also remained keenly aware of the underlying reality of justifying grace. She knew that the reason for having such a group is not to "save" these women. Their salvation, we were certain, was already accomplished in Jesus Christ; they were already held in the embrace of God and therefore did not need this group to somehow better merit God's love. Our pastor knew that the reason for gathering is to celebrate the Good News of God's grace in the midst of these women's lives, not to earn it. As she described it, there was great freedom in this. It meant that even if the group were to fail, God's love would not. For this reason, she could take risks in her leadership; she could be bolder in her interactions with various women as well as in her deliberations about room spaces and meeting times. Held in the grip of justifying grace, both she and the group would thus come to know the abundant life that flows from practices adorned in freedom.

I use this example because it vividly illustrates how both justification and sanctification can dispose one to look at a particular set of practices or a specific project. However, there is also another, slightly different way to think about the relation between these two and the logic of practices. As the committee contemplated the various projects we had envisioned (and the numerous practices included in each), we came to see not only that each project needed to be considered in terms of both excellence and freedom; we also saw that some of our projects embodied dynamics that leaned more toward the sanctifying character of grace and others more toward justification. This meant that in addition to seeing each practice as forming and freed, we needed to make sure that when all our projects were combined, there was a balance between those that emphasized formation and those that emphasized freedom.

To illustrate this briefly, recall our list of projects. On this list were a number of activities whose principal purpose was Christian formation, such as our children's education program and the women's spirituality group. Both of these projects take seriously the ways in which the Christian community serves as the place in which we learn to perform and be performed by grace. Both of these activities aim at adorning people with the garments of faith. There were also activities that aimed at pulling the church out of an exclusively internal focus and extending its work into the community it inhabits, practices that drive toward enactments of our freedom. Here I think of the community mentoring program, our decision to become a congregation officially "open and affirming" of lesbians and gays, and our decision to read parts of our liturgy in Spanish. As we considered each of these projects, we had to struggle against more traditional conceptions of our church's identity; we had to avoid setting in stone our previously formed identity in order to preserve the most fundamental characteristics of that identity, and in so doing we found strength in the freedom our justification afforded us.

Having made these distinctions, it is important to note immediately that the differences between these projects are much more blurry than may first appear. Each of these activities contain strong elements of both aspects of grace. For example, in pulling together the children's program and in forming the women's spirituality group — both of which aim at Christian formation — we had to struggle against previous conceptions of what such activities involve. We had to be creative and bold in our assessments of what was needed. Similarly, the mentoring program we wanted to start is itself a project that takes formation seriously. To help young children learn to read is to form them in a particular way, and to be involved in such an enterprise means that those who mentor are themselves transformed, reformed, and re-performed by their interactions with students. Likewise, as we began to speak Spanish in worship and to enact in our liturgy our gay-friendly policy, we weren't just being open to new ways of doing things; we were being reformed to new modes of being. The freedom afforded by justifying grace was reshaping the specific contours of the power of sanctifying grace in our midst. In this way, the dynamic play of adornment and freedom moved back and forth in all our projects.

Methodological Remarks on the Relation between Doctrines and Practices

Having delved into the world of Reformed ecclesiology and the doctrines of justification and sanctification, let me step back and offer a few clarifying comments about my understanding of what doctrines are and how, in general, they relate to practices. I turn to this topic (and the general theme of this volume) at the *end* of this essay because I believe methodological reflections are more useful when they have as their subject matter not a set of abstract claims about theological hypotheticals but rather a concrete set of substantive theological claims. As the reader will no doubt have noticed, when I use the term "doctrines," I refer to the historical loci that traditionally order Christian systematic reflection on the content of faith. These doctrines, I believe, are not only propositional statements affirmed as true in faith; more broadly, these doctrines function as conceptual arenas within which Christian identity is shaped and the contours of the Christian life are formed. To describe the nature of these arenas, I have found two images helpful, both of which have been alluded to in earlier comments: the images of doctrine as lived imaginative landscape and as drama.

As lived imaginative landscapes, doctrines serve as the conceptual territory within which Christians stand to get their conceptual bearings on the world and the reality of God therein. In this sense, doctrines are imaginative spaces that we occupy — we inhabit them and learn to negotiate the complexities of our living through them. The term "imaginative" functions to describe the role doctrines play in structuring the conceptual terrain of our thought and action. Saying these are imaginative landscapes does not imply, therefore, that the referents of doctrine are either fictitious or ideal. For Christians, these doctrines are believed to be true; in fact, they give us the "truest" account of reality. They are not, however, walled off from other imaginative constructs. Their borders are permeable. Yet within these borders, distinctive theological landmarks can be found, such as those that comprise the theological narrative in section one of this essay — claims like "God is the creator of the universe and wills to be in covenant relation with humanity, humanity has turned from God in sin, and God sent Jesus Christ into the world to redeem humanity from sin and promises the world forgiveness of sins and life eternal." These landmarks have a sturdy, resilient quality about them — they are truths we bump up against in the world of doctrine. They have an objective, non-negotiable character. However, as features of lived imaginative landscapes, they demarcate the interpretive field through which we view the world and ourselves and are not merely "truth claims" whose objective factuality demands our assent.

Doctrines are also "dramatic scripts" which Christians perform and by which they are performed, as I suggested in the section on sanctification. I like this second image because it captures (in a way that the landscape image does not) the person-shaping character of doctrine. When a Christian finds herself positioned in the landscape of doctrine, she does not stand there speechless and motionless. Rather, this landscape becomes the context within which her living unfolds. With doctrine as script, this unfolding occurs according to ruled patterns of thought and action. In this context, doctrines provide a scripted code for the motions of a Christian's life in much the same way that broader cultural codes and linguistic patterns structure the self she is always becoming. In the context of doctrine, these ruled patterns of performance craft the character not only of individuals but of entire communities as well, from the intellective dimension of living to the grammatical formation of such things as emotions and the gestural language of the body.

How might Christian practices be understood in light of this account of doctrine? Let me mention what I consider to be several important features of the relation between practices and doctrine. First, when doctrines are viewed as lived imaginative landscapes and dramatic scripts, the importance of practice within the world of doctrine becomes clear. Based on my account, it is impossible to conceive of doctrines apart from their relation to patterned forms of practice because, as territory and drama, doctrines are always occupied by and authoring the motions of those who live within them. For example, it is hard to imagine how one could conceive of the doctrine of providence without imaginatively construing a landscape wherein God's sovereignty is spatial and the character of human response to this sovereignty is dramatically scripted. In such a context, practices are an indigenous component of the doctrine itself, and not just something that one does after the fact of doctrinal assent. Another way of putting it is to say that doctrines "practice" us: Practices are not just things we do in light of doctrine; practices are what we become as we are set in motion in the space of doctrine.

Second, this understanding of doctrine highlights the relationship that exists between the imaginative intention of the person or community engaging in a practice and the visible grammar of the practice itself. Take the practice of hospitality (as Christine Pohl has eloquently described it): at one level, people can practice hospitality without being Christian and can do so in a manner that, at least in terms of the external character of action, appears to be identical to Christian practice.[13] What makes this same practice a practice of faith is the intent of the practicing subject. If one understands the patterned actions of hospitality to be caught up in the economy of God's gracious relating to the world, then the practice can be rightly called a "Christian" practice, even though it may appear no different from the hospitality offered by, say, a Buddhist. In other words, it matters what I think I am doing (what I believe) when I engage in a practice because believing is what makes it a practice of faith as opposed to another kind of practice. In this regard, practices, if they are Christian, can never be evaluated in isolation from the "lived imaginative landscape" that constructs the practitioner's intentions. Practices are thus dependent upon belief.

Third, the converse is also true: beliefs are often determined by (and therefore don't simply determine) the specificity of the practices that live within and through them. In the context of a Christian community, the self who is shaped in the space of doctrine is often a self who has already, at the level of daily practices, engaged in a form of living that makes one's subsequent knowing of doctrine possible. Similarly, it is often through practices that the self is structured in ways reaching beyond the ideational character of beliefs. Practices play a role in writing the unconscious and in ordering the non-conscious ways in which the body "knows"; and these, in turn, directly inform how we imagine the specifics of the doctrinal landscapes we occupy.

Two final comments about the relationship between beliefs and practices. First, both the doctrinal landscapes of faith and the performative dramas that unfold within them (through the logic of practices) do not exist in isolation but are constantly intersecting with and being remade through the multiple landscapes and dramas of selfhood and community that course through our varied cultures and structure the diverse contexts of our living. For this reason, it is hard to attribute a stable content to either. Second, beliefs and practices are spaces wherein relations of power are constantly being negotiated. At times, a specific doctrine may internally commend a model for negotiating these relations; at other times, a practice may have a strong rationale for a particular power relation internal to its own logic. For the most part, however, only in the interplay of

---

13. Christine D. Pohl, *Making Room: Recovering Hospitality as a Christian Tradition* (Grand Rapids: Eerdmans, 1999).

doctrines and practices can one determine the appropriate handling of power relations. And it is this interplay, finally, that must direct both our individual and our collective efforts to generate ever-new practices that share God's grace, God's form and freedom, with the world.

Deepening Practices:
Perspectives from Ascetical
and Mystical Theology

SARAH COAKLEY

In this chapter I would like to suggest some ways in which we can complexify our notion of Christian practices in order to do justice to the variety of different ways in which beliefs and practices are entangled with one another. My intention is to show that the richly coded term "practice" may be used with a number of discernibly different evocations in the religious sphere; and also that the logical relation of beliefs and practices may shift in different circumstances and in different stages of a Christian person's growth to spiritual maturity. Thus it is a vital part of this argument that the "deepening" of practices, so described, allows forms of belief to emerge that could not otherwise be accessed. It is with these complexities in the relation of beliefs and practices that this chapter will be concerned.

As Kathryn Tanner's chapter mentions, the word "practice" has become very much in vogue in philosophy, ethics, and anthropology of late,[1] and thus it is tempting to use it as a kind of methodological mantra, a concept arguably now acquiring explicative overload. But this undiscriminating use of the term may flatten distinctions that frankly need to be made theologically. Reformed theology has rightly stressed the "gift" element of

1. See Kathryn Tanner's chapter in this volume, note 1.

all practices flowing from the reception of grace at baptism,[2] and on this fundamental point Catholic theology concurs. But the Reformed insistence that Christian practices must always be read paradoxically and simultaneously using both the narrative of (unmerited) justification and the narrative of (responsive) sanctification[3] may actually iron out certain important complexities with which pre-Reformation Catholic theology struggled mightily, focusing as it did on the technical intricacies and distinctions of different manifestations of grace — "actual" and "habitual," "operative" and "cooperative" — and thus on the ways in which human responsiveness to the divine could have different shades or depths through a lifetime of graced interaction with divine love.[4]

In what follows I shall be exploring some of these different shades within the spectrum of Christian practices through the lens of traditions of ascetical theology, in both East and West. I shall be suggesting that Christian practices of at least three different sorts (roughly corresponding to the classical distinctions between the "purgative," "illuminative," and "unitive" ways) may be distinguished, and that they could be said to relate to three different levels of spiritual engagement. A disjunctive understanding of these levels, however, must be avoided at all costs: while the distinction between levels has important heuristic value, in the messy reality of life the levels may not clearly supersede one another but blend into a continuous whole. Moreover, as we shall see, the practices of earlier stages are never discarded but taken on, and taken for granted, in what follows. Only at the third level described, however, do deepened theological insights (re-minted beliefs) arise that are available only through prolonged engagement in practices — insights, that is, that could have been gained by no merely intellectual shortcut, however brilliant. These practices (supremely the practice of "infused contemplation") are the effects of a life of multiple forms of faithfulness, forging the participants by degrees into "the image of his Son" (see Rom. 8:29). Here the apparent extrinsicism of earlier forms of *imitatio Christi* gives way to a more explicit and conscious participation in that life.

---

2. This is especially underscored in Dorothy Bass and Craig Dykstra's chapter in this volume.

3. See John Calvin, *Institutes of the Christian Religion*, Book III.

4. An approachable account of a number of vying late-medieval theologies of grace is given in Alister E. McGrath, *Justitia Dei: A History of the Christian Doctrine of Justification* (Cambridge: Cambridge University Press, 1986), vol. 1, ch. 4.

But it is at this third level, I suggest, that even the skeptical outsider would be forced to acknowledge that the ostensibly bland term "practice" must give place to an overt theology of grace. And once this is realized, the question inevitably arises, retroactively, whether grace was not propelling the engagement in practices all along — a view readily asserted by the "orthodox" believer, of course (especially the Reformed one), but often far from manifest to the observer (or even initially, perhaps, to the believer herself). In short, there is a subtle sliding scale here: one starts from practices one might be tempted to regard as entirely self-propelled; but they are joined over time by practices that involve deeper and more demanding levels of response to divine grace and that uncover by degrees the implications of our fundamental reliance on that grace as initiated in baptism. In short, Christian practices do not happen on a flat plane. Since my examples in this chapter will largely be taken from the history of Christian monastic and ascetical theology, it will be instructive to compare this material with the emphasis on the Reformed doctrine of "sanctification" in other parts of this volume. We may ask in closing whether the implied theology of grace need necessarily diverge in the two cases, and if so, how.

If we return for a moment to a much-quoted definition of "practice" enunciated by Alasdair MacIntyre in *After Virtue*, we shall be able to make this point about the paradox of grace and "practice" a little more explicit. MacIntyre defines "practice" specifically in terms of "socially established" *human* projects: it is "cooperative *human* activity" resulting in an extension of "*human* powers to achieve excellence" and "*human* conceptions of the ends and goods involved" (emphasis mine).[5] If we were to go straight from this definition to an examination of distinctive Christian practices, we would run the risk of embracing an implicitly Pelagian understanding of the undertakings involved, or at least an account that sidelines a theology of divine interaction or cooperative grace. In order to offset this tendency, we shall here chart the progression from a level of practice that actively (and even aggressively) demarcates itself from non-Christian alternatives, through to the apparently passive practice of contemplation, in which an ostensibly time-wasting attentiveness is claimed to be the unimpeded receptacle of infused grace; and we shall attempt to explicate how an unfolding response to grace propels the whole. The stereotypical gender

5. Alasdair MacIntyre, *After Virtue* (Notre Dame: University of Notre Dame Press, 1981), p. 175.

evocations of these two poles should also not escape our notice: the unexpected power of the apparent "powerlessness" of contemplation is one that female writers in the contemplative tradition have drawn attention to, often with profoundly subversive effects; yet there is still the danger of trivializing their undertakings as mere feminine submissiveness. We shall return to this point a little later, for the question of the changing gender associations of these different levels is a highly revealing one for our theological task.

But how can the spectrum of cooperative grace-through-practices be given fresh attractiveness for today? Its modes of expression may seem arcane or elitist; it may smack of "works righteousness," or appear relevant only to "professional" vowed religious. In order to counter these objections at the outset we shall first look at a contemporary, humdrum example of this spectrum of beliefs and practices in operation. Then we shall turn back to more ancient traditions of ascetical theology for illumination.

"The Deep End"

The Anglican theologian W. H. Vanstone, who recently died, once likened the church (he had the Church of England in mind, of course) to a "swimming pool in which all the noise comes from the shallow end."[6] I think this ostensibly flippant remark bears some reflection: how much academic theology, and how much posturing in ecclesiastical politics, "comes from the shallow end"? What defensive practices are characteristic of that shallow end, and what are the signs that something different and more profound is occurring? And how much patient faithfulness, how much costly formation, how much waiting on the divine, are required of those who hope to enunciate beliefs "from the deep end"?

Vanstone's life is a good case for reflection on this point: he had a brilliant undergraduate and graduate career, but chose thereafter to labor entirely unnoticed for decades in a dreary housing-estate parish in Rochdale; here was his "practice" for most of his career. The parish was not in the sort of housing estate where there was great physical poverty (although it was the desperation and hunger of the Great Depression that had origi-

6. Much of the information here provided on Vanstone's life comes from his obituary in *The Daily Telegraph*, March 15, 1999.

nally elicited Vanstone's boyhood vocation to the priesthood), but rather a suburban development that manifested the more devastating spiritual poverty of a world "come of age" — without roots, traditions, or obvious hungers of the soul. Vanstone struggled on, and his parish grew from small beginnings. He spent a good deal of time simply walking around the streets of his parish and talking to passers-by. Otherwise he was visiting parishioners at home or was in church saying his office. He baptized, married, and buried people; on Sundays he broke bread with his congregation in the Eucharist. These were his repetitive, faithful practices as a priest. But it was a period of depression for him, and it was not obvious at the time that many of his efforts were bearing fruit. During this phase of his career he was repeatedly offered attractive academic positions, but he turned them all down; and when he was made an honorary canon of Manchester Cathedral, he never mentioned it to his flock (they continued to call him simply "Mr. Vanstone").

Late in life, however, after his first major heart attack, he wrote three short monographs into which he poured the condensed theological wisdom gleaned from his practices in the parish. The first, *Love's Endeavour, Love's Expense,*[7] a meditation on his work in the housing estate and its many difficulties, is about the costliness of love (the costliness of Christian practice, we might say) when it meets no apparent response. The Christian vision of love is held up before the gaze of secular indifference and goes unrecognized: "Hidden is love's agony, Love's endeavour, love's expense." The second book (not insignificantly for our theme, for it underscores that not all practices are physically active) is entitled *The Stature of Waiting.*[8] It is about the progressive, albeit slow, identification of the self with the "handing over" of Christ to his death that is so distinctive a mark of the passion narratives. The third, *Farewell in Christ,*[9] written not very long before Vanstone's own death, charts his acceptance of his own mortality, but is otherwise largely given over to an extended exposition of a Christic theology of grace.

7. W. H. Vanstone, *Love's Endeavour, Love's Expense* (London: Darton, Longman and Todd, 1977), published in the United States as *The Risk of Love* (New York: Oxford University Press, 1978).

8. W. H. Vanstone, *The Stature of Waiting* (London: Darton, Longman and Todd, 1982).

9. W. H. Vanstone, *Farewell in Christ* (London: Darton, Longman and Todd, 1997).

These were Vanstone's contributions to "theology from the deep end." He chose not to write them at all until he was ready to express them from that vantage point. In them, the most acute attention to the mundane (but sometimes tragic and sometimes glorious) stuff of parishioners' lives is elicited from his own unwavering disciplines of scriptural meditation, sacramental observance, and pastoral care (disciplines which he discreetly guarded at a time when their very usefulness was being radically called into question in the church at large). But at the deep heart of the exposition, as expressed in *The Stature of Waiting*, is the insistence on the unitive (and Christlike) "handing over" of the self. It is this contemplative heart that is seen, at the end of Vanstone's career, to have been beating through it all along, but to have come to full conscious appropriation only after years of painfully purgative faithfulness to practices that had only hidden efficacy.

What then does this particular life and example tell us about the relation of beliefs and practices? What it suggests is that the most purified Christian practice (from whence a theology of "the deep end" may be enunciated) is one of being "like God [in Christ], . . . *handed over* to the world, to wait upon it, to receive its power of meaning."[10] It is a passage into a peculiarly active form of passivity in which the divine pressure upon us meets not blockage but clarification. And this occurs — discreetly, quietly, and often even unconsciously in the recipient — through the "long haul" of repeated practices of faithfulness.

Purgative, Illuminative, and Unitive "Practices"

Vanstone's work, as I read it, is a kind of modern-day reformulation of the more ancient wisdom of ascetical theology, a theology that does not chart ascriptions of belief on a flat plane, but acknowledges the complexity of reformulation and personal appropriation of beliefs as the subject grows in spiritual stature. What then are the different levels at which practices may impinge on beliefs, or beliefs on practices? Traditions of "mystical theology"[11] within Christianity have spoken of three such stages of ascent:

---

10. Vanstone, *The Stature of Waiting*, p. 115.

11. I use the patristic language of "mystical theology" in conscious contradistinction from the modern appellation of "mysticism," which is much influenced by William James and subject to psychologized, individualistic interpretation with a focus on

the "purgative," "illuminative," and "unitive" ways. All of these presuppose, of course, the fundamental infusion of grace in the act of baptism; but its "unfurling," as I suggested earlier, may be perceived as occurring over time and through these three stages. Although it may be a little contrived to link these stages too neatly to particular practices, the idea seems worthy of an exploratory rehearsal.

At the first level, that of purgation, specific, external practices in virtue arise from the initial commitment to belief at baptism. Much of the emphasis is on setting one's life in a direction different from that of the world. For this reason, the rhetoric may be largely oppositional, and the practices remain somewhat legalistically construed: Christian *ethike* is being established. At the second level, practices start inversely to shape (or re-shape) belief, as a form of identification with Christ begins to flower and to unsettle the extrinsicism of the approach of the first stage. Finally, at the third stage, more arcane theological insights become available that are only the prerogative of those transformed by lengthy and painful practice.

Let me spell out these distinctions in types of practice a little further by presenting some graphic examples that seem to fit at the different levels.

Different Levels of Practice: Historic Examples

The work of Clement of Alexandria (c. 150–215) provides us in the *Paedagogos* ("The Instructor") with an almost perfect example of the first conception of practice we have outlined. The text is a guide for evidently privileged converts who need now to reconsider (and discard) elements of their former sybaritic lifestyle. Almost all of the examples of good Christian practices that Clement enjoins on us are matters to do with not embracing the practices of the world, and explicitly the practices of the rich and worldly. Clement is addressing those who are trying to sort out, as baptized people, which of the aspects of an earlier non-Christian life can or cannot be deemed appropriate to Christian virtue. He expatiates on everything from bed coverings to earrings; what would the "instructor" think of

---

fleeting high-point "experiences." For an excellent contemporary introduction to the ascetical tradition of mystical theology in its original (and very different) sense, see Andrew Louth, *The Origins of the Christian Mystical Tradition* (Oxford: Oxford University Press, 1981).

hair-plucking, makeup, body-piercing, gold jewelry, kissing your spouse in front of the "domestics," or appearing naked at the baths? These matters are clearly pressing for his audience: they need to know in precise, even legalistic, detail what will inculcate the virtuous life — hence the extrinsicism of the commands here, the representation of Christ as instructor, teacher, and restrainer ("Bridle of colts untamed, over our wills presiding," in the words of the famous hymn with which the text closes).[12] Little, if anything, emerges here about practices shaping belief; rather, the authoritative newfound belief is used as an ethical touchstone for distinguishing appropriate behavior (practice) from inappropriate.

It is particularly revealing here to note how Clement, in his initial restraining of his converts from "pagan" activities, is anxious too to emphasize the importance of clear gender binaries: this demarcation is seemingly all part of the order that the new life in baptism implies for the Christian neophyte. (A comparison with the material to be treated under the "unitive" way will be important here.) Thus Clement underscores, for instance, that, "A true gentleman must have no mark of effeminacy visible on his face, or any other part of his body. Let no blot on his manliness, then, be ever found either in his movements or habits."[13] Women, on the other hand, should not "smear their faces with the ensnaring devices of wily cunning" (that is, wear makeup), but be duly "subject to their husbands," and at all costs avoid "ogling" and "languishing looks."[14] The initial delineation of Christian from non-Christian practices, then, allows no unexpected forms of gender reversal; indeed, it is best for men altogether to "turn away from the sight of women." Practices here mark Christian purity over against pagan licentiousness, and any tendency to gender fluidity is firmly repudiated.

But we are in rather different territory, I suggest, with the implicit notion of practice in the sixth-century *Rule of St. Benedict,* which may form a suitable example of a second level of meaning. This short text, as so many commentators have justly remarked, is a document of great practical and spiritual subtlety; yet it contains no actual theory of the transformation of the monastic self, least of all with regard to sexuality. As R. W. Southern

---

12. Clement, "The Instructor," in *Ante-Nicene Fathers*, vol. 2 in *Fathers of the Second Century*, ed. A. Roberts and J. Donaldson (Peabody, MA: Hendrickson Publishers, reprint 1994; orig. 1885), p. 295.

13. Clement, "The Instructor," p. 289.

14. Clement, "The Instructor," pp. 286, 288.

has famously underlined, there is no "theory of the individual" in Benedict;[15] rather, the *Rule* simply lays out unsystematic advice for regulating a cenobitic house, with no eye to any specific charter of spiritual development. Rule 7, the crucial section on the virtue of humility, might appear to promise such a theory of ascent: "[Jacob's] ladder . . . is our life in this world, which for the humble of heart is raised up by the Lord unto heaven. Now the sides of this ladder are our body and soul, into which sides our divine vocation has fitted various degrees of humility and discipline which we have to climb."[16] On closer inspection, however, this is no ladder of logically-arranged stages, and the irony of Jacob's ladder is that one descends as easily as one ascends on it.

But herein lies the interesting rub for our purposes. The practices of Benedict's *Rule,* ranging from psalm-singing to harvesting to welcoming strangers, all quite explicitly mapped out so that "nothing will be [too] harsh or burdensome,"[17] are no longer so much ways of keeping the world at bay; but nor are they activities that will immediately (let alone invariably) produce an elevation on a scale of virtue. Rather they are to be followed in order that, over a lifetime, there may be a habituating of love, an imitation in a more than extrinsic way of the life of Christ, so that "we shall run with unspeakable sweetness of love in the way of God's commandments; so that, never abandoning his rule but persevering in his teaching in the monastery until death, we shall share by patience in the sufferings of Christ."[18] Here, it seems, there is the distinct suggestion that practices will re-modulate beliefs, that they will cause us to find Christ, for instance, in new and unexpected places — in the beggar at the door, in our own spiritual endurance, in the ministrations of the abbot. Christ is no longer, as in Clement, the "Instructor," reminding one, rather punitively, of one's new Christian duties. Christ does not dominate in Benedict, but is found more implicitly in postures of service.

Benedict's *Rule,* precisely because of its unsystematic nature, provokes reflection on the almost subliminal and unconscious way in which spiri-

15. R. W. Southern, *The Making of the Middle Ages* (London: Hutchinson, 1967), p. 213.

16. *The Rule of St. Benedict,* trans. Justin McCann (London: Sheed and Ward, 1970), ch. 7, 17.

17. *Rule of St. Benedict,* "Prologue," p. 4.

18. *Rule of St. Benedict,* "Prologue," p. 4.

tual re-modulation and transformation may occur over a lifetime through repeated practices. It is not obvious, for instance, why the daily and reiterated recitation in choir of psalmody should be either meritorious or life-changing ("Let nothing, therefore, be put before the work of God"[19]); boredom might be the more predictable outcome. Often it seems that there is a kind of consciousness-expansion that unfolds in the course of this repetition, but Benedict himself nowhere expatiates on this point. This alerts us to the importance of disciplined repetition in the fruitful interaction of belief and practice. Moreover, bodily acts of worship and attention (even if the mind is distracted) have their own integrity and effect; as the anthropologist Talal Asad has remarked, unbelief can be more truly the effect of "untaught bodies" than of uninstructed minds.[20] That Benedict gives instructions for bodies, and in particular bodies in necessarily — even uncomfortably — close interaction, is at the heart of his genius. It is through this endurance in community living, and not through virtuosity in private prayer (on which Benedict has remarkably little to say) that the "heart" comes to be "enlarged" "with unspeakable sweetness of love."[21] The enthusiasm with which Benedictine spirituality has been embraced by many non-"religious" in our generation perhaps reflects the desire for some bodily integrity of this sort distinguishable from the sexualized body emphasized by Western consumer culture. Moreover (and in strong contrast with the earlier Clement), Benedict nowhere expatiates on gender in terms, for instance, of appropriate "manliness." While "fraternal charity" is the goal, this is not described with the metaphors of gender stereotype, but rather with a deliberately counter-cultural stress on humility. Even the section of the *Rule* on dress manages to avoid all mention of gender expectations, something that would have been unthinkable for Clement. It seems societal gender expectations have been left behind in a curiously freeing way; yet there is still no hint of any positive upturning or subverting of gender binaries, as we shall find in developed "mystical theology."

This second, communal, interaction between practice and belief seen in Benedict undergoes a further twist, I submit, in a third level of engagement to which Benedict only briefly gestures (through the appeal to earlier

19. *Rule of St. Benedict,* ch. 43, 49.
20. Talal Asad, "Remarks on the Anthropology of the Body," in *Religion and the Body,* ed. Sarah Coakley (Cambridge: Cambridge University Press, 1997), p. 48.
21. *Rule of St. Benedict,* "Prologue," p. 4.

Egyptian sources). Here I shall concentrate on that minority strand in Christian theology and spirituality that has claimed that it is possible in this life to be incorporated *into* the life of the Trinity. And with this we arrive at a specific focus of this chapter's contribution: theological insights available *only* through practices — a contentious focus granted the smack of elitism that it inevitably suggests, especially to the suspicious Protestant investigator. It is the fourth-century Evagrius of Pontus, one of the earliest exponents of this claim, who writes: "If you are a theologian, you will pray truly. And if you pray truly, you are a theologian."[22] Not coincidentally, it is Evagrius who also writes, "We practise the virtues in order to achieve contemplation of the inner essences [*logoi*] of created things, and from this we pass to contemplation of the Logos who gives them their being; and He manifests himself when we are in the state of prayer."[23] Evagrius well stresses, however, the arduous process through which "pure prayer" in this sense is achieved: it is no beginner's prerogative, nor is it a possession that can be counted on to endure — the "cunning demon" is ever out to destroy or distract. Nonetheless, sustained prayer practices here are clearly the *prerequisites* of certain forms of theological knowledge — direct contemplative knowledge of the Logos. How do we assess this line of thought, apparently so differently expressed from the gentle assimilation to the human life of Christ sketched in Benedict? Is it necessarily tainted with the suspicious Platonism of Evagrius, with his distrust of the body and his less-than-robust appreciation of community?

Since Evagrius fell under the sixth-century ban of "Origenism," his reputation is overlaid with the charge of heterodoxy. His mixed attitude to the body and the material world, his doctrinal eccentricity, and his apparently individualistic emphasis make him an uneasy hero for one bent on explicating the doctrinally disclosing effects of practice through community as well as private devotion. Yet Evagrius is one of the most significant early monastic writers to discourse on incorporation into the trinitarian life, and with that on the vital, indeed logical, connection between the practice of "pure prayer" and that incorporation, that re-minted understanding of belief. Can this line of thought be re-expressed in a less heterodox mode? The answer is surely "yes."

22. Evagrius the Solitary, "On Prayer," in *The Philokalia,* trans. and ed. G. E. H. Palmer, P. Sherrard, and K. Ware (London: Faber and Faber, 1979), p. 62.
23. "On Prayer," pp. 61-62.

Much later, for instance, in the works of the sixteenth-century Carmelites in the West, we find a similar — indeed intensified — insistence on the lengthy and purgative process preceding the appropriation of beliefs in this mode. In the cases of Teresa and John of the Cross, we find an explicit account of incorporation into the life of the Trinity as a result of transforming union. But it is interesting to see how *corporeal* this transformation is in its effect. In Teresa's description (in the "Seventh Dwelling" of the *Mansions*), union does bring an intellectual understanding of the meaning of the doctrine of the Trinity, but it is an intellectual vision at a new and deeper level of response than previously known — "in the extreme interior, in some place very deep within."[24] It is earthed, embodied. This contrasts forcefully with the account of (so-called) "union" in the earlier *Life*, in which unitive states are brief, ecstatic, physically disabling, and not marked by recognition of doctrinal content[25] — in short, experiences of the sort now misleadingly termed "mystical" in the falsely-psychologized modern sense. This Teresa now eschews. The Teresa of the *Mansions* sees that it is a higher state to be able to withstand lasting union without physical ecstasy or collapse, and the acknowledgment of the trinitarian element is a concomitant feature of that more exalted position. The return to the quotidian, to "the pots and pans" of the kitchen, is incarnationally *required* of the one who passes into this union; any flight from the "ordinary," and thus from the continuing round of bodily practices in community that mark its Christian shape, would be a denial of the very trinitarian revelation just vouchsafed. This is no flight from the material, the everyday, or the chafing realities of the "other." Nor is this union a fleeting experience; it is a permanent, incarnate reality.

In John of the Cross's similar account of union in *The Spiritual Canticle*, the seemingly even more daring claim is made that the soul can actually breathe with the "very breath" of the Spirit that moves between the Father and the Son. The soul is actually knit into the life of God, its belief wholly internalized by the long practice of contemplation: "And thus the soul loves God in the Holy Spirit together with the Holy Spirit, not by

24. "The Interior Castle," VII:1, in *The Collected Works of St. Teresa of Avila*, trans. K. Kavanaugh and O. Rodriguez (Washington, D.C.: I.C.S. Publications, 1980), vol. 2, p. 430.

25. See, for instance, *The Life of St. Teresa*, trans. J. M. Cohen (London: Penguin, 1957), ch. 18.

means of Him, as by an instrument, but together with Him, by reason of the transformation, . . . and He supplies that which she lacks by her having been transformed in love with Him."[26]

The gender play in this third level of transformation is altogether different again from the preceding stages. Whereas in Clement the establishment of strong gender binaries was perceived as a bulwark against pagan immorality, and in Benedict gender seemed to become almost irrelevant to the program of subliminal community transformation, here the notable adoption of the "feminine" posture of the soul by John and the emergence of a strong voice of authority in Teresa (a contrast to her ostensibly self-belittling "rhetoric of femininity" in the *Life*) illustrate the characteristic gender fluidity of mystical theology's possibilities. Yet for both Teresa and John it is the *sui generis* responsiveness ("passivity" is too negatively-loaded a word) of the soul before God that is the hallmark of these states, in which contemplation is clearly now no *human* practice at all, but the direct infusion of divine grace.

Conclusions: Theologies of Grace

Clearly something crucial has occurred to the notion of practice in thus charting different levels of appropriation and relation to beliefs. At the third level described above, an approach to the Trinity is hazarded that, it is claimed by the contemplatives involved, can only be the epistemological preserve of those already transformed by divine grace itself to the point of "spiritual marriage." But what culminates in "union" has been sustained throughout, as can now be more clearly seen, by God's providence; even the ostensibly trivial acts of Christian self-definition in the neophyte (such as abandoning the wearing of jewelry, one of Clement's bugbears) have their "graced" dimension. But it would be odd, in view of the authors examined, to see this change in sartorial habit as *on par* with the final state of union; each may finally lead there, but the goal is a progressive purification of the self so as to become transparent to the divine.

We have seen, then, that "practice" may have a variety of meanings in the Christian context, and those meanings are significantly affected by the

---

26. "The Spiritual Canticle," Stanza XXXVII, in *The Complete Works of John of the Cross,* trans. E. A. Peers (London: Burns and Oates, 1965), vol. 2, p. 165.

depth of response involved in the believer. The contemplation of the Carmelites may be termed a practice, but strictly speaking it is done by God in the believer — from the human side, the *purest* act of willed "passivity." Still, the contemplative believer does not then give up practices of more mundane sorts that have formed and shaped her in the earlier stages of ascent; ostensibly trivial decisions about modest dress or habits of hospitality to the poor continue to be taken for granted, yet they get taken up and further transfigured. Just as a concert pianist never ceases from the mundane, and often tedious, practices of scales, so contemplation, as Teresa shows with such genius, is thrust back into the repetitive hurly-burly of the kitchen or the marketplace.[27] Even the hermit, as the literature of the Desert Fathers so memorably reminds us, goes back to basics of daily life as he is reminded of the frailty of his endeavors.[28]

Are then the traditions of contemplative ascent sketched here compatible with the Reformed reading of justification and sanctification? Here we have to face some hard questions in closing. Luther and Calvin of course both held Pauline-inspired views about the incorporation of the believer into the "body of Christ": christologically, they were in line with pre-Reformation tradition. But whereas Calvin was to work out his ecclesiology in terms of the paradoxical relation of the two narratives of justification and sanctification (a theme explored with contemporary application in Serene Jones's contribution to this volume), the material we have here charted was, in its Western medieval forms, undergirded by theories of grace that distinguished *different* levels and types of grace's effects. The danger of spiritual elitism in those theories that caused nervousness (if not outright rebuke) in the Reformers is hard to deny altogether in the material we have covered here. And the significant differences in emphasis, at least, between pre-Reformation and Reformed theories of justification are not ones that can be simply waved away, as the recent *Concordat* between Rome and the Lutherans amply shows.[29] It is not my purpose here to claim

27. "Interior Castle," VII:4, p. 448, on the importance of "Martha" in conjunction with "Mary."

28. See, for example, the sayings from the *Apophthegmata Patrum* in *The Wisdom of the Desert Fathers,* trans. Benedicta Ward (Oxford: S.L.G. Press, 1975).

29. See *Joint Declaration on the Doctrine of Justification* from the Lutheran World Federation and the Catholic Church (Grand Rapids: Eerdmans, 2000; also available on the Web at www.elca.org/ea/jddj/declaration.html), which does not attempt to obliterate the differences of emphasis between Catholic and Lutheran approaches.

that these historic points of division can be erased by an irenic smudging of them with the category of "practice," for that would be a mere sleight of hand. If the argument of this chapter has been successful, however, a theology of "deepening practices" may take from the insights of classic ascetical and mystical theology a message about the relation of practice and belief not obviously incompatible with the central instincts of the Reformers, although certainly questioning some of their rhetorical disjunctions. This position has been forwarded on the assumption (I trust sufficiently supported) that the monastic circles that spawned these traditions are not the sole preserve of their application; lay theologies of belief and practice are equally open to the transformative undertakings this literature proposes for body and soul, not least the vocation of a contemplative life.

To sum up: I have here suggested a spectrum of interactive forms of beliefs and practices through which, over a lifetime of faithful observation of both public acts of worship and charity on the one hand, and private devotions on the other, one might hope ultimately to come to "know" God in God's intimate life — to breathe his very Spirit, as John of the Cross puts it. I have proceeded on the assumption that this is the vocation to which we are all called, and I have attempted to give clarity to an admittedly complex and messy entanglement of beliefs and practices by suggesting a three-stage heuristic schema of the relation of belief to practice. At the first stage, when the neophyte sets out to delineate the differences between Christian and secular life, it is the public, given beliefs of the creeds that logically precede and substantially inform the initial practices of Christian life, and certain "pagan" practices are foresworn. This much we saw in Clement. But a devout life cannot stop with such externals, however meritorious; it engages in a whole web of interactive everyday Christian practices, such as Benedict prescribes, in which the logical relation of practices to beliefs becomes one of mutual interaction. More or less subliminally, and with a loosening of previous moral judging, the inner meanings of beliefs start to make their impact: Christ ceases to be merely an external model to be imitated, but is recognized in the poor, the stranger at the gate; creeds cease to be merely tools of judgment, but rather rules of life into which to enter and flourish; beliefs cease to be merely charters of orthodoxy dictating right practice, but rather practices start to infuse beliefs with richer meaning. Finally, the practices of prayer that have all along sustained this process may be purified and simplified, if the contemplatives are to be believed, into silent responsiveness, into an empty waiting on

God that precedes union in its full sense. This practice of contemplation is, strictly speaking, God's practice *in* humans — a more unimpeded or conscious form of that distinctive human receptivity to grace that has sustained the process all along and that is itself a divine gift. But it does not obliterate or invalidate all the other practices; rather, it sets them all in a new light, reversing more obviously now the logical relation of beliefs and practices as this practice finally discloses the *incorporative* telos and meaning of "beliefs." In particular, the Trinity is no longer seen as an obscure though authoritative ecclesial doctrine of God's nature, but rather a life into which we enter and, in unbreakable union with Christ, breathe the very Spirit of God.

Such a vision of the Christian life may still, to the Protestant, smack suspiciously of elitist progressivism, and that nettle has here been grasped. But what this vision most emphatically does *not* propound is the intrinsic spiritual superiority of any particular vocation, lay or ordained, let alone the necessity of high-point "experiences" of the divine, which are in any case in the Carmelite tradition treated with great reserve. That is why, in closing, it is worth recalling again the witness of Bill Vanstone, who — Anglican as he was — was profoundly affected by both Calvinist and Catholic theologies of grace, and who would have thought it absurd if someone had described him as a "mystic" in the modern, experientialist sense.[30] We should not presume, in this reading of ascetical and contemplative literature, that its insights about what Vanstone called the "deep end" are incompatible with a life of tough ordinariness, ministerial obscurity, and even a sense of human failure: "*Hidden* is love's agony, Love's endeavour, love's expense," as Vanstone reminds us. Even so, the "deep end" has been silently and powerfully explored over the years. The uncelebrated "mystical theologian" is no less a contemplative for being uncelebrated; the transformative stature of waiting (often affectively felt as "waiting without hope," as T. S. Eliot memorably puts it in the *Four Quartets*)[31] is a profoundly countercultural act, a practice mastered only over a lifetime, that nonetheless may bear away some of the world's pain.

---

30. See again my warning remarks about "mysticism" in note 11 above.

31. T. S. Eliot, "East Coker," III, from *The Four Quartets:* "I said to my soul, be still, and wait without hope, For hope would be hope for the wrong thing." *T. S. Eliot: The Complete Poems and Plays* (London: Faber and Faber, 1969), p. 180.

Is There a Doctor in the House?
Reflections on the Practice of Healing
in African American Churches

TAMMY R. WILLIAMS

My own interest in healing has emerged over the past few years as I have wrestled with the deaths of loved ones in their early thirties to cancer. My deliberations have involved attempts to "make sense" of their short lives, figuring out the implications of their untimely deaths for my own life and, of course, trying to understand where the God they loved was in the midst of these events. To ask these kinds of questions and to make connections between God, persons, and the meaning of events is to enter into theological reflection — a practice we will engage in throughout this essay. Unlike the way some theologians traditionally have approached their work, I did not begin my study by examining the biblical roots of "healing" and "sickness and health" or by analyzing what the church has believed about these concepts throughout its history. Because I took seriously my loved ones' testimonies about God's goodness and because I deeply respected the persons who cared for them, my point of departure was the communities of faith that nurtured my friends and the caregivers who loved them. I began by reflecting on those who "have church" and are immersed in its practices.

Special thanks to Robert Beckford, Wilfred Graves, Willie Jennings, A. G. Miller, Gail Nagel, Harold Dean Trulear, and Kevin Williams, who read earlier versions of the manuscript and made helpful suggestions.

94

This essay explores the practice of healing in African American churches.[1] The account I propose is interpretive and prescriptive. I offer an interpretation of healing by listening carefully to those engaged in ministries of healing and allowing them to speak for themselves through the time-honored practices of testimony, prayer, and song. I conclude prescriptively by suggesting how theological reflection and attentiveness to beliefs, particularly the work of the cross, can fortify the very practices of healing in which churches are already engaged.

An intentional focus on healing leads us to examine how theological commitments (such as "God is good") and social contexts profoundly shape the practice of healing in different church settings. I will attend to three broad approaches to healing — "care," "cure," and "holism" — that are paradigmatic of three tendencies within African American churches: traditional, Word of faith, and holistic, respectively.[2] "Traditional" refers to perspectives on healing that are characteristic of many non-Pentecostal mainline churches, such as my own Baptist denomination. "Word of faith" describes approaches by those Pentecostal churches that hold definitive views about divine healing in the form of *faith healing*. Since several Pentecostal theologies of healing exist, I isolate faith healing as a perspective that *some* Pentecostals adhere to, though many classical Pentecostals do not. "Holistic" identifies a multifaceted practice that seeks healing for the whole person; the wholeness I have in mind is rooted in the Old Testament understanding of *shalom* (well-being) as a social concept that encompasses health, salvation, and security. Holistic churches, which include both mainline and Word of faith representatives, offer a model of healing that is recognizably different in many respects than that of the other two approaches.

By comparing and contrasting these tendencies, we can observe how emphasizing certain doctrinal beliefs and minimizing others permit con-

---

1. C. Eric Lincoln and Lawrence H. Mamiya, *The Black Church in the African American Experience* (Durham, NC: Duke University Press, 1990), p. 1. I follow Lincoln's designation of African American churches as those "independent, historic, and totally black controlled denominations which were founded after the Free African Society of 1787 and which constituted the core of black Christians." This definition incorporates the historic black Methodist, Baptist, and Pentecostal denominations.

2. In actual practice, the fluid character of these communities makes their boundaries far less discrete. The "traffic" between communities and its resultant cross-fertilization suggest that a cross section of practitioners, both past and present, can have a dynamic influence on molding practices.

gregations engaged in a single practice — healing — to incarnate the practice in divergent, if not oppositional, ways. While sociologists of religion and others have interests in investigating healing practices, my purpose in observing these communities is to ask why and how healing matters *theologically*. How do understandings of God's person and activity in the world influence practices of healing? How do community members understand God's activity in their practices of healing? More broadly, my interest is in explaining how beliefs — the right kind of beliefs — get *used* in practices of healing. In particular, I am interested in explaining how right beliefs can not only be used to underwrite right practices but also how they can lead to *mal*practice.

As we shall see, problems exist in the healing practices of traditional and Word of faith churches. In the former, problems tend to arise from failure to properly fit practice to belief; in the latter, problems appear to stem from an inadequate theological understanding of healing. The holistic approach represents an alternative to both care and cure. I see it as the most adequate of the three, although I will also point out certain theological weaknesses that threaten to rob it of its promise and power. By analyzing healing in this manner, I hope to offer Christian leaders and Christians committed to healing ministries a theologically grounded way of formally and creatively reflecting on healing. Because healing is often practiced at the edge of life and death and often involves persons who are very vulnerable, it is essential that practitioners understand what they are actually doing and why they are doing it.

Social Context[3]

Christian beliefs and practices take specific form in particular social contexts. Although the three ecclesial settings we shall examine embody differ-

3. African American churches are socio-culturally heterogeneous and theologically diverse. In my analysis, I assume that African Americans from all social classes are represented in each ecclesial setting; therefore, I do *not* correlate a particular practice of healing or certain theologies of healing with a certain socioeconomic class. However, in light of the significant number of African Americans who are uninsured or underinsured, I highlight the marginality of African Americans in relation to healthcare as the social backdrop for all three ecclesial communities. What vary in the three church settings are beliefs about healing. Although class impacts healing (just as it affects all

ent approaches, it is important to note that profound belief in divine healing is characteristic of all. And for good reason. In a country in which forty-two million persons lack health insurance, twenty percent of whom are African American,[4] Jesus may be the *only* doctor that some African Americans encounter on a regular basis.[5] This critical contextual insight shapes healing as a theological event in myriad ways.

The marginality of many African Americans vis-à-vis the contemporary healthcare system, however, is only one facet of a much longer history of outright denial of healthcare to African Americans that can be traced back to slavery. Moreover, the withholding of beneficial medical treatment must itself be placed within the larger framework of the experience of African Americans with the medical profession, which has historically described blackness as pathological[6] and engaged in the classification and

---

practices), it does so in complex, unpredictable ways. What appears to be the more significant variable in healing practices is theological perspective.

4. Emilie Townes, *Breaking the Fine Rain of Death: African American Health Issues and a Womanist Ethic of Care* (New York: Continuum Publishing Group, 1998), p. 28. The uninsured figure of forty-two million persons is from 1996. The tragic statistic of the uninsured is underscored by the fact that fifteen percent of African American children were uninsured in 1990 and in that same year only 46 percent of all African Americans had private insurance (which often contains more comprehensive coverage and choices) compared to 77 percent of Euro-Americans.

5. Wilhelmina A. Leigh, "The Health of African American Women," in *Health Issues for Women of Color: A Cultural Diversity Perspective* (Thousand Oaks, CA: SAGE Publications, 1995), p. 8. Studies show that when medical care is sought, Euro-Americans are more likely to use doctors' offices for standard care. A significant number of African Americans, in contrast, seek medical treatment from emergency rooms or other hospital settings such as outpatient clinics. Lack of health insurance and difficulty keeping appointments during normal work hours (which may be difficult for the working poor or those doing shift work) often account for this tendency.

6. James H. Evans, Jr., *We Shall All Be Changed: Social Problems and Theological Renewal* (Minneapolis: Fortress Press, 1997), pp. 54-56. Evans discusses disease as rhetorical convention in which its language creates social reality. As a conceptual category, it can be defined in various ways and take on social meanings. Throughout history "disease" has been used to label the "other" that threatens us. In the case of American slavery, Evans argues that the perception that black skin was the result of pathology enabled the survival of American slavery. One popular hypothesis was that the phenotypical features of blacks were the result of congenital leprosy. Disease discourse also extended to psychological categories. During the nineteenth century, it was believed by some that the physiology of blacks predisposed them to mental illness. See Sander L.

objectification of black bodies.[7] According to one scholar, one of the most painful chapters in this history, the well-known Tuskegee Syphilis Study, "simply confirmed the historical assumption that black bodies could be sacrificed for the health of others."[8]

A byproduct of this tragic history is the great distrust and disgust that sectors of the African American community harbor toward the medical establishment.[9] Contemporary medical decisions that result in African Americans receiving less aggressive treatment for heart problems than Euro-Americans[10] and the exclusion of African Americans, particularly women, from important clinical trials[11] suggest that the suspicions of some African Americans are not unfounded. This historical and ongoing reality has led theologian James Evans to contend that "for African Americans the issue of their physical health is inseparable from the ravages of racism upon their humanity."[12] For those who have apprehensions about accessing the health system, divine healing assures them that Jesus is a doctor who can be *trusted*. To

---

Gilman, *Difference and Pathology: Stereotypes of Sexuality, Race, and Madness* (Ithaca, NY: Cornell University Press, 1985), pp. 137-39.

7. Cornel West, *Prophesy Deliverance: An Afro-American Revolutionary Christianity* (Philadelphia: The Westminster Press, 1982), pp. 47-65; Gilman, *Difference and Pathology*, pp. 79-93.

8. Evans, *We Shall All Be Changed*, p. 58. The Tuskegee Study was directed by the U.S. Public Health Service from 1932 to 1972 and involved four hundred black men in the South who were diagnosed with syphilis but never were informed that they were carriers. Moreover, the men were never treated in order that the project could study the natural progression of the disease. For an overview of the Tuskegee Study, see Townes, *Breaking the Fine Rain of Death*, pp. 88-100.

9. Townes, *Breaking the Fine Rain of Death*, pp. 126-27, notes how cynicism engendered by the Tuskegee Study colors how AIDS and public health officials are perceived in sectors of the African American community. An African American health educator from the Dallas Urban League observes: "'So many African American people that I work with do not trust hospitals or any of the other community health care service providers because of that Tuskegee Study. It is like . . . if they did it then they will do it again'" (p. 127). For an account of the frustration that the poor often experience when accessing the system, see Teresa Maldonado, "Sick of Being Poor," in *On Moral Medicine: Theological Perspectives in Medical Ethics*, 2d ed., ed. Stephen E. Lammers and Allen Verhey (Grand Rapids: Eerdmans, 1998), pp. 1001-4.

10. Townes, *Breaking the Fine Rain of Death*, p. 67.

11. Townes, *Breaking the Fine Rain of Death*, pp. 108-13, 136-39.

12. Evans, *We Shall All Be Changed*, pp. 45-46.

take this account seriously is to acknowledge that healing occurs and, at times, flourishes in African American churches not in spite of this context of racism, sexism, and classism, but *in the midst of* these evils as a way of dealing with them. As such, healing can be understood as a practice of justice.

Healing and Sickness Defined

It is important to make clear how I use the set of terms associated with sickness and healing in this essay. Disease, illness, and sickness — terms that we often use synonymously — are distinguished in medical anthropology.[13] The term "disease" reflects a biomedical perspective and refers to a dysfunction of biological and/or psychological processes that affects individuals.[14] It names the objective aspect of sickness; that is, the dysfunction exists regardless of whether it is culturally recognized.[15] "Illness" is a socio-cultural concept that pertains to the person's subjective experiences and social networks; both the affected person and her family are labeled ill.[16] Because it results from "personal, social, and cultural reactions to disease," "illness is the shaping of disease into behavior and experience."[17] "Sickness" is a blanket term that refers to both disease and illness, or to a combination of the two.[18] A parallel distinction is made between "curing" and "healing."[19] When a disease is effectively checked or removed, it is cured. When an intervention affects an illness, healing takes place, with implications for personal and social meaning.

13. Allan Young, "The Anthropologies of Illness and Sickness," *Annual Review of Anthropology* 11 (1982): 264-65.

14. Arthur Kleinman, *Patients and Healers in the Context of Culture: An Exploration of the Borderland between Anthropology, Medicine, and Psychiatry* (Berkeley, CA: University of California Press, 1980), p. 72.

15. John J. Pilch, "Sickness and Healing in Luke-Acts," in *The Social World of Luke-Acts: Models for Interpretation,* ed. Jerome H. Neyrey (Peabody, MA: Hendrickson Publishers, 1991), p. 191.

16. Kleinman, *Patients and Healers,* p. 73.

17. Kleinman, *Patients and Healers,* p. 72.

18. See Young, "Anthropologies of Illness and Sickness," pp. 269-71, for an alternate definition of sickness.

19. Pilch, "Sickness and Healing in Luke-Acts," p. 192; Kleinman, *Patients and Healers,* p. 82.

"Healing" and "illness," the primary New Testament categories regarding sickness, are also the guiding categories used in this essay. Biblical accounts of healing emphasize more encompassing concerns than the cure of individuals beset by objective disease. The significance of Jesus' healing of lepers, for example, was not only that he altered their physical condition; he restored them to purity, wholeness, and holiness.[20] Their new status allowed them to function as full members of the social order and the worshiping community.

This example points to a biblical view of healing as a practice that involves the whole person. The Old Testament concept of *shalom* best captures the concept of health.[21] It suggests the idea of completeness, soundness, well-being, and prosperity, and includes every aspect of life: personal, relational, and national. Because shalom entails living in covenantal relationship with God and others, holiness and righteousness are inherent in it. This view of shalom is reflected in the New Testament,[22] where healing consistently involves not only physical recovery from sickness but the renewal of relationships with God and others. The New Testament term *sozo* ("to save" or "to heal"), which is used for both physical healing and soul salvation, has a similar range of meanings. Therefore, from a Christian perspective, the aim of healing is the complete well-being of the person. It entails being in right relation to God, oneself, others, and the rest of creation. In light of its scriptural dimensions, healing can be understood as "a process of bringing or restoring wholeness and sound functioning to every aspect of human life, which includes bodily integrity, emotional balance, mental well-being, and spiritual aliveness."[23] This interpretation is

---

20. John J. Pilch, "Biblical Leprosy and Body Symbolism," *Biblical Theology Bulletin* 11 (1981): 108. Pilch argues that biblical leprosy (Lev. 13–14) is a repugnant skin condition and cannot be equated with the modern disorder known as Hansen's disease. It is not a "disease," but an "illness" that has important socio-religious implications for the sufferer and the entire community. See also Pilch, "Sickness and Healing in Luke-Acts," p. 207.

21. John Wilkinson, *Health and Healing: Studies in New Testament Principles and Practice* (Edinburgh: The Handsel Press Ltd., 1980), pp. 4-8.

22. Wilkinson, *Health and Healing,* pp. 31-33.

23. Edwin Huis, "Healing," in *The Complete Book of Everyday Christianity: An A-to-Z Guide to Following Christ in Every Aspect of Life,* ed. Robert Banks and R. Paul Stevens (Downers Grove, IL: InterVarsity Press, 1997), p. 478. Huis's definition captures the thrust of the definition adopted by the World Health Organization in 1946,

located within a very different world view than that of modern Western medicine.

The Practice of Healing in Traditional African American Churches

If you want your body healed, tell him what you want.
If you want your body healed, tell him what you want.
If you want your body healed, tell him what you want.
Jesus on the mainline now.

"Jesus on the Mainline"
(traditional gospel song)

Practices of healing not only reflect what we believe about human beings — both sick and healthy — but also what we think about their creator and redeemer. In traditional African American churches, understandings of God's *sovereignty* are particularly significant. In an insightful article on contemporary theologies of healing, Henry Knight III identifies two axes along which theologies of healing are often situated.[24] On one axis, God's sovereignty is understood as God's unconditional *freedom* to act for the good of God's creation. According to traditional churches, which tend to locate themselves on this axis, God is free to heal or not to heal. On the other axis, God's sovereignty is most clearly revealed by God's willingness and ability to honor God's commitment to heal. This conviction of God's unconditional *faithfulness to fulfill the promises of God's Word* is definitive for Word of faith churches. These two distinct understandings of what it means for God to be sovereign — namely, that God is free to act and that God is faithful in fulfilling God's Word — result in the distinctive practices of care for the sick and cure in these two types of congregations.

To observe how beliefs about God's person and activity shape practices of healing, we must first delineate the cluster of beliefs about God and

---

which speaks of health as "a state of complete well-being and not merely the absence of disease or infirmity."

24. Henry H. Knight III, "God's Faithfulness and God's Freedom: A Comparison of Contemporary Theologies of Healing," *Journal of Pentecostal Theology* 2 (1993): 65-89.

healing embraced in traditional African American congregations. By noting the content of these beliefs, we then can map out the logic of how an emphasis on God's sovereign freedom leads to a practice of healing that focuses on caring for the sick. The beliefs that traditional churches hold regarding the giver and the gift of healing include the following:

- God is sovereign and God is love.
- God loves and cares for sick persons.
- Healing is God's loving and concrete response to sickness.
- Healing is a gift that is wholly in God's hands. Its offer is conditioned by the divine will, and lived experience reflects that healing is not an inevitable outcome.
- God's faithfulness in being present to those who are sick *and* the faithfulness of the caring community are underscored. A belief in the possibility of cure, which is never abandoned, must be complemented by an emphasis on the necessity of care.

The other tenets highlight the work of God in Christ as the agent of healing:

- The cross teaches us that Jesus suffers with us and stands in solidarity with us during our trials.
- Healing is christocentric: In Jesus, God is both a doctor and a healer. The former designation, however, is determinative for the community's practice.

The starting point for the congregation's response to the sick is the undeniable reality of sickness and the way in which God relates to it. Healing is *God's* gracious response to the sick. God alone can be credited with healing. As the divine prerogative, God bestows it according to God's own purposes. These beliefs about how God acts make sense of lived reality in ways that both ease uncertainty and undergird personal pastoral care. First, a crisis of faith is avoided when some are not healed. Secondly, because a sovereign God often chooses not to heal, an emphasis on care must complement a belief in cure. Therefore, rather than "naming and claiming" healing, which, as we shall see, is the rule in Word of faith churches, these congregations literally name and claim sick *persons*.

Consonant with a belief in God's freedom are understandings of the person of Christ and the work of Christ on the cross that also support a practice of care. The cross teaches us that "Jesus knows all about our struggles." The one who identified with us and suffered for us on the cross is now present with us in our sickness and sufferings. Thus if a conquering Christ does not cure a malady, then a suffering Jesus will stand in *solidarity* with the sick. Traditional African American congregations highlight divine passion for the sick by speaking of Jesus as a doctor who never lost a patient. He makes house calls and treats patients with compassion. In short, he cares for them.

The Practice of Caring

Caring for the sick in traditional churches is a communal practice.[25] When Jesus does not bring about a physical cure, it is assumed that he chooses to soothe sick bodies through the healing hands of the nurturing community.

Along with various forms of hospitality, prayer is an essential part of this practice of care, and it functions as an act of solidarity. The reading aloud of a "sick and shut-in list" each week serves as a good illustration of how churches "name and claim" the sick among them. Although this ritual of naming the sick is often perceived as a formality, perhaps it is best understood as a ritual of defiance in a culture in which young, healthy, sexy, and white bodies count more than other bodies. By countering the temptation to forget those who are absent or rarely seen, naming is an act of remembering those who all too often — because of age or disability — are forgotten when they are *well*. Congregational intercession, which names the sick in the presence of God, counters the threat of invisibility and anonymity. It inverts the insidious process of classifying and objectifying black bodies by affirming that Sister and Brother Jones are subjects and not medical objects. By bringing them to the "throne" as daughters and sons of God, the congregation affirms their personhood. This is another way of describing communal prayer for the sick as covenantal. By committing itself to God, the community commits itself to be faithful to the sick. Through its perseverance it says: It does not matter how long you have

---

25. My claim is not that sick persons are not cured in traditional churches or that those who seek healing are not cared for in Word of faith churches. My purpose is to highlight what is *distinctive* in each church setting.

been sick or if you will ever recover. We will remember *you*, not only your sickness, in prayer. And we will care for you regardless.

Additional practices of care stem from the community's belief that sickness affects the entire family and not simply the afflicted member. This well-attested anthropological insight mirrors the Pauline understanding that when one member hurts, all are affected (1 Cor. 12:26). Therefore, various dimensions of hospitality, such as cooking meals, housecleaning, tending to children and spouse, and sending a benevolence offering, are also part of caring for the sick, although some of these actions were more prominent in the past than they are today.

It is important to recognize that a variety of factors tend to account for why some congregations pursue care. One determinant is "giftedness": because ministry to the sick in this setting does not require specialized skills or a certain level of spirituality, the entire community is able to participate. Another factor is age: generally speaking, congregations with older members are more likely to engage in a ministry of care.[26]

Evaluation of the Care Response

Embedded in the practice of caring for the sick is a theological account of healing that seeks to do justice both to God's character and work in the world and to human experience. The strengths of the care response lie in its communal response to sickness and its pastoral ability to contend with the ongoing presence of sickness while fully affirming the sick person as a member of the community.

One might ask, however, if a care response unwittingly privileges the experience of sickness more highly than that of being healed. At times, the

---

26. My attempt to isolate a population of the sick is to illustrate a demographic factor that may account for why some congregations tend to gravitate more toward care than cure as a means of addressing specific needs. Churches with older members are an example. Some of the sicknesses that plague the elderly are incurable chronic illnesses. Since osteo-arthritis, rheumatism, failing vision and hearing, and impaired mobility are commonly associated with the aging process, they are often considered the "natural" results of growing old. Moreover, because these ailments are often not life-threatening, they are rarely the objects of petitions for miraculous healing. They are reluctantly, though tacitly, accepted as part and parcel of what it means to have the same body for roughly eighty years.

acknowledgement of sickness as a universal condition can result in responses of *resignation*, which are often communicated through the language of spirituality. For example, some believers speak of sickness as the "cross" that they bear for Jesus, or as God's way of "trying to tell them something." No doubt many of these believers are attempting to express a conviction that the Christian tradition has held throughout its history: sickness and suffering can be a means through which God works God's purposes in our lives. At the same time, it is important to recognize that an overemphasis on care can unknowingly overshadow cure as divine possibility and human hope. When this happens, believers can overlook that God can sovereignly choose to heal just as God can exercise freedom to be present in compassion and nurture.

Herein lies a danger of any one-sided care response to sickness: caring for the sick, particularly those with chronic illnesses, as part of the church's ongoing ministry, can lead to an unreflective acceptance of sickness and suffering as inherent in daily living or as part of God's divine will. Belief that "it is God's will that some are not healed" can become *mal*practiced or enacted as the conviction that "it is God's will that some are sick." A validating, caring embrace of sick persons as a long-term practice can evolve into a misshapen practice of care that accepts sickness and suffering too readily as God's will for our lives rather than as results of human fallenness.

Word of Faith Responses to Sickness

He healed my body and told me to run on,
He healed my body and told me to run on,
He healed my body and told me to run on,
He's my friend.
[That's why] Can't nobody do me like Jesus . . .

"Can't Nobody Do Me Like Jesus"
(traditional gospel song)

This stanza of a popular gospel song suggests the point of departure for a Word of faith understanding of healing. Although many may "call him up" and request healing, as we saw in the previous section, not all who do so can testify: "I once was sick and couldn't get well. But he *healed* my body and now I can tell." Anyone can make the claim that "Jesus is a doctor"; what really counts is whether your doctor can make you *well*. Therefore, the healing power of Jesus is prominent in these churches, and "cure" is the normative vision for healing. And for good reason: divine healing may be the only option many sick African Americans have, when one considers that their death rates exceed those of Euro-Americans in all major disease categories.[27] Refusing to believe that medical science should care for sick bodies while the church ministers to sick souls, *cure* takes seriously the urgency of the healthcare crisis in the African American community and the intractable failure of the medical bureaucracy to solve it.

Divine Healing as Faith Healing

When asked how God is at work in the world, Word of faith churches (which belong to the Pentecostal tradition) characteristically respond that God's care for creation is best demonstrated by God's integrity in honoring God's Word. Scripture is used to formulate two critical elements in a theology of healing. The first is the decisive role of Jesus' atoning death in securing healing for all believers. The additional component is the primacy of the believer's faith. Both constituents — atonement theology and faith — require further elaboration. They are the scaffolds for a theology of healing, which includes the following principles:

- God is good and desires well-being for God's children.
- Healing is God's loving and concrete response to sickness and demonstrates that God wants to offer us the very best.
- God desires good for all of God's children; therefore, healing is a gift that can be appropriated universally. This is the divine intention.
- The cross teaches us that Christ took upon himself our sins and infirmities on the cross to make us whole. Salvation *and* healing are provided for us through Christ's atoning death.

27. Leigh offers statistics from the National Center of Health Statistics that show higher 1992 death rates for black women in the categories of heart diseases, cerebrovascular diseases, cancer, diabetes, and HIV/AIDS infection ("Health of African American Women," pp. 122, 124). See Townes, *Breaking the Fine Rain of Death,* pp. 65-72, for mortality rates for the entire community.

- It is God's will to heal. Experience shows that those who exercise faith can and will be healed.
- Healing is universally accessible to believers; therefore, cure is the operative paradigm.

The atoning death of Jesus as an expression of God's will to heal is the foundational event that makes healing a possibility for all believers. Although most Pentecostals believe that God has sovereignly provided for healing through Christ's atoning work ("by his stripes ye were healed," 1 Pet. 2:24, King James Version), a considerable number of Word of faith adherents believe that it can be appropriated in the same manner in which justification is received.[28] Therefore, believers can boldly petition God for healing unconditionally and receive it by faith. Since a person would not pray for salvation conditionally by pleading, "if it be your will, save me, Lord," then a believer should not pray for healing by adding, "if it be your will, Lord."[29] The cross, wherein healing has already been secured, reveals God's will to heal.

If Jesus' work on the cross is the decisive divine act through which healing is realized, then faith is the activating principle that appropriates healing. According to a Word of faith understanding, through faith believers can obtain God's promises, particularly health, wealth, and salvation, which are also known as the "blessings of Abraham."[30] Making a "positive confession," that is, believing scriptural promises of healing by faith and then acting on that faith, is indispensable to healing.[31] Believers are empowered to confess and act by appropriating "spiritual laws" that God has placed in the universe for the benefit of all. Moreover, believers have been granted divine authority to claim biblical promises. The power of positive confession, according to Word of faith adherents, is not merely declarative, it is performative: it creates and fashions the reality of believers. This power is not limitless, to be sure; believers can obtain only those promises, such as healing, that are biblical. However, if one confesses that she has

28. Miroslav Volf, "The Materiality of Salvation," *Journal of Ecumenical Studies* 26 (1989): 458.

29. Volf, "Materiality of Salvation," p. 458.

30. I rely on Knight, "God's Faithfulness and God's Freedom," pp. 65-68, for this paragraph.

31. See also Frederick K. C. Price, *Is Healing for All?* (Tulsa, OK: Harrison House, Inc., 1976), pp. 75-82.

been healed, despite physical evidence to the contrary, then healing will follow.[32]

The Practice of Faith Healing

The approach to healing in Word of faith churches is pneumatic and tends to be more individualized. A privileged role is accorded to the Holy Spirit. The Spirit heals through distributing gifts of healing to members of the body, working miracles, providing some with special prayer gifts, and giving others endowments of supernatural faith. Accordingly, the Spirit is understood here to work in the community through individuals — particularly through sick members and those with gifts of healing.

One way in which faith healing seeks to empower believers is by teaching them that they have the authority to take control of their lives by exercising faith through prayer. Battling the healthcare establishment often reinforces feelings of powerlessness; but faith healing, through its focus on the divine availability and willingness to heal and its emphasis on the positive confession of the believer, inverts the power structure of healthcare politics. Because the divine doctor has already provided a cure, the believer no longer has to be at the mercy of overworked healthcare staff. She no longer comes before God "in the most humble manner in which she knows how" but as a conquering prayer warrior who takes authority over the enemy's strongholds by claiming the promises of God by faith. Since healing is an *accomplished* fact that the believer can attain by exercising her own "ever-increasing faith," ongoing congregational prayers for the sick tend to become less important. Although others can pray for the sick member, some adherents believe that faith by "proxy" still requires the faith of the sick person in order to be efficacious. New prayer methods and special healing prayers figure prominently in this setting.[33]

32. Knight notes positive confession adherents make a distinction between "revelation knowledge" and sensory knowledge. When one's perceptions cause one to question that healing has taken place, one must affirm Scripture and look beyond one's senses. To do otherwise is to risk the loss of one's healing.

33. An example of Word of faith perspectives regarding prayer can be found in selected excerpts from the foreword and introduction of Word Ministries, Inc., *Prayers That Avail Much: An Intercessor's Handbook of Scriptural Prayers,* vol. 2 (Tulsa, OK:

Growing reliance on giftedness or "specialization" is also a feature of a Word of faith emphasis on the role of the individual. Members are often encouraged to discover and cultivate their spiritual gifts. Those who have special prayer gifts, gifts of healing, or prophetic gifts are sought out to minister personally to the sick. This is often done through the laying on of hands accompanied by anointing with consecrated oil. Specialized healing practices, such as these, can ensure the kind of attention that is lacking in many HMOs. For those who have experienced long waits in clinics, being summoned to the altar to have their illnesses rebuked signals that God's specialists take sickness and healing seriously.

Evaluation of the Cure Approach

The Word of faith practice of healing has a high view of biblical authority and demands that human experience be interpreted in light of Scripture. It seeks to make sense of particular biblical passages that emphasize God's sovereign healing power and human reception. It also upholds God's fidelity to God's Word as the means in which the divine will is exercised: God's Word *is* God's will. Pastorally, the practice seeks to empower and equip sick believers to take control over their lives by appropriating healing.

The practice, however, is not without weaknesses. First, an appeal to "universal" spiritual "laws" that appear to be inclusive and egalitarian results in a generic practice of healing: one faith principle works for all. This principle ignores the very particular bodies that particular persons inhabit. The obvious distortion in this enactment of healing is that those who remain sick are often viewed as less spiritual than those who are healed. Strict adherence to a Word of faith understanding can result in

---

Harrison House, Inc., 1989). "*Talk the answer, not the problem. The answer is in God's Word.* You must have knowledge of that Word — revelation knowledge (1 Cor. 2:7-16)" (p. 10). "Believe you receive when you pray. Confess the Word. Hold fast to your confession of faith in God's Word. Allow your spirit to pray by the Holy Spirit. Praise God for the victory *now* before any manifestation. *Walk by faith and not by sight* (2 Cor. 5:7)" (p. 11). "*Prayer does not cause faith to work, but faith causes prayer to work.* Therefore, any prayer problem is a problem of doubt — doubting the integrity of the Word and the ability of God to stand behind His promises or the statements of fact in the Word" (p. 18).

"blaming the victim" — holding the sick responsible for not getting well. Although faith appears to be the great equalizer that ensures healing, since all have the potential to possess "the God kind of faith," what seems to matter in this framework is faith plus results. Leaving the sick to their own devices — their own faith — at a time when they are most vulnerable can increase emotional distress and prolong illness. Moreover, it can weaken faith.

Second, Word of faith congregations' emphasis on the specialization of gifts can lead to the exclusion of the majority of the congregation from healing ministry. Stated differently, would-be participants run the risk of becoming spectators of the "special event" of healing. More importantly the tired, yet willing, hands of the *many* are no longer deemed to be healing hands. *Helping* hands, yes — but not healing hands. Mundane facets of communal care such as bringing meals and watching the children of the sick fall outside the sacred canopy of healing. For some in this setting, the very need for such "auxiliary ministry" displays the fact that many people of God lack the power to succeed in their primary task of healing sick bodies. They reckon that in light of the church's call to lay hands on the sick that they might recover, cooking chicken and greens is a sorry concession to the church's failure.

The most critical and ironic outcome of individualization can be detected in how issues of identity and respect are reconfigured in this framework. Sickness is now often associated with one's spirituality. Therefore, the longer one remains sick, the more likely it is that one's faith will be called into question. The best illustration is that of the "sick and shut-in list" that we highlighted in traditional churches. Keeping names on a sick list for a long period of time in a Word of faith setting often takes on a different meaning: it publicly identifies those who have not taken authority over their illnesses and claimed their healing. It no longer affirms the dignity of the sick, as in traditional churches. In like manner, sick members, in some settings, are discouraged from returning to the altar each Sunday for prayer. They are told to "claim their healing" and "count it done." For some faith healing advocates, to pray once for healing is an act of faith, but to pray repeatedly is to question God and undermine one's blessing — which is on the way.[34]

34. Knight, "God's Faithfulness and God's Freedom," p. 68, observes that some Word of faith practitioners believe that a single prayer is efficacious. Praying twice is

Those who have experienced the shortcomings and failings of both traditional and Word of faith responses ask if there is a doctor in the house: "Is there no balm in Gilead? Is there no physician there?" (Jer. 8:22 NRSV). The limitations of both approaches demonstrate the importance of an alternative ministry of healing.

The Holistic Response to Sickness

There is a balm in Gilead
To make the wounded whole.
There is a balm in Gilead
To heal the sin-sick soul.

"Balm in Gilead"
(African American spiritual)

In many African American churches, a practice of holistic healing has emerged that seems to be attracting increased interest on the part of both traditional and Word of faith congregations. The term "holistic" reflects an integrative view of well-being that embraces the entire person, including her relationships and the larger environment in which she lives. So defined, the practice of healing extends into many areas of life. The most common biblical perspective on health and healing articulated by practitioners of this approach is that of human responsibility or stewardship. Beliefs in this approach to healing often include the following tenets:

- God responds to sickness in a variety of ways; therefore, believers should avail themselves of all God's means of healing.
- The body is the temple of the Holy Spirit (1 Cor. 6:19).
- Safeguarding our health is a Christian duty because our bodies are the sites through which we glorify God.
- Only as we care for our bodies can we be effective in ministry.

---

tantamount to disbelief. He quotes Kenneth Hagin, a leader of this movement whose works are influential in some African American circles, as saying: "I don't believe I prayed more than half a dozen times for both of them [referring to his children] in all these years. Why? Because you can have what you say."

Like the other approaches, the holistic approach incorporates Scripture and prayer.[35] However, its contours are much broader and its strategies are more diverse, encompassing many aspects of human well-being: individual psychotherapy and fitness classes, for example, would come under its umbrella. I will highlight those ministries that emphasize physical well-being and will narrow my focus to three features that characterize the holistic response: a diagnosis of communal sickness, the prevention of sickness, and programs for recovery and nurture.

Holistic Healing Approaches in Local Churches

Proponents of holism presume that sociopolitical contexts and communal cultural values shape individual health and must therefore shape healing interventions.[36] While traditional churches assure the sick believer that she will be cared for and Word of faith churches teach her that she need not remain sick because God has defeated the enemy, many holistic churches make the personal and social roots and causes of illnesses an integral concern of their healing ministry. How and why the believer became sick is the question that is often raised in this approach. Not surprisingly, congrega-

---

35. See website of West Angeles Church of God in Christ. West Angeles Church of God in Christ in Los Angeles, CA, is an example of a holistic church "concerned with the wellbeing of the whole person," which has both extensive prevention and recovery programs. The programs, which are based upon Scripture and prayer, include a Weight Watchers community meeting and fitness classes. The nurture and recovery focus includes a fathers' fellowship, ministry to single parents, a twelve-step program for substance abusers, ministry to the hearing impaired, and marriage recovery. Prayer and Scripture are foundational for these programs. For example, the counseling department is committed to helping Christians learn how to apply the Scriptures to individual situations, "establish a power base through Jesus Christ," and view themselves from God's perspective. With respect to the fitness classes, one instructor spoke of his class as a form of evangelism inasmuch as gospel music is used, scriptural passages are called out during the workout, and prophetic prayer is offered for members at the end of each class (telephone interview with Minister Walter Goode).

36. See Townes, *Breaking the Fine Rain of Death*, pp. 154-55, for a discussion of health as a cultural production. In contrast to a biomedical model of health that emphasizes "curing" sick "individuals," this perspective analyzes how "health behaviors are culturally produced," that is, how a variety of social factors and group values shape sickness. As such, it is sensitive to culturally relevant responses to sickness.

tions are beginning to make connections between social factors, such as lifestyle choices and income, and the health of their church community. Sickness, churches in this category agree, is a communal phenomenon that has the capacity to impact groups of persons. The insidious reality of HIV/ AIDS and the heightened prevalence of other life-threatening illnesses among African Americans belie any notions that sickness is an aberration that affects a select few.

In cases in which the entire community is impacted by pathology, macro-level changes need to occur before individuals can overcome their afflictions. Illnesses resulting from environmental pollution offer a prime example. If sickness in the community results from the presence of a local toxic waste dump, praying for persons on weekly sick lists (traditional practice) and anointing with consecrated oil (Word of faith practice), however Spirit-directed, will neither resolve the problem nor get at its source. In order for members to recover fully, the dump must be removed.[37] One implication for the practice of healing is that identifying and changing those structures and institutions that are the root cause of illness become important aspects of caring for the sick.[38]

Another means of combating illness at its source is to employ a strategy of prevention, which can spare church members from the painful consequences of ill health or premature death. Therefore, practices of caring for and honoring the body[39] are incorporated into healing practice at the earliest stages. Although families in traditional and Word of faith churches no doubt also practice prevention to some degree, what differs in this setting is that prevention is undertaken primarily as an ecclesial act to safeguard the health of the body of Christ and that of the larger community. Numerous churches have undertaken special programs to draw attention to health concerns, such as diabetes, prostate cancer, and obesity, that plague African

---

37. See Emilie M. Townes, *In a Blaze of Glory: Womanist Spirituality as Social Witness* (Nashville: Abingdon Press, 1995), pp. 55-60. Townes refers to toxic waste landfills in minority neighborhoods as a contemporary form of lynching.

38. Short of social analysis, grassroots organizing, and political engagement at various levels, internal healing ministry will be insufficient to deal with the structural and systemic roots of the illness. The point is not that healing prayer is limited to a certain "sphere" or that prayer is an apolitical practice. Rather, practices must be connected with other kinds of activities in order to address structural injustice.

39. Stephanie Paulsell, "Honoring the Body," in *Practicing Our Faith: A Way of Life for a Searching People* (San Francisco: Jossey-Bass Publishers, 1997), pp. 13-27.

Americans disproportionately. In this light, issues of diet and exercise, often perceived as matters of individual preference, are now addressed as critical ministry issues. To bolster prevention efforts, more African American churches offer gospel aerobics and fitness classes, monthly blood pressure checks, cancer screenings, and nutrition counseling.[40]

When prevention efforts are unsuccessful, congregations offer a variety of counseling options. Acknowledging that we have been created as complex creatures with profound emotional needs, these congregations affirm that healing often occurs through relational means, such as support and recovery groups, including those for bereavement, divorce, and substance abuse. Nurture groups that focus on singleness, marriage enrichment, and parenting are also common in many churches.

In contrast to other responses to sickness, holism integrates both generalists and specialists in its practice. It expands the idea of giftedness to include professional expertise and specialized training and thereby incorporates a number of health professionals, such as psychologists and nurses, into congregational ministries. At the same time, it also privileges the hands of the sick. Enabling the sick to "lay hands" on each other in therapeutic settings is one way of giving tangible expression to the work of support and recovery groups.

Evaluation of the Holistic Approach

Holistic healing rightly seeks to address the very nature of healing and therefore envisions whole persons as those who are rightly related to God, themselves, others, and the rest of creation. We must ask, however, if the practice is faithful to this vision. I believe that holism is the most viable approach and the one that holds the most promise for the future, yet it is not

40. Body and Soul of Pasadena, CA, is an example of a ministry engaged in preventive care. It is a partnership of six African American churches from various denominations that collaborates with the Pasadena branch of The American Cancer Society, the Pasadena Public Health Department, and other groups. The coalition is committed to implementing "a program of nutritional, physical, and spiritual education" through weekly church activities such as pastors promoting healthy living through sermons and teachers including nutrition information in Sunday School and Bible studies. The various churches participate in a variety of programs that include fitness walks, distributing information on nutrition, gospel aerobics, and planting community gardens.

without significant deficiencies. Since many African American churches are gravitating toward holism, I will devote attention to its strengths, weaknesses, and promise, with the intent that the analysis will address issues that are prevalent in most churches and implicit in other approaches to healing.

Of the three approaches, holism offers the most comprehensive definition and practice of healing. Its multifaceted nature accounts for its strength. The practice's diversity allows it to respond to a greater range of human needs, to better attend to the complexity of human experience, and to be more sensitive to the health needs of different age groups and various sectors of the African American community[41] than alternative healing practices. It also brings healing into closer cooperation with Christian and everyday practices. As a result, the practice tends to be more fluid and versatile than other approaches, and in many instances more inviting.[42] Holism's willingness to consider the causes of illness and to pursue prevention is important as well; it has the ability to avert the unnecessary loss of African American lives. This feature of holism cannot be taken lightly — especially when I consider the experience of the loved ones I mentioned in the introduction. While the church rightly offered them radical hope in a healing God and hands-on care for their exhausted bodies, I cannot help but wonder what might have been had a prevention ministry been in place in their churches.

Yet despite much to commend it, holism does have its shortcomings. It is interesting to observe that the strength of the holistic approach does not appear to be rooted in the cogency of its beliefs; in fact, it is not always clear how holism holds together its diverse elements. Furthermore, it is somewhat difficult to *locate* primary beliefs in the practice. Unlike care and cure responses to sickness, the holistic approach does not readily articulate explicit beliefs about God's nature when it discusses its understanding of

41. It appears that women's health concerns can be better addressed by holistic healing than other approaches. See Teresa Fry Brown, "Avoiding Asphyxiation: A Womanist Perspective on Intrapersonal and Interpersonal Transformation," in *Embracing the Spirit: Womanist Perspectives on Hope, Salvation, and Transformation,* ed. Emilie Townes, The Bishop Henry McNeal Turner/Sojourner Truth Series in Black Religion, vol. 13 (Maryknoll, NY: Orbis Books, 1997), p. 90, for a discussion of a church-affiliated womanist (black feminist) group that addresses black women's health concerns.

42. See Kathryn Tanner's chapter in this volume for an account of the fluidity of practices, pp. 229-30.

healing. This is not to say that believers in holistic churches do not hold robust beliefs about God's love, sovereignty, or redemptive activity. Rather, practitioners speak more readily of the need to care for their bodies as good stewards (which is not surprising in a framework that stresses human effort in the form of prevention) than of God's ongoing nurture and sustaining of their bodies as God's good creation. Whereas traditional and Word of faith practitioners essentially "do what they believe" in their healing practices — offering care and appropriating cure — it is more difficult to discern what practitioners of holism believe about God by observing their pluriform practice. In short, it appears that sustained and formal reflection about God's nature and activity is missing from holistic practice.

The failure to explicitly articulate how *God* heals through the practice of holism might suggest that the viability of holism, in some settings, stems from its productivity and effectiveness[43] rather than its robust beliefs and practice. The absence of explicit beliefs about God is not problematic at a practical level, for little if any theological reflection is needed in order for the practice to function initially.[44] Diet and exercise *work*. Certain forms of counseling are *beneficial*. In fact, one might argue that lack of theological attentiveness permits holism to borrow activities from the wider culture eclectically and uncritically. Thus an activity such as exercise can be adopted from the larger society and easily adapted to a church setting. With the right music and instructor, a worldly workout is transformed into "gospel aerobics." However, this apparent benefit can also be a problem: because so many non-Christians do the same workouts in other settings, it is not readily apparent and immediately identifiable how God is at work in a routine of push-ups and why this everyday activity is in fact part of a larger practice of healing.

Therefore, the very ambiguity of certain features of this practice requires that holism engage in theological reflection (figuring out what one has been doing, why one does it, and how it fits with other beliefs and actions)[45] and set forth explicit beliefs about God (for example, why the God

43. If doing a practice *well* is inextricably bound with "that which makes the practice itself good," namely its ability to point to and reflect God's active care for the world, then effectiveness (as manifested in such things as lowered cholesterol rates and weight loss) fails to define fully what it means to have a successful healing practice. See Christine Pohl's chapter in this volume for a discussion of the goodness of practices.

44. See Tanner's helpful discussion of theological reflection and practices, p. 230.

45. Tanner, p. 232.

that Christians worship cares about bodies) if the practice is to minister to its participants with integrity. When detached from theological convictions, the holistic approach risks becoming a merely pragmatic church-based program of health-related activities rather than a specifically Christian practice of healing that points to the transformative power of God. Nevertheless, holism, which is still in a relatively nascent stage, has the capacity to be a life-changing practice in spite of its limitations, once it gets its theological bearings.

Theological Reflection, Beliefs, and Practices

I want to suggest how tending to beliefs can empower practices by demonstrating how a particular belief that we have already encountered, namely, the work of the cross, can be reconfigured to bolster the practice of healing. Moreover, I want to indicate how the process of theological reflection can enable holism to function as a potent practice of healing.

When we compare the three approaches to healing, it becomes clear that *practices are subject to distortion if theological accounts are indiscriminately abridged in ways that lose sight of the belief's purpose and end.* Just as care and cure practices would benefit from cultivating full-bodied accounts of the doctrines of incarnation and faith,[46] so too would the holistic approach benefit from cultivating a more expansive exposition of beliefs. I offer the work of the cross, which confirms that a gracious God is at work in the world to do good, as one example. Although the care practice speaks of

---

46. In the care response, solidarity with the sick is valued as an important dimension of Jesus' healing activity. Yet the logic of the doctrine of incarnation that informs this perception suggests that Christ's identification with our weaknesses and his assumption of full humanity is in service to redemption: Christ assumed our humanity in order to *heal* us in the fullest sense. This seems to imply that the aim of congregational solidarity with the sick requires openness to healing and redemption in its manifold forms. With respect to the cure approach, the practice must make reference to a fuller doctrinal account of faith, including its use of Scripture. Faith, which has a long history in the Christian tradition, has been understood as both a gift of God and a matter of the will, as both objective and subjective, as assent to truths *(assensus)* and as trust *(fiducia)*. As a relational reality, Knight reminds us that "[o]ur faith is not in a promise to heal but in a God who is love and has demonstrated that love even unto death on the cross" ("God's Faithfulness and God's Freedom," p. 88).

Christ's sufferings as a sign of solidarity with his people, and the cure practice views healing as a benefit of the work of substitutionary atonement, none of the approaches articulates how "the foolishness of the cross" (1 Cor. 1:18-31)[47] subverts and deconstructs deeply-ingrained cultural "wisdom" associated with body, health, and healing. In the mystery of the cross, we are confronted with a weakened, wounded, and disfigured body — which was given for us. How does this body speak to our own bodies, that is, to our own notions of strength, beauty, autonomy, longevity, and fear of death?[48] In a culture in which some pursue healing because they lack primary healthcare, while others are obsessed with cultivating the "body beautiful," strengthening Christian practices of healing will necessarily entail discerning what is inadequate, and at times wrongheaded, about our own health-related practices as well as those of the wider society.[49]

For practitioners of holism, this kind of critical questioning could lead to revisiting the practice more attentively, which might lead adherents to recognize and name implicit beliefs about God and how they relate to the actions of practitioners. In effect, this would amount to compiling a more complete list of beliefs than the one I offered earlier. In this vein, practitioners could connect prevention efforts with God's activity of preserving and sustaining creation, and associate support groups with God's redemptive and restorative activity. In like manner, practitioners might draw closer ties between creation and stewardship of the body, with the result that caring for one's body is understood as a concrete response to receiving

47. See Richard B. Hays, *First Corinthians*, Interpretation: A Bible Commentary for Teaching and Preaching, ed. James Luther Mays (Louisville: John Knox Press, 1997), pp. 36-39, for pastoral and ethical implications of this passage.

48. For example, the subversive nature of the cross calls into question dominant standards of beauty, which tend to be Eurocentric, as well as distorted African American cultural expectations such as the myth of the "longsuffering, strong black woman." The latter concept often contributes to African American women suffering from preventable illnesses due to denial. See Karen Baker-Fletcher and Garth Kasimu Baker-Fletcher, *My Sister, My Brother: Womanist and Xodus God-Talk* (Maryknoll, NY: Orbis, 1997), pp. 143-48.

49. Of course, Christian practices and those of the wider society mutually condition and correct each other. It may be the case that some societal healing practices, such as those that care for persons with HIV/AIDS or serve victims of domestic violence, have prodded the church to better understand its own beliefs and deepen its own practices.

it as a gift from God. Reflecting on the way certain beliefs fund the practice of healing could then raise different kinds of questions, such as holism's relationship to other practices. One might ask, for instance, how holistic healing differs from "wholeness," "wellness," and other manifestations of "spirituality and health" that are so widespread in our culture.

By continually engaging in this kind of analysis and reconfiguring the practice in ways that accord with Christian beliefs, practitioners could work toward a more fully developed holism that will have the capacity to offer an integrative response to sickness — one that incorporates the strengths of care and cure approaches. This envisioned approach would theologically and practically affirm that in healing God acts through the sovereign exercise of freedom *and* through honoring God's Word, esteems both faith *and* faithfulness, and works through both individual persons and community.

There Is a Doctor in the House and Jesus Is His Name

Can't nobody do me like Jesus,
Can't nobody do me like the Lord,
Can't nobody do me like Jesus,
He's my friend.
He healed my body and told me to run on . . .
He's my friend.
[That's why] Can't nobody do me like Jesus . . .

"Can't Nobody Do Me Like Jesus"
(traditional gospel song)

Not only must healing practices define and foster healing, they must also spell out the *purpose* for which Christians are to be healed. For what will Christians live once they have recovered from sickness?[50] How edifying is the practice of healing if Christians lower their blood pressure and become "healthier" merely to pursue materialistic lifestyles of acquisition and consumption that conflict with the values of God's reign? If the cross deconstructs our false notions of "healthy living," then Jesus' ministry of healing,

---

50. Walter J. Hollenweger, *Pentecostalism: Origins and Developments Worldwide* (Peabody, MA: Hendrickson Publishers, 1997), p. 238.

119

which encompassed forgiveness, reconciliation, and the promise of God's coming reign, can reconstitute the church's practice. What Jesus offered the sick was not a different interpretation of healing but the opportunity to experience a *qualitatively different* kind of life, one the gospels refuse to romanticize as a life of unending health or idyllic happiness. Rather, the life Christ presents to us is one that inverts all of our domesticated notions of well-being and prosperity: for in it, true strength is imparted in real weakness; receiving one's life results from risking it; and abundant life is promised, although long life is never ensured.

Those who embrace this life of discipleship can testify that *there is a doctor in the house.* To be healed by him is to be beckoned by the resurrected body of the Crucified One into a life of unconventional beauty in which our tired and wounded bodies are no longer classified and objectified but are embraced and made whole. Because the healing Jesus offers us is rooted in his ministry of redemption, its aim is the healing of our "sin-sick" souls. Therefore, healing as spiritual transformation can take place even when cure or physical recovery does not. Conversely, it is possible to experience physical restoration and still remain unhealed.[51]

And Jesus is his name. This doctor in the house is a peculiar kind of doctor, whose aim is not to cure and then disappear but whose healing more profoundly consists in our knowledge of him and his presence with us. If healing essentially concerns our relationship with God, then the aim of healing is "getting to know the doctor better" and honoring our relationship with him in "sickness and in health," in "life and death" (Phil. 1:20). It is the *kind* of doctor Jesus is that characterizes the nature of Christian healing. The gospels not only highlight Jesus' prowess as a healer but also his empathy for the sick. In African American church tradition, Jesus not only treats the sick but also comforts them with a compassionate bedside manner. He remains at their side as a companion when other caregivers leave. His abiding presence as a "friend who sticks closer than any brother or sister" assures the sick that they will not be neglected or abandoned. And for scores of African Americans who desperately seek to be cared for, cured, or made whole, this doctor is one who can be trusted.

51. Huis, "Healing," p. 478.

A Community's Practice of Hospitality: The Interdependence of Practices and of Communities

CHRISTINE D. POHL

Walking into the community's kitchen at 5:50 a.m., I found six people busy with their early morning tasks. The coffee, eggs, sausages, and grits were ready, and the oranges were sliced. Several of the workers had already been up for hours, preparing a warm breakfast for the 150 people who were sleepily lining up outside in the early morning darkness.

Partners in the house, volunteers from churches, local schools, and agencies, and people who had only recently moved off the street mingled easily among the pots of steaming food and the piles of dishes waiting to be laid out. At 6 a.m. more volunteers arrived, and we sat down in a circle in the homey dining room that would soon seat shifts of thirty-six hungry people at a time. After several announcements and the distribution of serving assignments, we read from the Scriptures.

Over the course of three days we looked at the story of Abraham, Sarah, and the three strangers/angels (Genesis 18); the instructions in Hebrews 13:2, "Do not neglect to show hospitality to strangers, for by doing that some have entertained angels without knowing it" (also Romans 12:9-13); and the story of Bartimaeus' persistent cry to Jesus and Jesus' hospitable response to the blind beggar (Mark 10:46-52).[1] Part of my responsibil-

---

1. All Scripture quotations are taken from the New Revised Standard Version of the Bible.

121

ity that week was to lead a time of devotion and reflection each morning, which I did by offering a few comments on the verses and then inviting responses.

The circle — whose makeup changed somewhat each day — included teachers and students, retired people and youth, Christians and non-believers, lawyers who worked on death penalty cases and seminary professors who taught preaching and New Testament, African-Americans, Asians, Caucasians, the formerly homeless and the very well-housed. As they responded to the readings, the depth and diversity of their insights made each morning's reflections fresh and challenging. On the third morning, when we discussed Jesus' gracious response to being interrupted by Bartimaeus, a lawyer with no religious background wondered whether her work on behalf of prisoners facing the death penalty might be understood as her way of interrupting the machinery of the legal system. A man who had moved into the house just a few days earlier identified with Bartimaeus in a different way, responding to the Scripture with special personal urgency. Like Bartimaeus, he wanted to be heard, and he wanted to be able to see — to see the people around him and to read the pages of the Bible. He needed a pair of glasses and wondered whether this community of Jesus' followers could help him get them. Community leaders assured him that they would.

After reflection time, we shared prayer concerns and prayed. We offered gratitude to God for a new day and for resources to share. We prayed about an ongoing court trial that involved the death penalty; we prayed for a man in the house who was dying from AIDS; we prayed that God would give us hearts that were ready to welcome. The prayer and devotion time did not end at that point, however, even though it was time to take up our breakfast responsibilities. The community had established a pattern of reflection-meal-reflection; all of us knew that we would return to this circle after the meals were served. Thus we knew that the serving time itself was inseparable from our prayer and reflection on Scripture. As the leader of the reflection, I asked people to be thinking about certain questions as they hosted breakfast that morning: Where were they encountering Jesus? Where did they find holy ground? What gestures of respect and welcome did they notice? How might they understand the interruptions they were likely to experience?

As guests entered the dining room, partners and regular volunteers greeted many by name. Each was handed a bowl of sausages and eggs and was invited to sit down at a table covered with a red and white checked tablecloth. On each table, the guests found bread, jam, peanut butter, hot grits, and a vase of fresh flowers. The setting was quiet, almost sleepy, and relatively unrushed.

The people who came through the door for breakfast were looking for food, friendship, a comfortable seat, and a change of socks. Some checked for their mail, others visited with people in the house or read the morning paper for a few minutes in an upholstered chair. Some, when pressed, told of serious medical or legal problems that needed immediate attention. Because the practice of hospitality in this community is multi-layered, guest/ host roles often intermingled. The people in the house regularly offered food and other forms of aid to the homeless people of the city, but the partners in the house also invited some homeless persons to live with them in community if they were willing to try to live within the disciplines of community life — no alcohol, drugs, TV, or paid work outside the house. Those who became residents received shelter, food, shoes that fit, a routine that shaped their days, friendship, and a place to serve others. Partners — those who had committed themselves to long-term responsibility for the house and ministry — also welcomed resident volunteers, individuals willing to make a six-month or yearlong commitment to living in the house and sharing in the ministry. The resultant community of partners, resident volunteers, and residents who had recently left the streets served those who were homeless. Beyond this, they also offered hospitality to hundreds of day volunteers who came to work but who were also the resident community's guests, since they needed to be welcomed, instructed, and nurtured as well. These volunteers were invited into the relationships and daily practices of an ever-shifting community organized around offering hospitality to strangers and friends.

I recently spent five days at the Open Door Community in Atlanta in response to an invitation from the partners who had read my work on the hospitality tradition.[2] This community possesses a deep, lived knowledge of hospitality, but its members were eager also to engage in more systematic reflection. They hoped that my presence for several days would help them to sharpen their theological and biblical insights regarding the difficult practice to which they were committed. They saw my visit as an opportu-

2. Christine D. Pohl, *Making Room: Recovering Hospitality as a Christian Tradition* (Grand Rapids: Eerdmans, 1999).

nity for sustained conversation and for mentoring residents and volunteers in the practice that is central to their life as a community. Attentive to the importance of the historical tradition of Christian hospitality and to its biblical foundations, but also aware of the complex social structures and interests that make hospitality to the poor both urgent and difficult, this community engaged the biblical text and tradition with critical intensity.

My experience in the community that week intertwined various roles: volunteer and stranger, teacher and learner, guest and host. It was interesting to note that much of what I had to offer I had, in fact, learned first from the Open Door and similar communities. While doing research on hospitality, I had visited several communities, participating in their shared life and talking with both hosts and guests. I had also read extensively about other Christian communities and churches from past centuries that had lived in ways that embodied this particular practice. During my previous visit to the Open Door, I had seen how a practice that was crucial to Christian identity in the ancient world could also be lived out today. What I had seen persuaded me of the beauty and fragility, the mystery and difficulty of this practice.

My visits to the Open Door and other communities of hospitality opened windows onto a single, central practice of the Christian life. But the experiences were simultaneously windows onto a whole way of life, because the practice of hospitality can never stand alone in the life of a Christian community. It is necessarily supported and sustained by other practices and commitments, just as it supports and sustains them. Yet close observation of these communities also brought into view the difficulties, failures, and deformations to which every Christian practice is prone.

An intentional Christian community provides something of a microcosm of how practices work in the lives of faithful Christians. In looking at a single practice as it is embodied in a small Christian community, this essay attempts to tease out significant understandings and tensions regarding practices more generally. In particular, it explores the interdependence of practices — how the practice of hospitality is complexly connected with other Christian practices — and the interdependence among Christian communities of various kinds. Some individuals, churches, and communities excel in one practice more than others; this is also therefore a reflection on the role of specialization and complementarity in the encompassing body of believers.

In almost every community I encountered, the practice of hospitality centrally involves common meals and conversation between hosts, guests, and strangers around a table. In this context, food, shelter, attention, and respect are shared. Hosts make room for those with no place, sharing themselves and their lives rather than only their skills. They offer hospitality in response to the people and needs they have encountered — needs for nourishment, place, safety, justice, friendship, and the knowledge of God's love and grace. But they also offer welcome as a way of responding to the gospel, and especially to the witness of Jesus and the Scriptures to the centrality of hospitality. Additionally, hosts offer welcome because of its importance to their own lives; as one commented, "without hospitality, our souls would wither."

Many practitioners describe offering hospitality to strangers as "the best and hardest thing" they've ever done. It is "the best thing" because the practice is so central to Christian faith and identity and because they so often find God present in it. Hospitality is at the center of such communities because it is at the center of the gospel. One of the founders of the Open Door explains:

> We speak, sometimes softly, sometimes shouting out (Isa. 58:1), of our life together. Out of the hunger, desire, and the need to build a Christian life in the center of the city, out of a call to be witnesses and to give testimony, out of the thirst to say "Yes, yes!" we proclaim to those who are hungry, "There's plenty of food!" We stand in jails and prisons promising "Yes, yes!" to those who are in prison: "There is a promise of liberty to captives!" "Yes, yes!" to those who work and cannot earn enough to pay both room and board: "There is an abundance at this table! Enough for all. Our God is a God who keeps promises! Yes, yes!" Out of this vocation we move into a mission — a love in action — for we have been taught by Jesus and Martin and Willie Dee Wimberly: the only solution is love. That is what we're all about![3]

Hospitality is "the hardest thing" because work, strain, and hard decisions are so often involved. One morning during my visit, there were enough volunteers that one could be freed from kitchen duty to play the piano. Live music added to the welcoming setting. Michael played a soulful

---

3. Ed Loring, *I Hear Hope Banging at My Back Door: Writings from "Hospitality"* (Atlanta: The Open Door Community, 2000), p. 5.

version of "Bridge over Troubled Water" as other volunteers distributed vitamins, socks, and toothbrushes. In that context, it seemed somehow fitting to think about bridges and troubled waters and how all of us needed friends. But the experience was also troubling. Despite the respectful demeanor of volunteers, one could also sense the quiet, long-term humiliation of men whose circumstances forced them to ask well-intentioned strangers if there were any underwear available and of women who discreetly inquired about personal hygiene items. The awkward and painful dimension of hospitality was more apparent in these encounters than during meals, because even when the items were available the small indignities of life on the street hit home powerfully. Gracious hosts and pleasant music could not fully obliterate the differences in power and resources between those who served and those who came as needy guests.

After the morning guests had left, the breakfast workers cleaned up. Then we sat down for our own breakfasts. We were hungry, tired, and closer to each other from our shared efforts. We prayed, laughed, ate, and read again the morning's Scripture. I repeated the questions I had raised earlier in relation to the Scripture passage and asked for additional responses based on the morning's experiences. We also reviewed how the breakfast had gone. Responses came quickly and intensely.

We talked about Jesus and gestures of welcome, about holy ground and a shortage of socks, and about ways we welcomed or disregarded one another as we responded to guests. That morning several of the homeless people had asked about showers. It had been hard for volunteers to say "no" — the showers weren't open because there were not enough resident volunteers to oversee them. For a homeless person, an opportunity for a shower is a crucial experience of hospitable welcome and human dignity, but because of a shortage of experienced volunteers, there could be no showers that month.

Another morning, shortly after breakfast, community members and volunteers went out into the front yard of the house for a worship service with people who found daily refuge in the yard. One of the volunteers, an older African-American man who had been active in the Civil Rights Movement and who had recently arrived to prepare lunch, led out in song. Most of the people in the circle joined in quickly:

Pass me not, O gentle Savior, Hear my humble cry,
While on others you are calling, Do not pass me by.

Savior, Savior, Hear my humble cry;
While on others you are calling, Do not pass me by.

He did not know that we would be reading about Bartimaeus and his cries to Jesus, but careful planning could not have resulted in a more fitting hymn. So we sang in the yard, slowly, plaintively, calling on Jesus not to pass us by. Then, shouting above the noise of morning traffic, I read the story of the blind beggar (Mark 10) to a group of men and women generally as scorned and rejected as Bartimaeus had been. One of the partners preached, emphasizing the importance of crying out until we're heard. After the brief street sermon, one of the men who regularly slept in the yard began to sing, "I Want Jesus to Walk with Me." The familiar song seemed disturbingly fitting in that setting — homeless people spend a lot of time walking.

This worship service was itself a powerful experience of hospitality and welcome, even though it took place outside the doors of the community. The circle grew larger as more homeless people became interested and joined the group. This worship had grown from a ministry of hospitality, but more importantly it embodied and proclaimed welcome itself. The transcending of social status boundaries in worship was brief but very good. I wondered what morning commuters saw as they drove by on their way to work. Did they see only an oddly mixed ragtag circle of folks carrying on about something, or did they catch a glimpse of the kingdom of God?

The hunger of some of the Open Door's guests to hear and to understand the Word of God was deeply moving. Many of those who had come in off the streets or who slept in the yard had at one time been part of church communities. They were familiar with the stories of Scripture, and they knew the words to the old hymns we sang. Many had been baptized; some congregation had once recognized them as children of the covenant family of God. Even so, now these baptized brothers and sisters slept outside, far from the shelter of family and church. The contrast prompted difficult questions about the meaning and significance of baptism for Christians and about how sacraments connect with our practical and spiritual responsibilities to one another. For leaders in the community of hospitality, promises made in baptism raised acute concerns about churches that built fences and hired security guards to keep their sanctuaries and parishioners safe from "the homeless."

Worship and the sacraments sustain the life of this community. Bible study, reflection, and prayer frame each breakfast and lunch, and Sunday worship services are a high point of the week. On Sunday afternoons, the dining room is transformed from one kind of sanctuary to another, as the regular place of eating becomes also the place where community members and friends feed on the Word. Here homeless people, pastors, students, professors, children, and teens join together with community members around the welcome table. It is unusual to worship in a heavily used dining room, but in this case the setting serves as a helpful reminder that community, hospitality, food, Eucharist, and worship are closely tied together. The weekly Eucharist follows the singing and preaching, and then worship spills into the evening meal, a time of joy and sharing open to all.

Worship in this context was never divorced from concerns about justice. Prayer and reflection necessarily attend to the inadequacy of minimum wage, the exploitation of poor people by unjust labor practices, the ever-changing rules surrounding healthcare and prescription drugs, and more. That these issues have very personal human consequences is always clear. In communities of hospitality such as the Open Door, partners live alongside people who experience daily injustice; injustices, big and small, happen to people they know and love. In the case of a homeless man with advanced cancer in his leg, their concern was not only that healthcare was inadequate for indigent people, but also this particular man's lack of healthcare was threatening his already precarious life.

"Justice is important, but supper is essential," argues one of the community founders.[4] For this community of hospitality, justice is terribly important, and their work for it keeps their hospitality from reinforcing the injustices of the larger society. However, it is their suppers together that turn needy people into friends.

One Community among Many Communities

The longing for friendship at table, the capacity to feel compassion for those in need, the grace to follow Jesus' way of welcome to the outcast — these and many other gifts, mysteriously supplied and sacrificially cultivated, have led hundreds of small communities around the world to orga-

---

4. Ed Loring, "Bandaids and Beyond," *Hospitality* 8/2 (March 1989): 2.

nize their lives around the practice of hospitality, singling it out from among the many practices that belong to Christian living as their central calling. The pursuit of justice is important, to be sure; but for such communities that pursuit is decisively shaped by specific friendships forged within the practice of hospitality.

Few Christian communities organize their lives this thoroughly around a single practice, however. Most are like the two congregations whose hospitality is described in Gilbert Bond's chapter in this volume: their worship gatherings incorporate some aspects of hospitality, and certain members support hospitality ministries on a part-time basis by distributing food or volunteering at a shelter. These ministries are important, but they do not require the congregations to organize nearly all their time and resources around the difficult demands of offering welcome to people who have no other place to go for the most basic needs of life.

What are we to make of the sacrificial emphasis on a single practice embodied in the Open Door and other communities of hospitality? Some observers turn it into an impossible ideal — a model of the Christian life that makes other models seem tepid and lackluster by comparison. However, to segregate these admirable communities from larger currents in the whole Body of Christ — which spans many denominations, continents, and generations — would be to misunderstand both the gifts they offer to the whole Body and the gifts they receive from it.

For those who find nourishment around its tables, the Open Door may seem to be an oasis in the inhospitable desert of American society — a desert, indeed, into which most American churches have themselves been absorbed. In fact, however, the Open Door and other communities of hospitality have little chance of flourishing when cut off from other Christian communities, including some in which the sacrificial service that shapes the Open Door is rarely on plain display. Some of the reasons for the mutual dependence between the larger church and this highly committed community are obvious: communities that welcome significant numbers of strangers need volunteers, food, and other kinds of support. The members of many congregations, as well as many who are not members of any congregation, come to the Open Door on a daily, weekly, or monthly basis to serve meals, to produce the newspaper, and to join in the ministry to prisoners. One woman faithfully brings fresh flowers every week and arranges them for each table in the dining room. The Open Door depends on volunteers and on the generosity and resources of churches, friends, and the denomination to which the Open Door is connected. It also relies on the formation in hospitality that volunteers have received in other settings, even relatively unchallenging ones. If churches were not introducing members to grace-filled practices of service, generosity, and discernment, the volunteer supply would wither, and with it crucial dimensions of the Open Door's hospitality. There would be less frequent meals, no showers, and fewer resources to distribute.

The Open Door relies on the larger Body of Christ in less tangible ways as well. Its focus on the practice of hospitality allows it to draw wisdom and guidance from multiple theological and ecclesial traditions. Although connected to a Protestant denomination, its identity and practices have also been profoundly shaped by the writings and experiences of Dorothy Day and the Catholic Worker Movement. Peter Maurin, co-founder of that movement, drew heavily from the hospitality tradition embedded in ancient Irish monasticism. In this single example, it is clear how a particular practice spans many centuries, traditions, and locations, and how attention to practices opens up opportunities to draw from the riches of various traditions.

In turn, communities of hospitality, with their experienced practitioners, have significantly contributed to the recovery of the practice of hospitality and have helped to keep it alive and fresh for the whole church. While their challenge to the larger church to become more hospitable can cause discomfort, it also provides glimpses into the mystery of God's gracious presence in the guest-host relationship. Within this often flawed but nonetheless vibrant practice, people are able to see aspects of the kingdom lived out.

Experiences at places such as the Open Door also shape volunteers and affect how they are involved in their home congregations. On several nights each week, volunteers from around the city bring dinner to the community. Often it is a suburban congregation that cooks the food and sends a few representatives to help prepare and serve it. Once the food is laid out, these volunteers sit down to the meal with community members and sometimes develop close ties across significant social boundaries; some become advocates for hospitality and justice in their churches and in the larger society. They go home with different angles of vision and different sensitivities, thereafter looking at budget allocations and building decisions differently because of their friendships and experiences within a community of hospitality.

Moreover, practitioners and communities that excel in a single practice are essential to sustaining the practice across generations. Often, they play a central role in transmitting the practice to the next generation. The wisdom and wonder of a practice is communicated through stories that are told and retold within the community of faith, and these stories become more vivid when encountered in the midst of contemporary practitioners and in the face of contemporary need. In the last few centuries the practice of hospitality to strangers as a specific dimension of Christian identity was nearly lost, and with it the skills, commitments, attitudes, and stories that sustained it earlier in the church's history. The renewal of this practice in recent decades is largely due to the small contemporary communities that visibly embody it.

Not every community, church, and family can or will do every practice well; what each emphasizes depends on gifts and resources, on context and needs. When a community does live a practice well, however, people notice. Communities of hospitality welcome homeless people, refugees, persons with disabilities, or students and seekers. But they often also welcome an enormous number of other guests — people who come to visit or volunteer because they sense that there is something true or authentic within these communities.

Jubilee Partners is a particularly strong example of this. A Christian community in rural Georgia, it welcomes twenty to twenty-five refugees at a time in two-month cycles. By providing a safe and secure environment and teaching the rudiments of English and the tasks of daily life in the U.S., community members and volunteers welcome refugees from around the world into their shared life. Common meals, worship, celebrations, and work in the large gardens and on various projects for justice anchor the community. The shared life that they have created is so winsome that in addition to the refugees, Jubilee Partners now annually welcomes almost three thousand people as visitors or short-term volunteers.

One Practice among Many Practices

Toward the end of my visit to the Open Door Community, two of the partners left for their days off. As they departed for the community-owned farm an hour from the city, they anticipated a time to garden, rest, and read. Because the work of welcome can be unrelenting and the needs of guests can press in from every direction, practitioners wear out quickly. In the midst of significant need, communities of hospitality come to recognize the necessity and blessing of some form of sabbath-keeping, some rhythm of rest and renewal. Indeed, most communities insist that workers take time off and get away at regular intervals. The importance of this practice is often hard-learned, however; in a number of cases, it was only after people had burned out, grown ill, or begun in their exhaustion to offer grudging welcome to their guests that communities realized the need for regular rest.

But rest and renewal come at a cost; when some hosts are absent, hospitality usually needs to be reduced. The provision and testimony of gracious welcome can seem compromised. If the practice of hospitality by its very nature led practitioners to the practice of sabbath-keeping, both together lead practitioners to the practice of discernment, as they make difficult decisions about when and how to "close the door." Tensions related to these difficult decisions can erupt in anger; practitioners learn the need for practices of confession and forgiveness as they continue in their common life. One by one, the difficulties of welcoming poor people and strangers lead practitioners to most of the practices named by Dorothy Bass and Craig Dykstra in their chapter.

Meanwhile, the joys of offering welcome to homeless people draw practitioners into other practices. For example, during my time at the Open Door I encountered once again the importance of the practice that church musician Don Saliers has called "singing our lives to God." Although so many of their connections to organized Christianity have been lost, homeless men and women still sing the songs of faith; they are still connected with the promises of God through music handed down through the generations. Their songs are often the gifts that they bring to their hosts. In the practice of shared singing, we were reminded that the Body of Christ, though broken, is also whole.

Even communities that excel in a single practice necessarily engage in many other practices. Indeed, practitioners learn that faithful attention to many practices is crucial to keeping a single practice from deformation or failure. But it is also the case that faithfulness in one practice helps persons to recognize the deformations in other practices. For example, the concrete character of hospitality — beds to be made and meals to be prepared — provides frequent earthy reminders that testimony about loving the neighbor is inadequate unless actual neighbors are welcomed into daily activities and valued places.

Practices are distinguishable by their meaning and history, as well as by their requisite behaviors and skills. But practices are also profoundly interrelated. For testimony to be fully truthful, especially in contested situations, the environment must be hospitable. Archbishop Desmond Tutu and other members of South Africa's Truth and Reconciliation Commission sought to provide such an environment when eliciting the painful testimony they had been charged with gathering; inhospitality could smother testimony. Conversely, a community of hospitality that was unwilling to hear the testimony of its guests would not be truly hospitable. Over and over again, guests in communities of hospitality have explained to me that they knew they were welcome because hosts offered attention to them and took time to hear their whole stories.[5] Practices do not always fit together easily. But faithfulness in one practice requires and elicits increasing competence in other practices, and tensions internal to a single practice press persons to learn other practices.

At least two kinds of interdependence, then, sustain the practice of hospitality at a community such as the Open Door. The first is mutual reliance between this community and other communities of faith. The second is mutual reliance between the privileged practice and the other practices of the Christian life.

First Corinthians 12 includes an image of interdependence that has long informed Christian reflection on the nature of the church. Just as "the body does not consist of one member but of many" — foot, ear, eye, and so on — so all who belong to Christ are one body: "now you are the body of Christ and individually members of it." Paul goes on to list some of the gifts that individuals — "members" — bring and some of the offices they hold. His image of a single body, the Body of Christ, suggests the character, quality, and source of the unity that ideally prevails among Christian communities and among the several practices that constitute the Christian life.

---

5. On the crucial importance of sympathetic, engaged listeners in the face of testimony about trauma or grave wrongdoing, see Shoshana Felman and Dori Laub, *Testimony: Crises of Witnessing in Literature, Psychoanalysis, and History* (New York: Routledge, 1992), pp. 41, 53, 58, 68.

The Interdependence of Communities
and of Practices in the Body of Christ

The theological and biblical understandings that undergird the practice of hospitality in communities such as the Open Door become explicit in two other central practices that shape their common life and are intrinsic to their identity. These communities engage in critical theological reflection, and they worship God together around the table where Christ is both the host and the feast.

To resist distortions and misuses of welcome, practitioners reflect critically on their own activities and try to attend to the relation between their theological commitments and their practices. On the wall of the dining room at the Open Door, the members have posted a copy of an ancient Celtic Rune of Hospitality which ends with: "Often, often, often, goes the Christ in the stranger's guise." Part of their regular discipline is to ask whether they have treated difficult strangers the same way they would treat Jesus. In weekly or monthly meetings, partners also reflect on what is happening as a result of their practices. How are volunteers, residents, and guests being influenced and perhaps re-formed by the breakfasts or lunches they serve or share? What does it mean that someone who was recently homeless is now serving breakfast and supervising volunteers? Have harsh words and hasty decisions undermined other expressions of welcome in this place? Study of the changing economic and political situation within which they serve — considering the implications, for example, of new pressures being brought to bear on poor people and new opportunities emerging in their city — also informs the community's ongoing reflection on practice. Moreover, vital connections to the biblical stories that shape the practice are woven into worship, as well as into regular and special occasions for reflection.

The critical theological reflection of these practitioners also includes the movements of confession and repentance. Hosts are aware of all that they fail to do as they observe the limits on hospitality that make it possible to offer any welcome at all. They practice hospitality in a situation in which disparities of power and resources are visible in painful ways; congregations that send volunteers may also be congregations that do not make room for the baptized homeless persons they feed at the Open Door's urban location. Moreover, partners and longer-term resident volunteers come to know their own weakness and frailty in the midst of daily exposure to the needs and wounds of others.

These hosts thus bring their own needs for healing to the Eucharistic table, a table where both they and homeless persons are the guests of Christ. When the community's eating place is transformed each Sunday afternoon in preparation for the sharing of the Lord's Supper, the connections between the common meal and the Eucharist become obvious. The two are so spatially and temporally proximate that daily meals literally flow into the feast Jesus shared with his disciples, the feast he now shares with those gathered in this place. One of the community's greatest strengths is that the flow between worship and daily life will continue, as the sacrament informs the convivial Sunday evening supper that follows and then all the other meals of the next six days. Ed Loring of the Open Door writes, "We understand that every meal we eat is related to the Eucharist, to the eschatological banquet — that promise by which we live that there is enough for everybody, and that when we obey God's Spirit who is moving across the earth there will be no hunger."[6]

In worship, the connections between a community's responses to God and its responses to other persons are acknowledged, repented, celebrated, and renewed. A certain kind of worship — the Eucharist — and a certain kind of activity — the shared daily meal — combine to form the heart of the Christian practice of hospitality at the Open Door and other Christian communities that excel in this practice. In the Eucharist, Jesus' sacrificial welcome is continually reenacted; in the daily meal, practitioners remember and recognize God's generous and gracious provision, as they enjoy one another's company and feed one another's bodies.[7] Each evening's meal — Sunday and everyday — is the high point of the day; "if you miss that, you miss everything," practitioners reported again and again.

Most Christian congregations do not emphasize the importance of hospitality to needy strangers. As we have seen, however, many recognize that communities that do offer such hospitality are a powerful testimony to a practice deeply embedded in the narratives and teachings of the Christian tradition, a practice that recognizes the vulnerability of strangers, the dangers of exclusion, and God's special presence in the guest-host relationship.

6. Ed Loring, *I Hear Hope Banging at My Back Door*, p. 6.

7. See Jualynne E. Dodson and Cheryl Townsend Gilkes, "'There's Nothing Like Church Food': Food and the U.S. Afro-Christian Tradition: Re-Membering Community and Feeding the Embodied Spirit(s)," *Journal of the American Academy of Religion* 63 (Fall 1995): 519-38.

Attending to this testimony should encourage other communities to reflect on practices in their own lives. First, they might consider whether they have a calling to excel in a particular Christian practice. Second, they might examine how the several practices of the Christian life mutually sustain and support one another. Just as the Open Door draws on the gifts of, and contributes to the awareness of, many congregations, so other congregations can seek to make distinctive contributions that are finally woven together within the worldwide church's service to God and neighbor. In doing so, however, it is important to remember that emphasis on one practice to the exclusion of the full range of practices that constitutes a whole and holy way of life cannot be sustained for long.

Beyond this, the testimony of communities of hospitality calls to every community that gathers at the Lord's table to remember the poor, the stranger, the needy. By crafting a way of life that is admittedly limited in its ability to meet overwhelming need but that is nonetheless generous in material and spiritual things, these communities have renewed and made visible a central aspect of the ministry of Jesus and of the holy, catholic, apostolic church across the centuries. "Wherever, whenever, however the kingdom manifests itself," Krister Stendahl has said, "it is welcome."[8]

8. Krister Stendahl, "'When you pray, pray in this manner . . .': a Bible Study," in *The Kingdom on Its Way: Meditations and Music for Mission*, RISK Book Series (Geneva: World Council of Churches, 1980), pp. 40-41, quoted in Letty Russell, *Household of Freedom* (Philadelphia: Westminster, 1987), p. 76.

Liturgy, Ministry, and the Stranger: The Practice of Encountering the Other in Two Christian Communities

GILBERT I. BOND

This essay examines two Christian communities — one Anabaptist, the other Afro-Baptist — and the practices by which each encounters the stranger at the boundary of its collective body. The shape of these encounters, we shall see, discloses not only the distinct outlines of each body's borders but also the less readily discernable outlines of Christ's identity. Like other Christian communities across a spectrum of somatic and ecclesial articulations, these communities sometimes articulate their understanding of self, other, and God in Christ in formal statements of doctrine and dogma. However, they also enact their tacit understandings bodily. By considering specific acts of ministry undertaken by these two communities, we shall see how practices enact definitions of self, other, and God in Christ, thereby developing an approach to identifying and naming the implicit theological sensibilities embedded in a collective body's acts of faithfulness.

The methodology employed is an intentional field approach. I employ the term "field" in two senses of the word. First, the practices examined in this essay are found in the field of their enactment. These two examples of Christian practice were chosen because they exist on the edge of the encounter between the welcoming members of a community — its agents of hospitality — and the stranger who is ushered across the threshold between inside and outside. The text of each scenario is a transcription made on the basis of my own actual participation and studied attention as informed by participant/observer methods.[1] Second, by juxtaposing practices from two different communities, both of which attempt to welcome strangers into their midst, I attempt to create an interactive textual field that invites the reader to enter a theological conversation regarding the meaning and transformative possibilities of practice, not only in these two communities of faith but also in the reader's own.

The methodological question placed before each practice is, "What is the relationship between a community's worship and the manner in which the community engages the outsider?" Worship is a practice that is enacted by members with one another, with and before God; worship is insiders' work. How does a practice enacted among members on the inside of the sacred cultus inform the same members' practice of encountering the stranger when that stranger comes seeking to join in the service of worship or to receive the service of ministry?

"Liturgy is a common art of the people of God in which the community brings the depth of emotion of our living to the ethos of God," Don Saliers has written. "In these acts we discover who we are, but also and primarily, we discover who God is in this act."[2] Christian worship is an intensive enactment of both communal self-identity and divine identity; worship presents the body to God, claiming the body's presence before God. In the following scenarios, I attempt to identify normative practices of communal self-understanding as they are manifest in worship, in order then to explore the relationship between sacred ritual and the manner in which the formative practices of worship shape or disfigure a community's encounters with those who are met at the boundaries of the sacred cultus. By holding worship in conversational tension with ministry I hope to reveal how one set of bodily enactments informs, or fails to inform, another. The dialogue between worship and ministry speaks across the distance between God and self through the other. In order to clarify this dialogue, it

---

1. See *Journal of Ritual Studies* 2:2 (1988); the entire issue is devoted to fieldwork. See also Tom F. Driver, *The Magic of Ritual: Our Need for Liberating Rites that Transform Our Lives and Our Communities* (San Francisco: HarperSanFrancisco, 1991), and Don Handelman, *Models and Mirrors: Towards an Anthropology of Public Events* (Cambridge: Cambridge University Press, 1990).

2. Don E. Saliers, *Worship as Theology: Foretaste of Glory Divine* (Nashville: Abingdon Press, 1994), p. 27.

will also be important to consider the tradition-specific interpretations of Christ, church, and ministry that inform each community.

Anabaptist Covenantal Community: Exclusive and Inclusive

Anabaptist communities,[3] which emerged during the Reformation, with few exceptions did not accept Luther's view that justification by faith alone is central to and sufficient for salvation. Instead, they affirmed that believers must manifest the fruits of obedience to Christ in covenantal community across a lifetime, through acts of loving submission even unto violent death, which was frequently their fate. Salvation was not a singular moment or action, but a day-to-day commitment in the face of uncertainty.

Anabaptists eschewed creedal and systematic formulations of their faith, emphasizing instead the collective enactment of belief. Theology became that which the body *does*. In order to do theology, we must first become a theological community, for it is through the brother and sister that one comes to God.[4] Theology, in this tradition, is the body becoming wholly articulate across a continuum of verbal, chirographic, typographic, and bodily articulations and enactments.

In place of sacraments, whose efficacy they denied, they upheld "ordinances." Similar to the Jewish *mitzvah*, an ordinance was a service required by God which was, when lovingly obeyed, a blessing. This emphasis on obedience led some Protestants to accuse Anabaptists of Pelagianism, but the charge made sense only to outsiders. To believers, ordinances brought one into conformity with the truth of Jesus Christ, whose life, crucifixion, death, and resurrection had so fundamentally altered all of humanity and creation that human beings were now capable of works of loving obedience that revealed the indwelling presence of God in Christ in all people. The result was a radical communal mystical theology that affirmed the direct communion with God of the gathering of believers, or holy *Gemeinschaft*.

---

3. Anabaptist understanding of the centrality of praxis rests upon a communal mystical experience and the collective appropriation of mystical theology. See Steven Ozment, *Mysticism and Dissent: Religious Ideology and Social Protest in the Sixteenth Century* (New Haven: Yale University Press, 1973), and George H. Williams, *The Radical Reformation* (Philadelphia: Westminster, 1962).

4. Robert Friedman, *Theology of Anabaptism* (Scottsdale, PA: Herald Press, 1973), pp. 80-81.

Communal practices thus became central in the Anabaptists' understanding of Christ and church, because they believed that Christ was manifest in (not mediated through) the practices of this holy *Gemeinschaft*. Practices were therefore understood as forms of communion, since they were enacted by communities of believers and were understood as acts through which believers both participated in the presence of Christ and made him manifest among themselves and in the world.[5] The community of believers became simultaneously the manifestation of the Kingdom and the material body of Christ sent to serve an unregenerate world, with the accompanying disruption of social and theological structures.

This framework provides the historical theological context for the late twentieth-century encounter we shall examine, in which Anabaptist self-understanding and the practice of ministry to the outsider collided.

Scenario I

Chicago First Church of the Brethren sits at the intersection of the Eisenhower Freeway and Congress Boulevard, which leads into the heart of East Garfield Park. East Garfield Park is Chicago's most impoverished neighborhood, with an excessively high unemployment rate among its mainly black population. The Eisenhower, which runs through a concrete canyon gouged into East Garfield Park, allows the residents of Chicago's near western suburbs to travel in and out of the city without ever glimpsing the evacuated carcasses of tenement buildings standing charred and hollow next to empty lots, commemorating moments in time frozen by fire.

The neighborhood ignited on April 4, 1968, in response to the assassination of Martin Luther King, Jr., who temporarily resided in the area during the Southern Freedom Movement's campaign in the urban North. Investment capital left and never returned. By the 1980s a population of over 250,000 residents did not have a single bank, savings and loan, credit union or any other means of accumulating capital for neighborhood improvement.[6]

---

5. Gilbert I. Bond, "The Role of Liturgical Forms in Early Anabaptist Worship: Toward an Anabaptist Liturgical Theology," *Studia Liturgica* 30 (2000): 196-225.

6. Check exchanges — which take money out of impoverished communities, thereby looting the poor — were the only means of tending bank drafts and transfer

First Church of the Brethren was a remnant congregation that had shrunk to a fraction of its former pre-exodus size. Once part of a complex of Brethren institutions that included a nursing school for training overseas missionaries, Bethany Hospital, and Bethany Theological Seminary, the church remained while its three-hundred-plus membership followed the relocated seminary to the near western suburb of Oak Brook. After the move, sixty members remained, among them birthright Brethren and converts; affluent, working class, and poor; college-educated or beyond and high-school educated or less; urban and suburban; black and white — Anabaptists all.

The poverty surrounding this island Anabaptist community deepened as the United States exported millions of entry-level industrial manufacturing jobs overseas; as the majority of voting Americans took up residence in suburbs; and as citizens turned cynical towards a disposable, economically unnecessary, and largely unwanted population. By the time the Reagan administration began slashing federal expenditures for impoverished children, ketchup had been officially designated a vegetable in the federal school lunch programs. This same administration also promoted the distribution of surplus agricultural commodities, including powdered milk, processed cheese (often referred to as "Reagan Cheese" by the recipients), corn meal, honey, and butter.

Churches and community organizations located in target areas served as distribution sites. Chicago First Church of the Brethren was one of them. Dutifully, its members would travel to the warehouse on one Friday each month to collect surplus food commodities and then distribute them early the following morning, in season and out, right through the bitter months of Chicago's infamous winter. As assistant pastor of the church, I participated in the ministry with unsophisticated enthusiasm. Ten of our sixty members would ready the church for distribution day by following a ritual of preparation. The three males in the group would descend into the basement fellowship hall, where as a church we spent as much time sharing food and conversation across the table as we spent worshiping in the

payments. By 1985 citizens began to organize a grassroots investment corporation that resulted in a community bank, the only one in the entire area. See Nicholas Lemann, *The Promised Land: The Great Black Migration and How It Changed America* (New York: A. A. Knopf, 1991), which describes this area of Chicago in relation to the other neighborhoods.

sanctuary, and carry one of these tables up to the narthex. There we would set it in place between the recipients and the distributors. On our side were the stockpiles of USDA brand commodities; on the other side were the lines stretching down the stairs to and through the doors of the church and out onto the street.

At precisely 9:00 a.m., the doors of the church would open, the hungry would come in, and the distribution would begin. The residents of East Garfield Park also participated in a monthly ritual. The table held room for two stations. At each was a sign-in sheet that requested name, address, phone number, and type of identification. The last category was somewhat misleading, since the purpose of the request was to force the recipient to prove his or her impoverished status. This was always an awkward moment, for the government's demand for demonstrable evidence of one's eligible poverty seemed to combine the absurd with the obvious and the insulting. Most of the residents of the neighborhood carried a "green card" (unrelated to the card issued to immigrants allowing them to qualify for jobs) that was issued to those poor enough to participate in the government Medicaid program serviced by a local HMO. It was the most common form of proof that one was poor enough to qualify for free cheese.

The comic absurd part of the requirement became apparent when one reflected upon who else would wait in the Chicago winter outside a church for several hours to receive a five-pound brick of processed cheese if they could afford to buy it or a better grade of cheese in a grocery store. Those who did come through the doors were part of a population whose highest form of income was a transfer payment, and whose lives were enrolled in a tangled web of institutions that heaped insult upon inefficiency with each encounter. While services to the poor in East Garfield Park were highly unreliable, some things could be counted upon: one could expect to be asked to prove that one was, indeed, poor enough to reside in and receive "benefits" designated for the eligible poor.

Something kept subverting our best intentions. For some reason unknown to us, the majority of the recipients were neither pleased nor grateful for all of our sacrificial labors on their behalf. Not only did the hours we spent lugging cheese and honey up and down stairs and faithfully attending to each portion passed across the table fail to convey the sacrificial servanthood that was so crucial to our Anabaptist identity, this work was also generating a seething underbelly of resentment, which manifested itself in the righteous indignation of those we thought we were serving.

One fateful Saturday morning, these contradictions unfolded with what now seems to be ritualized predictability. Two young men entered the church and ascended the stairs toward the table as I was finishing Miss Saunders's parcel. These two young men walked up to the station of Sister Holmes. She was one of the tent-poles of the church — Brethren churches don't have pillars — faithfully present every distribution Saturday, a member of the fellowship commission, a friend to every member, and a watchful guardian against disrespectful outsiders. My good sister requested to see documents proving the indigent eligibility of these two potential recipients of government largess. Only one could produce the proper papers.

"I must have forgotten mine," said the other.

"Then I can't give you any food," my sister responded. An angry silence ensued. I could feel the tension down at my end of the table.

"God gone bless you sure as the day is long, young man. You just don't know what a difference this makes. About this time of month there's never enough for me and my grandchildren — but God sent you, yes he did, and he's gone bless you," Miss Saunders was saying.

Please, don't bless me, I wanted to tell her. We haven't done anything worth blessing. I don't want to be impolite, but I'm worried about my sister who is facing the angry silence of a young man who failed to prove that he had failed, a young man who could not show qualifications that he had disqualified for everything else except a bag of surplus cheese and powdered milk on a freezing Saturday morning. In the name of Jesus. The angry silence — my gut told me — was about to erupt.

"What in the [blank — blank] do you think all these people come here for? [His reference was Oedipal.] Everybody lining up here is poor. If we weren't poor we wouldn't be here." He spoke as a prophet.

"You can't speak to me like that," my sister retorted.

"I wasn't talkin' to you; I was talkin' to my partner." (He was signifying.)

He turned and walked down the stairs to the front doors of the church. Then he proceeded to perform the one deed Brethren find very hard to forgive. Members of the Church of the Brethren have maintained a witness for peace in many different arenas of violence for centuries. They have taught love of enemies to their children for many generations. Members of my church have testified and pleaded before judges and juries, asking that they show mercy and spare the lives of murderers who have taken the lives of their parents. But if you smoke cigarettes, there is very little forgiveness for you in the Church of the Brethren, and if you light up inside a church, you are going to Hell.

He lit up; and my good sister ignited. She came from behind the table and headed down the stairs to confront this chimney from Hades.

"Thank you so much, young man, God going to bless you, yes he is . . ."

No, God's not going to bless me or us; or if he is he shouldn't — please don't thank us, please. . . . I was trying to be polite and bring my blessings to a halt, trying to get my body from behind the table and place it between my good sister and the smoking demon she was about to confront, without leaping over the table and prematurely sending the oracle of my undeserved blessings to one of those rooms in her Father's house. The table was a barricade, an impediment.

I couldn't move fast enough. My good sister yelled, "You can't smoke in here! This is a church." She grabbed the demon. I saw the end. This was Chicago, Chicago's West Side. You don't grab angry, despised, young, smoking men in Chicago, or anywhere else, and my good sister knew better, but she had lost this knowledge along with her survival instincts, at least for the moment.

He was kind; he reared back and hit her with an open hand instead of sinking his fist into her face. Her glasses bounced off the wall; he flew out the door. I was too slow and too late. But she was all right. I helped her up the stairs and into the pastor's study.

After tears, angry and sorrowful, prayers halting and hurting, we closed the food distribution ministry down. It had become too dangerous, too volatile. With painful discernment and honest conversation and confrontation, the members of the ministry realized that in spite of our best efforts, our ministry was inherently violent. This was an agonizing confession for Anabaptists, who are historically dedicated to nonviolence as the fruit of loving obedience to Jesus Christ. The table we used to distribute the food belonged to the church; the federal government, however, defined its function. Anabaptists have been historically suspicious of the worldly *Gesellschaft*, not only because they were themselves persecuted by macro-institutions of the church and the world, but also because they contended that certain institutional structures were incapable of manifesting or mediating the Kingdom of God. First Church's naive enrollment in the federal government's food distribution program subverted and distorted the relationship between our ecclesial identity as a holy

Geimeinschaft and our relationship with those in need outside of our covenanted boundaries. We had incorporated those structures that earlier in our history had been judged profane and incapable of manifesting the relationships that revealed Christ among us. The *Gesellschaft* had displaced the holy *Geimeinschaft*.

The most dramatic enactment of this *Geimeinschaft*'s identity is the Love Feast. Historically, in the Church of the Brethren as well as other Anabaptist bodies, the occasion is not found on a liturgical calendar, because it is governed not by a regular cycle but by the condition of the community's relationships. Believers would only celebrate the Love Feast when the community was reconciled to itself and to God. The Love Feast did not mediate grace but rather manifested the Christ who already resided in the community. Alienation would prevent the presence from being fully manifest and discernable to all. If the elders discerned that alienation and conflict were present, the Love Feast would be postponed until relationships within the community allowed for the fullness of Christ to be seen by all.

While outsiders may be present to witness the ordinance, only believing members of the community are allowed to partake in the three-part movement of the Feast: foot washing, agape meal, and bread and cup. The work of reconciling within the community is part of the work of preparation for the Love Feast, which includes weeks of planning, organizing, and making ready the meals and the meetinghouse. The day of the feast begins with a full worship service, after which the members prepare for the Love Feast. The foot washing comes first; men and women divide into separate groups and the collective singing of hymns begins. Each man removes his suit jacket, rolls up his sleeves, and removes his shoes and socks. Then he proceeds to pour the water, tie the towel around his waist, get on his knees, and immerse and individually wash and towel dry each foot of his brother. This brother then washes the feet of the one who washed him. Both stand, embrace, and say, "I love you, brother." Then the last one washed commences to wash the next brother's feet. A washes B, B washes A, then B washes C, who washes B in turn. The point is not efficiency, and therefore the logic is not linear. The point is community; the progress is slow, folding back in on itself in reciprocal loops, until all are interconnected in the touching, the washing, the embracing, and the confessing.

The agape meal is served after the basins and towels are stowed away and all are at table. Prayer and the reading of the Scripture accompany the meal, which is a solemn occasion. The passages read remind the community of Jesus' last acts of ministry before going to the cross: the feast, the washing, and the cup. The third and concluding movement is the sharing of bread and cup. Brethren prefer not to celebrate this movement apart from the preceding two, and therefore "communion" services are not a weekly or monthly part of traditional Brethren services. Reconciled community is the context within which the bread and cup are celebrated. Bread and cup do not a community make.

While this religious drama intensifies the covenantal bonding within the community, it also creates a powerful and clearly defined boundary between members and "the world." Historically, in the Church of the Brethren and among other Anabaptists, the set-apart community is called out of the world in order to reshape the relationships among themselves in incarnational communion with Jesus Christ. They do not expect the reciprocity and mutuality that define the interior life of the community to be experienced with those outside the community of faith. They wash one another, but they do not expect their feet to be washed by Friends, the traditional designation of those who are not Brothers or Sisters.

Having been called out of the world, however, Brethren also understand themselves as being then sent into the world as suffering servants. Brethren ministries have not been barricaded or well defended. The witness of the Heifer Project, C.R.O.P., Brethren Disaster Relief, and other ministries created by the Church of the Brethren have embodied dimensions of suffering servanthood. They also represent movements toward reciprocity between the holy *Gemeinschaft* and the suffering people of the world.

What was needed in East Garfield Park were the very gifts we shared as a community of believers. When members of our church were hungry, we ate together. Food was always served within the context of relationships: struggling, painful, playful, prayerful, loving, sometimes hurting, but always committed relationships in Christ. That was who we were. At a church retreat, a leader once asked us to draw the church of the future, the church we would envision had we resources and people enough. We all came up with differing visions of educational space, new sanctuary, parsonage — but when we had to draw the one part of the church we could not live without, all of us eliminated the sanctuary, the education rooms, the pastor's office, and the parsonage, while no one eliminated the kitchen and the fellowship hall: a place to prepare the Love Feast, a place to wash feet, share the agape meal, and pass the bread and the cup. That was who we were.

That violent Saturday called us to ourselves. We eventually took the long table from the top of the stairs and carried it downstairs to the fellowship hall. And we contacted some of the people who used to line up outside the church for cheese and powdered milk and invited them to a meal, a meal that members of the church prepared. And with some fear and trembling, we sat and ate with people who were very much not like us, people who knew little about being Anabaptist or Brethren; but in eating together, we discovered we were very much like each other. Eventually members of the community and members of the church prepared neighborhood fellowship meals together, cooking and eating and praying together. Eventually neighborhood children started coming to church. It was very frightening to be for outsiders what we had been for each other: a fellowship of believers who washed one another's feet and shared common meals.

Not all of the members adjusted to our new relationship with the unwashed. My dear sister who had been battered in her attempt to remove the smoking ember from our midst eventually came, sat, ate, and listened. At the end of a neighborhood fellowship meal, she approached me and said, "Brother Bond, this is a wonderful ministry, and I am thankful that you seem to be able to talk to anybody. But I can't sit across the table from somebody and hear that they haven't paid the rent in three months."

"Well, Sister Holmes, if we ever start a housing ministry, we won't put you in charge of collecting rent. I'm sure there are other gifts you can share in the Kingdom."

My sister was telling me that the years of sacrifice and discipline that enabled her and her husband to move out of poverty into the middle class remained too close and unhealed for her to be reminded of them at table.

If we carried the logic of our most powerful, liturgical enactments to their conclusion, we could define our practice of encountering the stranger as an effort to create the conditions that would enable us to wash one another's feet. Receiving from those we were supposed to serve, from those outside of our community, stretched, painfully, the boundaries of our understanding of ourselves and our perception of others.

Afro-Baptist Liturgies of Communion and Contagion

The dynamic dialogue between worship and ministry in African American Christianity in North America emerged out of the ethos of slavery. Within this context, the very act of gathering together became central to the indigenous practice of this community, whose origins belong to slavery, African American Christianity, and God.

"Throughout the history of African American worship, the need for sacred space both evolved from and enhanced the opportunity for ministry," writes Melva Costen.

> Corporate worship was and remains the foundation and context for the ministry of mutual pastoral care and nurture in the faith. Initially, the immediate corporate missional task was to seek ways to survive and attain justice and freedom, which the Word of God had declared was rightfully theirs. This mission was often realized and actualized following worship in political revolutions and insurrections. While these might not represent traditional understandings of missional acts or service they represent for an oppressed people empowered engagement in the struggle for liberation. A very important mission for a people who claim mutual "pilgrim's journey" in God's story is to render service by engaging in efforts to reconstruct an unjust society.[7]

The historical experience of African American families made the church's role as gathering place even more important. While slavery grossly distorted economic and political macrostructures, the family was the site of primal injury for enslaved Africans and their African American descendants, whose bodies supplied slavery with its raw material. After the legal end of the slave trade in 1807, slavery in the U.S., unlike South America and the Caribbean, was not replenished by a constant supply of fresh imports, and the family became the source of supply for the ever-expanding slave market.[8] Violation of conjugal and familial bonds among the slaves, therefore, became normative as families were created only to be dismembered.

7. Melva Wilson Costen, *African American Christian Worship* (Nashville: Abingdon Press, 1993), p. 125.

8. Robert William Fogel, *Without Consent or Contract: The Rise and Fall of American Slavery* (New York: W. W. Norton & Co., 1989), pp. 17-154.

After the Civil War, Cheryl Sanders notes, the church became the place wherein displaced and dislocated slaves could seek out lost or missing relatives in an effort to reunite families. Rituals of hospitality and welcome were therefore integral to the condition of their lives and the character of the church community.[9] Hospitality as an African American Christian practice thus addressed an array of overwhelmingly urgent social and historical conditions.

Rituals of hospitality have found a place in Afro-Baptist liturgy as well. Rituals of hospitality testify not only to the importance of being acknowledged and welcomed in a country that remains hostile to the presence of African Americans, but also to the Good News of God's unconditional welcome to strangers. In many cases, such rituals have become quite elaborate.

The following scenario examines two moments in one church's ministry of hospitality — the first enacted within the sanctuary, the second within the church's shelter for homeless men. My focus is upon a particular part of the body in its metonymic relationship to both the personal and collective body of the church: the gloved hand. By juxtaposing two scenarios from the church's ministry of hospitality, I hope to explore the gestures' tacit theologies, drawing on Antoine Vergote's argument that "the ritual gesture reveals and unfolds the intentions of the body as lived. It inserts itself into the space of the humanized world, concretely links the subject to the human community, and attaches it to the Other who is source and ultimate meaning of its existence."[10]

Scenario II

Immanuel Missionary Baptist Church, which was established in 1825 by slaves, is the oldest African American church in New Haven, Connecticut. Today its membership of approximately eight hundred is composed of middle and working class families. The narthex of Immanuel Missionary

9. Cheryl Jeanne Sanders, *Saints in Exile: The Holiness Pentecostal Experience in African American Religion and Culture* (New York: Oxford University Press, 1996).

10. Antoine Vergote, "Symbolic Gestures and Actions in the Liturgy," in *Liturgy in Transition*, ed. Herman Schmidt, S.J., *Concilium* 62 (New York: Herder & Herder, 1971), p. 46.

Baptist Church is busy and noisy, though it is not a particularly interesting space. Its virtue lies in its unadorned spaciousness, which allows it to serve as a transitional decompression chamber between the mechanical bustle outside its doors on Chapel Street, which takes traffic one-way west toward downtown and beyond, and the stillness of the carpeted and hushed nave, which lies just through another large set of doors on the opposite side. The liturgical scholar James White notes that the architectural design of many contemporary church buildings does not identify the narthex as part of worship space and argues that it should be taken more seriously as such:

> Gathering for worship is an important socializing occasion; its humanizing function ought not to be overlooked. The body that takes shape on Sunday morning is a body already discerning the presence of the Lord in the flesh even as it gathers for worship. Therefore, let us not be disturbed by the noise and shuffle of people arriving. Meeting is important; assembling is part of Christ's work among us. It deserves to be recognized with sufficient time and space.[11]

On a Sunday morning at Immanuel, the narthex is full of arriving members and welcoming ushers, whose immediate interactive responses to all who enter shape the narthex into just such a place of proto-worship. Ushers are immediately identifiable by their uniforms and their gestures. The men are dressed in black suits, the women in white nurses' uniforms. Both women and men are bedecked in soft white cotton dress gloves. Scenes of affirmation are enacted both among arriving members and between them and the ushers. The narthex is a space of intensive tactility as men offer their hands for extended handshakes that are noticeably free of the ritualized vernacular gestures found outside the sanctuary, on the streets, in barber shops, athletic fields, collectively known as "dap."[12] Here, gestures of affirmation include extended embraces, comments upon sartorial stylizations, details of beauty and barber shop outcomes, and overall evaluations of family presentation.

In the midst of this activity and noise, the ushers are a carefully coor-

---

11. James F. White, *Christian Worship in North America: A Retrospective, 1955-1995* (Collegeville, MN: The Liturgical Press, 1997), p. 301.

12. Clarence Major, *Juba to Jive: A Dictionary of African-American Slang* (New York: Viking/Penguin, 1994). See also Thomas Kochman, *Rappin' and Stylin' Out: Communication in Urban Black America* (Urbana: University of Illinois Press, 1972).

dinated unit that performs as a body within the body to shape and shepherd those arriving into a body whose first contact with officials of the church's ministering body announces and bodily articulates the tones of welcome that will resonate and echo throughout the service. Ushers gently insinuate themselves into this interactive ritual and redirect its energy with gesture, word, and presence. They greet each member by name and hand her or him a bulletin with one hand, then touch the member gently with the other hand, indicating it is time to move toward the nave in order to make room for the narthex to absorb those still arriving.

Upon my arrival, several members of the ushering unit visually evaluated me, and then turned to one another to check if any one of them knew me. After silent nods indicated that I was a stranger, one usher came forth and directed me to a visitors' registration table to complete a small card providing the welcoming committee with sufficient information to introduce me to the church during the "Right Hand of Fellowship," which I saw listed in the bulletin as a rite within the worship service. With a gentle touch and nudge, I arrived at the table, completed my abridged autobiography, and, again, was gently touched and pointed to the next set of doors where my gentleman guide would take me into the sanctuary. After asking if I could take a back pew, I was handed over to another usher, who looked radiant in white and who, again, touched my arm and silently guided me to my seat by extending her hand to that part of the pew wherein I should settle.

Once seated, I was approached by another uniformed male in white gloves, this one bearing a pencil whose eraser had been covered with bright red cellophane wrap tied with a yellow ribbon. I was asked to hold on to this item during the "Right Hand of Fellowship" or to wear it in my suit pocket. When I lifted its red veil, I noticed that the pencil was crowned with an eraser shaped like a dollar sign, while the pencil was imprinted with a reproduction of a twenty-dollar bill bearing the likeness of President Andrew Jackson, an avid supporter of the American Colonization Society, an organization that sought to "solve" the problem of slavery by deporting African Americans to Africa.[13] Jackson was also the owner of two hundred slaves.

Once the service began, the nine ushers stood at their positions —

13. Monroe Lee Billington, *The American South* (New York: Charles Scribner's Sons, 1971), p. 105.

four on the outside aisles, four on the inside, and one at the doors of the sanctuary, all with the left hand behind their back in a posture of uniform vulnerability and openness. As the service commenced, the ushers continued to play an active role in the unfolding religious drama. They moved, turned, and acted as a body. During the prayer chant, which followed the processional, they turned and faced the pulpit. Since their backs were turned to the narthex doors, the sanctuary was closed for that period in the service. At the conclusion of the prayer chant, the ushers turned in unison, each with the left hand still behind the back, and faced the doors to the narthex. Some ushers then greeted the late arrivals and guided them to the other ushers, who formed a human channel through which the latecomers had to pass to take their seats.

During the prayers, the ushers folded their arms across their chests and bowed slightly forward. At the "Right Hand of Fellowship," they removed their right gloves in order to shake hands. Visitors were welcomed by name and asked to stand as their names were called. Members identified us by our red cellophane pencils, and we were greeted vigorously. The pastor admonished those who joined the church on this day: "If you are not in church, these deacons will follow you, they won't lose sight of you, they will follow you all the way into heaven. There are other deacons who will watch out for you. They will call you to see what the problem is that keeps you from church."

As the pastor began his sermon, the ushers removed both gloves, took their seats in the pews, and resumed their identity as members of the body. As the pastor concluded his sermon on fellowship and reconciliation, he invited others to come forward. "You are no longer a stranger; you're a child of the Most High. My father who is rich in housing will welcome you there." At the invitation to discipleship, the ushers came forth, once again, to sit on the side of the church in folding chairs. Their gloves were back on.

As the service moved toward the ordinance of the Lord's Supper, I realized that the cloth used to cover the bread and wine was white, the same color as the gloves the ushers wear. The ushers had brought the congregation and visitors to this moment of connection through word, deed, and sign, forming a visible and tactile unity. Their soft white touch, contrasting white gloves, and white nurses' uniforms had signaled to all that this is a safe and healing place, and these corresponding signs of connectedness and community were now leading to communion. Both elements were served in the pews by gloved ushers and deacons. After communion, male and female ushers led the pastors out of the sanctuary during the recessional. As worshipers passed into the narthex and beyond it to Chapel Street, the pastor and associate pastor stood on either side of the doors shaking hands.

Later that day, I visited the shelter for homeless men that bears this church's name, though it does not occupy its building. This visit was also shaped by rituals of greeting. I arrived an hour before the shelter officially opened in order to talk with the director, who is also a deacon at the church. This gentle man greeted me warmly, and we spoke at length about the shelter's operation, clientele, funding, and staffing. Our conversation concluded in time for me to take my position outside the shelter, where a growing number of men were lining up outside the doors. I noticed, all of a sudden, the complete absence of transitional space at the shelter. One is simply outside or inside. The beautiful autumn day made standing outside a pleasant experience, save for the long line of suspicious glances and glares. I began working the line, finding those who would return my greeting and speak with me.

When at last the doors opened, we were called in two by two. Once over the threshold, the men were asked to state their names, which were written into the book by a shelter employee. We were then asked to provide a mandatory donation of three dollars to the shelter for an overnight stay. This is standard policy at all shelters in New Haven — which, according to those men who would speak with me this evening, is a far more attractive place for homeless people than other Connecticut towns. I was appalled, however, at the three-dollar charge; I now understood why so many men and women beg in downtown New Haven. The policy turns the homeless into beggars of necessity.

Upon paying the three dollars, each man was asked to step away from the desk and to spread his legs and raise his arms, so that a man wearing yellow latex gloves could examine his body through the clothing. The process was not only sterile but also sterilizing; the effect of being touched in this manner was alienating and socially isolating. Moreover, the power of this ritual multiplied as it was repeated again and again, the same set of actions upon forty men, isolating each one as a potential contaminating presence. The movement across the boundary from outside to inside made each man an inside alien, as each received the confirming touch that marked his presence as a potential source of contamination, so dangerous that his hosts were required to don protective equipment.

153

Those admitted went directly to the showers and then emptied into the television pool, where each overnight resident took a seat gazing into the football game underway that Sunday evening. I sat in the midst of this glassy-eyed and growing community of men and watched the welcoming procedure continue. When I asked one of the men watching TV if he would mind talking to me, he eagerly turned from the screen and became a willing informant.

"Would anyone miss you if you did not show up here?"

"Say what?"

"Does anyone ever ask about men who might show up on a regular basis, but one day might be absent?"

"Hell, no."

"Do you ever wonder what has happened to the familiar faces when they don't show?"

"Sometimes. But it's like this: there's only so much room, and he might be standing out there now, next to the cut-off man."

"Where does he go then?"

"He'll have to find a steam grate for the night."

"Do you ever have a chance to offer suggestions concerning the way the place is operated?"

"Oh, yeah."

"When?"

"Twice a year."

"How often?"

"Once every six months, they ask us some questions."

"Is this what the men usually do, come in and watch TV?"

"Yeah, until the food comes. Then we eat."

By this time a small group had gathered within earshot, forming a small circle of listeners around us. The men were simply hungry for someone who took an interactive interest in them. The subject of conversation itself was not a priority.

The food arrived, provided by a volunteer church group. One of its members offered thanksgiving prayers. The men lined up again. Dinner was served. We ate as we sat alone in our seats.

As I ate, I thought about First Brethren Church in Chicago. Like my former congregation, Immanuel Baptist Church was beset by contradictions between worship and ministry that prevented it from sharing its best gifts with those whom it would serve. On Sunday morning, the ushers who greeted both members and visitors were representatives of the hospitality of God. They not only greeted the stranger but also accompanied him or her on the way to an encounter with the divine in the midst of the worship service, in the heart of the sanctuary. In other words, the first invitation into the sanctuary had been followed by an invitation into the re-conjoined and re-membered family of God, where the healing presence of God could restore the relationships of persons who encountered Jesus and chose to commit both to Christ and to that particular local community of faith. Christological signposts declaring the Good News of God's unconditional welcome to the stranger thus guided the liturgy at Immanuel Baptist. On Sunday nights at the shelter, however, much different signposts were in place. What could help heal the rupture between the ritual of hospitality that invites communion and community within the sanctuary and the ritual of contagion enacted at the shelter?

Concluding Reflections

In this essay I have attempted to explore the relationship between sacred ritual and the manner in which the formative practices of ritual shape encounters with those who are met at the boundaries of the sacred cultus. In trying to identify normative practices of communal self-understanding and identity, I have also tried to hold in tension the relationship between the enacted identity of worshiping communities and their perceptions of and responses to those identified as outsiders.

Christian practices are inherently ambiguous. Yet it is precisely in their intrinsic weakness that their strength is located. They lack the clarity of a fixed and stable determinacy, but, ironically, efforts to reduce their ambiguity by making them more reliable and determinate also render them more fragile. Within their ambiguity resides their capacity to be transformed.

I have assumed much as I have proceeded across each communal terrain. In a hermeneutics of generosity, I have affirmed that each Christian community retains within its practiced self-understanding an identity that participates in the truth of Jesus Christ as one who dwelt among us. I have identified this as the community's enacted understanding of self, Christ, and other. Guiding this hermeneutic is an informed Anabaptist perception that emphasizes bodily enactments of faith over its verbal or semiotic articulation. I discern related sensibilities at work within both of the communities discussed here. By providing comparative scenarios, I intend to invite other communities of faith also to rethink and reenact the encounter with the stranger in ways that reflect their own traditions and respect the integrity of their communal identity.

Practices are part of an ensemble of articulations that belong to Christian bodies. They do not exist in isolation. The second scenario discloses the need for a Christian community's various practices to stay closely connected to one another. An individual's or community's movement toward the holy vulnerability of Christ is never progressive, linear, or undeterred, however, nor is movement toward the integrity of Christian practices a straightforward matter. We all struggle with the tension between self-preservation and the inherent risks we face as human beings and as Christians. Yet Christ beckons us, against our own judgments of reliable self-preservation, to avail ourselves of the grace that allows us to lose our lives and remove our outer garments, to wash the feet of even those who would betray us and to allow them to wash our feet as well.

One can imagine the latex-gloved examiner at the entrance of the shelter greeting each homeless man, asking for his name, revealing his own . . . and then asking to be forgiven by the one whose body his gloved hands will search within the trembling terrain of faith and fear: another site and moment of potential transformation.

Little Moves Against Destructiveness:
Theology and the Practice of Discernment

NANCY E. BEDFORD

The grandiose cinemas of a time not too long ago in Buenos Aires, with their marble stairways and shiny brass fittings, have suffered a process of postmodern fragmentation. Most of them have been chopped up into multiple shoeboxes with small screens; indeed, the only intact, old-time movie houses in the city have been turned into post-Pentecostal or neo-charismatic places of meeting. The religious beliefs and practices emanating from these new houses of worship tend strongly to condition the theological questions — and answers — being formulated at present in the context from which I write.[1] But it was what I saw in one of the shoe boxes, not too long ago, that triggered for me the question about the relationship between theology and the practice of discernment: a film called *La Nube* ("The Cloud"), directed by Pino Solanas.

The film is heavily symbolic. It depicts a Buenos Aires where it has been raining for over 1600 days and where people walk or drive backwards most of the time. Amidst the pelting rain, a small group of friends is struggling to save a playhouse from being demolished and replaced with a shopping mall. They are told not to worry, because the mall would be equipped

---

1. For more on this, see my article "Tres hipótesis de trabajo en busca de una teología. Vías para la renovación de la teología latinoamericana," in *Cuadernos de Teología* 18 (1999): 41-51. My own context is that of the South Cone, and within it, of the River Plate area, focusing mainly on its various forms of Protestantism.

with a space reserved for the performing arts — although of course the small print specifies that any play presented would have to be lucrative and conform to aesthetic standards set by the mall owners. The characters involved in the struggle walk forwards when they are consistent with their commitment to justice and truth; much of the time they walk backwards, just as the masses of people depicted in the film do. Given the immensity of systemic injustice and their own personal ambiguities, none of the characters is able to achieve more than small victories, yet several of them are willing, in different ways, to "work and look hard for ways, for opportunities to make little moves against destructiveness."[2]

Virtual Reality and the Virtues of Reality

Solanas's film ends with a rather Sisyphusian call to resistance. This is bracing, but the film's response to evil is finally individualistic, silent about the reasons for resistance, and devoid of eschatological hope. The film fails at these points; the Christian faith, on the other hand, does not. Even in the face of rather discouraging odds, Christian communities are called to resist evil through steps consonant with God's kingdom and God's justice; this is at the heart of Christian hope. Yet figuring out which steps to take, and how to take them, is a tremendously complex matter. In this essay, I shall argue that the Christian practice of discernment can be centrally important to communities struggling with this complexity within the contemporary Latin American context. By discernment I mean figuring out what to do, all together as a church, with the help of God's Spirit.

In this context, and also more generally in Christian history, discernment is a practice that plays an important role in theological reflection on every other practice of the Christian faith. I define "a practice of the Christian faith" as a purposeful, creative outworking of a sequence of steps that empower persons in community better to proceed [pro-seguir] along the way of Jesus Christ. Negatively, to be engaged in such a practice means resisting evil. Positively, it implies the process of being drawn by God's Spirit ever more deeply into a life pattern that responds to the rhythms of the

---

2. André Trocmé in Philip Hallie, *Lest Innocent Blood Be Shed* (New York: Harper and Row, 1979), p. 85; see Christine Pohl, *Making Room: Recovering Hospitality as a Christian Tradition* (Grand Rapids: Eerdmans, 1999), p. 184.

dancing dynamic of the Holy Trinity. Both a sense of spontaneity and constant innovation and a sense of discipline and joyful conformity to the "mind of Christ" are inherent in any practice understood in this way. Similarly, ambiguity (which is common to human beings and all of their manifestations of religiosity) is an inherent part of every practice of the Christian faith, even the best-intentioned ones. Both the innovative discipline and the inherent ambiguity of the practices of the Christian faith make the faithful practice of discernment a necessary component of every other practice, inasmuch as discernment is a practice that embodies a recognition that all practices (including itself) are "penultimate" and not "ultimate." In other words, the practice of discernment incorporates a hermeneutic of suspicion and retrieval (Ricoeur) into every practice, in order to help people in community figure out which moves seem faithfully to resist evil and to address concrete needs amidst the multiple ambiguities of life. The practice of discernment entails both following creatively in the way of Jesus Christ and taking into account personal, social, and structural dimensions of reality.

Beyond this role, moreover, the practice of discernment would seem to be particularly central when people who live under a great deal of pressure from structural injustice find it necessary to decide which "little moves against destructiveness" really promise to advance in a fruitful direction. This is the situation of the Christian community to which I belong. To understand our situation as one that requires "little moves" is to undertake a different theological discourse than that which accompanied the sense of an impending and triumphal Exodus in some early Latin American liberation theology. An exploration of the difference may prove helpful.

A comparison with Gustavo Gutiérrez's magnificent *Teología de la liberación: Perspectivas,*[3] brings to the forefront both differences and similarities between the contexts and tasks of theologians in Latin America in 1971 and those we confront today. At that time, Gutiérrez — along with

---

3. I will be quoting and translating from the Spanish edition of Gutiérrez's book (Salamanca: Sígueme, 1972). There are many depictions of the origins and history of Latin American liberation theology; one useful article among many is the essay by Roberto Oliveros in *Mysterium Liberationis,* ed. I. Ellacuria and J. Sobrino (Madrid: Trotta, 1990), pp. 17-50, although it concentrates almost exclusively on the Roman Catholic aspects of the story.

many other thinkers, both Christian and non-Christian — believed that the process of liberation as it was manifested in the so-called Third World was the major event of the time (p. 39). The social praxis of contemporary people seemed to be taking on an adult character that meant that they saw themselves as active historical subjects, able to decide lucidly to resist social injustice and help transform social structures (p. 75). In that context, theology was not to limit itself to *thinking* about the world, but was to situate itself as a moment in the process of the world's *transformation* (p. 41). The category of *history* was seen as central to theological praxis and thought; history was understood as a unified process, in which salvation history and secular history were not divorced (p. 200). Human history seemed to have defined contours and a significant direction. At the same time, the theory of dependency was a major factor in understanding Latin American history and reality (pp. 118ff.). In the face of dependency and oppression, revolutionary change — that is, liberation — and not cosmetic reform was perceived as the necessary answer (pp. 126ff.). The God of justice desired this liberation for God's people in a triple sense: an economic sense, a historical sense, and a human sense. All three levels of meaning were part of a singular complex process that "finds its deep sense and its full realization in the saving work of Christ" (pp. 67ff., 238ff., and 315ff.). In the conclusion of his book, Gutiérrez wrote:

> Liberation theology, which seeks its point of departure in the commitment to abolish the present situation of injustice and to construct a new society, must be verified by the practice of that commitment, by its active and efficacious participation in the struggle that exploited social classes have taken on against their oppressors. Liberation from all forms of exploitation, the possibility of a more human and more worthy life, the creation of a new human being, are dependent on that struggle (p. 387).

Thirty years later, structural injustice in Latin America not only continues but is even more pronounced. The need for liberation in its widest sense continues to be acute. However, the exhilarating sense of impending revolutionary change is long since gone. The category of "historical agents" or "subjects" applied to persons has fallen into relative disrepute.[4]

---

4. See, for example, the incisive article by Hugo Assmann, "Apuntes sobre el tema

History itself is now seen as too anthropocentric a category to stand alone; the dimension of creation and its crises has emerged as another central category for liberation. The theory of dependency has become too blunt an instrument to measure reality. Certainly, many people continue to understand the theological task as *orthopraxis* and not only as *orthodoxy:* not only as discourse but also as action, and as the rich interaction between both. However, the actual praxis capable of bringing about substantive change is rather difficult to determine, with no real consensus. Perhaps the problem in a nutshell is that as a result of globalization processes, reality has become so complex that — as anthropologist Néstor García Canclini puts it — David no longer knows exactly where Goliath is.[5]

Classic Latin American liberation theology depended to a great extent on one metanarrative: that of liberation attained in history and in fact to be attained soon. Goliath could be readily identified and the correct pebbles for the sling seemed at hand. To be sure, there is a sense in which Christian hope is inevitably a metanarrative; however, it is a metanarrative that only God can see in its entirety, and which we anticipate but darkly and in part. In recent Latin American theology, the sense of the provisional quality of all discourse and practice has begun to be felt more strongly.[6] Yet does this necessarily mean that post-globalization liberation theology is condemned to concentrate exclusively on "small stories," so that the sense of a wider story is lost? García Canclini is helpful here in understanding the dynamics between the great and the small when he postulates that one reason it is difficult to come up with a unitary theory of globalization is not only because of deficiencies in the state of our knowledge, but also because fragmentariness is a structural characteristic of globalizing processes. In other words, globalization is on the one hand a series of homogenization processes and on the other a fragmentation of the world, in which differences and inequalities are reordered without being suppressed. To speak only of the macro-process of globalization without seeing the fragments and small stories would be to give a partial explanation, as would

---

del sujeto," in *Perfiles teológicos para un nuevo milenio,* ed. J. Duque (San José: DEI, 1997), pp. 115-46, which includes criticism of his own former use of the category.

5. See Néstor García Canclini, *La globalización imaginada* (Buenos Aires: Paidós, 2000), pp. 26ff.

6. On this see also Elsa Támez, *When the Horizons Close: Rereading Ecclesiastes,* trans. Margaret Wilde (Maryknoll, NY: Orbis Books, 2000).

the inverse. García Canclini argues that perhaps the only way to speak significantly of these complex and sometimes contradictory processes is by using metaphors.[7]

The last few years have been a time of theological deconstruction and searching for ways of (re-)construction able to integrate the best insights of the first liberation theology into its new manifestations.[8] Perhaps the use of creativity and imagination — gifts of God's Spirit, after all — and a willingness to play with metaphors are ways in which to start discerning how to overcome this time of parenthesis in which Latin American theology has been getting its bearings. One image for the practices underlying a realistic Latin American theological discourse that comes to my mind at present is not so much the metaphor of the Exodus as the humble image of Jeremiah when he bought Hanamel's property in Anathoth. When he handed over his seventeen silver shekels and obtained his property deed, he "put them in an earthen vessel, that they might last many days" (Jer. 32:14). He invested what he had on a very long-term project. He knew — no one knew better — that desolation was at hand (32:25), but trusted in a vision of hope (33:9-12). The same sort of commitment to God's justice under overwhelming odds can be found in the central symbol of the Christian faith, the cross. The difficulties in living according to this sort of pattern are not imaginary. As John Yoder puts it, the cross is not a "peculiarly efficacious technique . . . for getting one's way. The key to the ultimate relevance and to the triumph of the good is not any calculation at all, paradoxical or otherwise, of efficacy, but rather simple obedience. Obedience means not keeping verbally enshrined rules but reflecting the character of the love of God."[9] This would seem to be a key for faith and theology

---

7. Canclini, *La globalización imaginada,* p. 49. He mentions several that he has heard in reference to globalized society: amoebic society, global village, global Disneyland, third wave, global shopping center, new Babel, technocosm.

8. See Enrique Dussel, "Transformaciones de los supuestos teológico de la Teología de la liberación" (Las "trece tesis de Matanzas para ser debatidas") in *Perfiles teológicos para un nuevo milenio,* ed. J. Duque, pp. 29-39.

9. John Howard Yoder, *The Politics of Jesus* (Grand Rapids: Eerdmans, 1972), pp. 244-45. He continues: "The cross is not a recipe for resurrection. Suffering is not a tool to make people come around, nor a good in itself, but the kind of faithfulness that is willing to accept evident defeat rather than complicity with evil is, by virtue of its conformity with what happens to God when he works among men, aligned with the ultimate triumph of the Lamb."

in Latin America at this time: it is imperative to look for ways to be faithful and persevere, even though hope for positive and substantial structural changes has waned in society at large.

Yet Yoder's words, even if one is in agreement with them, open up a whole set of further questions: How do we know when our particular actions of obedience are faithful to God's character? How do we even know what God's character is? How do we know God? Can anything significant be said about God? Christian theology, as I understand it, devotes much of its energy to trying to answer such questions, in the confidence that in Jesus Christ a word has been given that allows for significant, if provisional, answers to such questions. Theology also is — or should be — aware that discourses about obedience or about buying fields in the name of the Lord can easily lead to quietism, to corruption, to direct or indirect complicity with injustice. That is why the questions of theology are questions of *discernment* as well: if one understands theology as reflection born of *fides, spes, amor quaerens intellectum* — faith, hope, and love seeking understanding — then the practice of theology and the practice of discernment, though not identical, will be so intertwined as to be inseparable.

As I left the cinema after watching *La Nube,* questions such as these were buzzing around on the edge of my consciousness, vaguely provocative yet not fully formed. The urban, apocalyptically-tinged scenario appeared disturbingly similar to the images in the movie: several very dirty persons were purposefully rummaging in the garbage; a pair of young children languidly and grotesquely danced the tango for tourists and then passed a hat around; anxious pedestrians wanting a ride met the gazes of frightened taxi-drivers, each wondering if the other might be a potential mugger; an apparently deranged street preacher was shouting about the coming wrath; the cold comforts of virtual reality flickered behind the barred windows of an electronics store. It was raining. Living in a reality such as this, one at times feels an acute desire to say, with Mother Goose, "Rain on the green grass/And rain on the tree/Rain on the housetop/But not on me." Yet in this society there is no effective waterproofing of any area of life for the likes of a theologian: if rain during over 1600 days symbolizes structural injustice, as I take it to in *La Nube,* it is impossible not to be permeated by its effects. From this perspective, the old saying "Lo que mata es la humedad" ("What kills you is the humidity") takes on a sharp new contour: it points to the *hellishness* of a city such as this: you can't get away from the humidity and the trash and the chaos and the poverty and the noise and the problems. And yet — as should not be surprising in the light of the Incarnation — this very hellishness actually can act as a blessed *kairos* for theology. An environment soggy with Solanas's sort of rain can serve to keep theology honest, focused on the basics. It is very difficult to avoid the centrality of topics such as theological anthropology, personal and structural sin, and the need for God's grace, living amidst the dregs of "mammonic" idolatry. In Ignacio Ellacuría's rather graphic terms, a society such as this provides the "coprology" for the world; the analysis of the refuse produced by capitalist globalization allows one to recognize the larger sickness of the world as a whole.[10]

The Process of Community Discernment: Little Moves Against Destructiveness at the *Betel de Floresta* Community of Faith

Theology, if it desires to be relevant and honest, has no alternative but to deal with the facts presented so graphically by reality. Moreover, Christ's love compels it to do so (2 Cor. 5:14). And yet, a reality that makes quasi-apocalyptic scenarios and magical realism[11] into part of one's daily routine

10. Ellacuría's stark image is often used by Jon Sobrino, as in "Los pueblos crucificados, actual siervo sufriente de Yahvé," chapter 4 of his book *El principio-misericordia. Bajar de la cruz a los pueblos crucificados* (Santander: Sal Terrae, 1992), pp. 83-95. Along the lines of this metaphor see I. Ellacuría, "Quinto Centenario. América Latina, ¿descubrimiento o encubrimiento," in *Revista Latinoamericana de Teología* 7 (1990): 271-82. On discernment in Ellacuría's theology, see my article "Teología y discernimiento. En homenaje a Ignacio Ellacuría en el 10° aniversario de su asesinato-martirio," in *Proyecto* 11 (1999): 209-23.

11. This literary tradition is more properly known as the "miraculously real" ("lo real maravilloso"). It is probably more popular in North American universities and their Latin American studies programs than in Latin America itself; at the same time, what is studied in the United States at these programs, whose libraries contain the best collections of Latin American sources, is often re-injected into Latin American cultural life. At any rate, "magical realism" is a meaningful category to convey to North American readers the sense of surreal juxtaposition of unexpected elements common to a city like Buenos Aires. Neil Larsen, in "Preselective Affinities: Surrealism and Marxism in Latin America," *Cultural Logic* 2 (1998), argues that this sort of fiction is nothing other than the conversion of surrealism's strategy of prescribed dosages of "shock" into literary form. The problem with this sort of montage esthetics is that "even the most violent juxtaposition, once it is registered and the initial shock dissipates, has nothing

and discourse can become morally deadening. Just as people exposed to loud noises from factory machines, tractors, traffic, or musical amplifiers often slowly lose their hearing, at least partially, one's outrage and sensitivity can be dulled by constantly confronting the multiple tragedies triggered by systemic injustices. In this situation, people who consciously try to live in Christ-like ways not only find themselves wondering how to *discern* what to do and what decisions to make as individuals and as part of larger groups, but also — particularly if they are involved in the theological task — begin to realize what tenuous, ambiguous practices both theology and discernment actually are.

Historically in Latin American theology, some of the best insights have been born out of the life of concrete communities of faith. In this sense, one result of understanding theology as "reflection on praxis" has been a more inductive than deductive sort of theology.[12] Since a driving interest of this essay is to try to see how the practice of discernment might provide the means of identifying "little moves against destructiveness" that could illuminate theology and theopraxis in times of capitalist globalization in Latin America, it may prove useful to examine an actual process of community discernment and its effect on the theological practices of those involved. The case I have chosen is my own community of faith.[13]

Iglesia Bautista Betel is a small, urban church in a quarter or *barrio* lo-

---

to save it from its own rapid routinization." This is precisely the problem one faces in Latin America: because they are so pervasive, structural injustice and violence can begin to lose their shock value, thus becoming "naturalized." When this happens, injustice no longer seems sinful or changeable; it just "is." This is one of the main pitfalls that a discerning theology must avoid.

12. The experiences and struggles of real people shine through the work of theologians such as Gutiérrez, Sobrino, Segundo, L. Boff, or Míguez Bonino. This is probably one reason why some of their writings have such an abiding appeal: it is a "situated" theology. An interest in narrative and metaphor is already implicit and sometimes explicit in their work. Their references to persons — to Monseñor Romero, for example, but also to unnamed *campesinos* in Sobrino — are thus not "anecdotal" but actually quite central to their insights.

13. I might add that this community has never been very involved with the insights of liberation theology as such; in fact, most of the members would either not recognize the phrase or, if they did, would probably mistrust it. One of the important challenges to Protestant/evangelical theologians in Latin America is how to re-actualize the best insights of (often, though not always, Roman Catholic) liberation theology in a way that also values their own Protestant theological traditions and insights.

cated in the Western area of the Federal Capital, or Buenos Aires proper. One hundred years ago, Floresta, as its name implies, was still a green area flush with natural beauty, where rich people had weekend homes. In time, the old villas were surrounded by high-rise buildings, sold, and reconverted into retirement homes or clinics, and the area became a middle- to lower-middle class neighborhood. It is home to recent Ukrainian and Bolivian immigrants, as well as to the usual melting-pot sort of Argentine best known to the census. In the last decade, Floresta has frayed considerably around the edges, as unemployment and impoverishment have advanced. Many small businesses and family manufacturing concerns have collapsed under the pressure of unregulated dumping practices by large supermarkets and by a flood of cheap imported goods. In the heart of Floresta, not far from onion-shaped towers of the Ukrainian Catholic Cathedral of Buenos Aires, is the International Baptist Seminary, in the chapel of which Betel church was born some thirty-five years ago. The church eventually moved into its own building — a rather shabby reconverted house two blocks away — but has lately taken to meeting on Sundays in the seminary chapel, because the "temple" (as church buildings are called in evangelical circles in Argentina) is badly in need of repairs and structural reform.

Church attendance runs about seventy to eighty persons on a Sunday. The group is quite heterogeneous and is growing slowly but steadily. Five years ago there were no young families in the church, but now a dozen smallish children run up and down the aisles — and even behind the altar — during the Sunday service. Several immigrants from neighboring countries, especially Peruvians, make the congregation more ethnically integrated than other types of gatherings in the neighborhood, such as social clubs or amateur soccer teams. Among the church members are unskilled laborers, domestic help, crafts- and tradespeople, office workers, teachers, professionals, university students, and several persons involved in formal theological education, either as students or as professors. What almost all the people of working age in our church have in common, regardless of their occupation, is the lack of an "assured income." Some have job stability but are underpaid; others have no stability though a better salary; others have a meager wage and no stability; and still others are unemployed, either chronically or intermittently. Whenever congregational prayer requests are mentioned, joblessness or the fear of losing jobs is mentioned as a main concern.

This new vulnerability of lower middle- and middle-class evangelical church members has caught many of them by surprise. They had tended to assume that their sense of responsibility and God-fearing ways ensured if not necessarily prosperity, at least a certain stability and well-being. During the first half of the twentieth century, the common route for converts from nominal Roman Catholicism to an active evangelical faith had been an enhanced interest in reading the Bible (and therefore an increased involvement in practices that promote literacy and articulateness) and the reinforcement of a somewhat austere work and worship ethic that tended to lead to savings and eventually greater material accumulation as well as a higher education for the next generation. Now, for the first time, second- and third-generation evangelicals with a university education — just to name one subgroup represented at Betel — are faced with massive underemployment, unemployment, or inhumane working conditions. Their new social and economic vulnerability leads them to ask new questions, not so much about a theoretical "option for the poor"[14] as about how to practice their faith when poverty or impoverishment is creeping up on them, creating structures that seem to force their options. This is the *kairos* in which a new interest in the practice of discernment in the face of great need has sprung up within the church, though the actual word "discernment" is rarely mentioned.

Linking the questions of this *kairos* to the historic Christian practice of discernment is complex. In popular Argentinean evangelical speech, the word "discernment" has taken on a peculiar and almost magical coloratura. It seems to evoke something along the lines of individually practiced divining. At Betel it was therefore necessary at first to define the word every time it was used, as in: "By discernment I mean figuring out what to do, all together as a church, with the help of God's Spirit."

It is difficult to determine exactly the process whereby a church such as Betel begins consciously to exercise the practice of discernment. In this particular case, three events in the life of the church were important. The first was the effort made by the church to respond to the massive flooding in Northern Argentina by sending powdered milk, diapers, canned goods, and clothing to the refugees. The second was the visit and

---

14. The phrase "option for the poor" is usually perceived in evangelical churches such as this one as the discourse of a somewhat suspect leftist intelligentsia far removed from their own lives and piety.

message of a representative of "TEAR Fund," a British evangelical relief agency. His sermon made clear both the biblical imperative for social justice and the fact that many church people similar to those at Betel were "doing something" about it rather effectively. The third was that a group of twenty-somethings from the church began reading and studying a translation of the book *Justice for All,* by John Perkins, an African-American minister from Mississippi. These three factors promoted what one might call consciousness-raising among laypeople used to thinking primarily in terms of the salvation of the soul, but whose individualistic, immaterial theological categories were already being shaken by the structural socio-economic changes brought on by the globalization of capitalism and neo-liberal economic measures.[15] It was not uncommon to hear comments after the service such as, "We need to do something to respond to human needs. But what?" Slowly, consensus began to arise on the necessity of making this question a priority in some systematic way. At that point, however, the thought process lacked concrete means of implementation.

As a theologian interested in the practice of discernment, I realized that something significant was going on in my own community of faith.[16] It seemed to me that God's Spirit was raising this question insistently in many of our lives, often using the voices of children to do so.[17] In search-

---

15. Echoes of Paulo Freire, *Pedagogy of the Oppressed* (New York: Herder & Herder, 1970) come to mind here.

16. Part of the methodology used by the group writing this book was for each person to try to become immersed in a particular practice while reflecting upon its relationship to beliefs and theology.

17. I would hold that the questions of young children — when taken seriously — are often among the most important catalysts in the process of discernment, especially in societies where small children and their conversation are valued highly, as in Argentina. Their questions are insistent, often incisive, and display an unconscious hermeneutic of suspicion. Some questions posed by my oldest daughter, three years old at the time, that were significant to me in clarifying my priorities were: "Does that woman sleep outside at night? Why? Shouldn't we find her a place to stay?" (observation made on the street). "Does God give all people food or just some?" (asked after giving thanks for the food). We also held the following conversation:

Day One: "Mommy, we can't see God." "Well, not right now, but we know what God is like because Jesus showed us." "Yes, but he went away and now God is not here." "God's Spirit is here, even if we can't see God. It is like the wind. We

ing and praying for a way that might help us move forward, eventually some of us stumbled upon a church-based community development course that had originated in Southern Africa. We suggested to the church that those interested might work through the course together. Immediately, a group of about fifteen committed persons of various ages and backgrounds was formed. Those of us with formal theological training began to translate the text and adapt the materials from rural Africa to urban South America, with the help of friends knowledgeable in economics and law. The course included biblical themes and practical suggestions. The fact that it came from the "periphery" and not from the affluent North was regarded very positively by the group.

The group meets every other Saturday. Different members of the group have taken on different roles in the discussions. These are not set or obligatory, but seem to emerge naturally from the gifts and disposition of a given person. One person, for example, prepares assiduously for each meeting, working through the biblical texts to be treated beforehand. She is, however, anything but an enthusiast — more of a pragmatic skeptic, constantly questioning the viability of any given idea. By so doing, she often points out real weaknesses and stimulates others to try to respond to her concerns. Another person, who has been in the church for over thirty years and remembers most of what has gone on in that time, functions as the group's historical memory, pointing out what has been tried in the past. A third person has become very interested in liberation theology and insights from Marxism. A few years ago, quoting Lenin from the pulpit (as he has been known to do) would have likely led to scandal; now Lenin's

---

can see how the wind works, but it is invisible." "Mommy . . . [in a condescending tone] That is just your imagination!"

Day Two: "Mommy, you know how you said that you can feel God's Spirit in your heart?" "Yes." "Well, last night when I was sick I felt God's Spirit saying to me that we need to find a place to live for those people that sleep outside and get coins to give them and teach the bad people to be good and share with the poor people."

Other members of the church also reported on the comments of their children. One father commented, sadly, that although his son had earlier shown a lot of sensitivity to social injustice, in time this had been blunted. This father felt that he himself had blunted it by not putting into practice what he preached about justice. Again the question was raised: "What should we do?"

words are discussed in the group. Another member is involved in party politics. He rarely speaks, but when he does, it is from direct knowledge of how the public sphere works. In short, each member of the group speaks from his or her own reservoir of experience and wisdom, and each listens to the others. The pastor does not push the discussion or try to manipulate conclusions, but he does sum up what has been said and try to reduce the anxiety levels of those who are overly eager to reach immediate conclusions despite the complexity of the issues discussed. The group believes that the main question to be discerned is *What is the calling of our community in response to human needs within it and without?* The corollary question is *What particular project would be the most faithful way to fulfill that calling?*

Several important ideas expressed at the very first session reappeared in subsequent meetings. These can be identified as specific "moments" in the process of discernment. They do not appear in a particular order but rather tend to resurface in different guises:

- *Empathy:* For the first time we are realizing that we are not that different or that far away from those we consider indigents.
- *Constructive criticism of our tradition:* It was wrong in the past to do nothing holistic in response to human needs. We have wrongly emphasized a disincarnate "salvation of the soul" to the detriment of what the Bible actually says.
- *Admission of our limitations:* We cannot do it all. There is more poverty and more need out there than we can address. We feel overwhelmed when we think about resolving everything ourselves.
- *Learning how to listen actively:* It is very important that each person express herself or himself freely and also listen respectfully to what the others say. These discussions usually seem more focused than those the same people might enjoy in other contexts. Each member seems to want to avoid unnecessary or unhelpful talk.
- *Contextualization:* Our urban reality frames our discernment. This is not a rural context. For example, in an urban context it might be more important to help people offer services rather than manufacture goods.
- *Insight into structural dimensions:* Structural political and economic conditions require our attention. We need to question the wider system that leads to specific cases of suffering. If we are to make a differ-

ence, we will have to network with other groups that share our interests.

- *Practical ecumenism:* Many of the groups with experience in developing projects of the type we are considering belong to other Christian confessions. The Roman Catholics have much experience in this area and are excellent dialogue partners. For some members of the group, to learn from Catholics how to do anything in church is a novel and even trying experience, but it is leading to new perspectives on the church universal.
- *Biblical hermeneutics:* Reflecting on these issues and trying to plan concrete moves teaches us to read and understand the biblical text in new ways.
- *Awareness of the human tendency toward self-deception:* This is understood by the group as a particular danger in "discernment," especially when recourse is made to phrases such as "God told me this or that."[18]
- *Pneumatological sensibility:* The feeling of the group is that it came into being by the leading of the Spirit and that the Spirit of God will eventually disclose through prayer, Bible study, discussion, and experimentation the concrete paths we should tread.

The group, and through it the church, is still in the midst of this process of discernment. It is still too early to predict exactly which project(s) will be carried out. It seems likely that the first step will be developing a nongovernmental organization able to give micro-credits for micro-businesses, possibly following a modified version of the Grameen Bank methodology. Some members of the group see this as a first step that does not go far enough, because its methodology does not sufficiently question structural injustice. However, this method does work to help people help themselves and become self-employed. The group hopes eventually to move to higher levels of project complexity, for example by helping to form cooperatives that could produce goods for alternative, ecologically sound foreign trade. That this sort of project would collide both with deeper anthropological problems (the problems of greed and self-centeredness) and with higher structural hurdles is clear to the group.

18. This point is made more than once by Frank Rogers Jr. in his chapter on "Discernment" in *Practicing Our Faith: A Way of Life for a Searching People,* ed. Dorothy C. Bass (San Francisco: Jossey-Bass Publishers, 1997); cf. pp. 107, 109, 113.

Most of the group yearns to contribute to the "big picture" (what early liberation theology called *transformative praxis*) but believes such a contribution cannot be attained unless "small moves" are first learned and put into practice. While some might argue that this stance leads to quietism or a narrow focus, I believe that it is teaching the group gently but firmly how to transcend its former spiritualistic tendencies and defeatism. Latin American theology needs to be involved in and enriched by such stories of community growth while it insists at the same time on pointing firmly toward the wider horizons induced by eschatological hope. The small steps Betel is taking are giving it a desire for larger strides, while keeping the community rooted in modest but real experiences of success[19] that continually kindle further hope and imagination.

The group wishes to achieve full consensus before deciding the exact profile of the project to be attempted. What can already be seen, however, is that the process of trying to "discern" what to do in the face of a given situation has affected many areas of the life of the church. From a pastoral perspective, it is evident that some people are praying regularly for the first time, that biblical narratives seem more alive than previously, and that the theology of the sermons (preached by the pastor and various church members) is permeated with biblical themes of justice, with heavily Christocentric elements.[20] Moreover, deeper relationships are

19. Though not a formal project of the community, the experiences of some unemployed members of the group in deciding to pool their talents to prepare and market food on a small scale has been one of the encouraging instances to be born of the process of discernment.

20. This is no coincidence. As Jon Sobrino puts it: "If being a Christian is to come to be sons/children in the Son/Child *(hijos en el Hijo),* then Christian discernment will have a structure similar to the discernment of Jesus, something only achievable by following him. . . . The *structure* of Jesus' discernment must be re-created throughout history according to the Spirit of Jesus." See "El seguimiento de Jesús como discernimiento" in *Jesús en América Latina. Su significado para la fe y la cristología* (Santander: Sal Terrae, 1982), p. 210 (this article also appeared in English in *Concilium* in 1978). At times, the Third Person of the Trinity is explicitly present, while the Second Person is only implicitly present; this is a reversal of the dynamics one usually finds in trinitarian thought. I would indeed hold that the practice of discernment practically forces trinitarian, and more specifically pneumatological, reflection. It is worth pointing out that José María Castillo, drawing on Jesuit traditions of discernment, argues somewhat analogously that whereas Jesus is the most perfect example of one who discerned wisely, the only criterion that allows Christians to know whether or not they have dis-

forming between the people in the group; the children are visibly happy to see the adults "planning something" that will help people; and a renewed sense of hope has been kindled in some who are imagining new work possibilities. Those involved are excited about working together and about the possibility of developing a web of similar groups, especially throughout the Southern Hemisphere, using e-mail to communicate quickly with each other. To have received the course from Africa is highly symbolic: Southern Africa is just across the ocean from Buenos Aires, but it has always seemed more like something in the antipodes. For this group, this is no longer so.[21]

From a more theoretical theological perspective, the difficult structural socio-economic situation has allowed an *epistemological rupture* with a twist. In the past, old thought categories have burst when the wealthy have encountered the poor; but within this group it is the forced encounter of many with their own near-poverty or poverty that has changed their perspective. This new, more vulnerable position has allowed greater openness to the Holy Spirit's voice (sometimes heard in the voices of the children and of the very old) and a greater empathy for those whose needs are even more pronounced than their own. Assumptions have also been challenged by an incipient hermeneutic of suspicion and retrieval regarding the ministry practices inherited from missionaries, the question of whether customary evangelism has been too one-sided, and a return to the Bible to verify whether a more holistic understanding of ministry is scriptural.[22] This process requires interdisciplinary analytical tools and the

---

cerned accurately is the fruit of the *Spirit* (as in Gal. 5:22) — that it to say, the manifestation of love in our life with one another. Moreover, he argues, since the fabric of our life in society is complex, we need cultural, historical, economic, and socio-political instruments of analysis in order to make sense of purported manifestations of love and to discern wisely about them. See Castillo, *El discernimiento cristiano. Por una conciencia crítica* (Salamanca: Sígueme, 1989), pp. 154-55. Here too appears the primacy of the Spirit's work alongside the inevitable socio-analytical mediations required by theology. The classical Latin American liberation theology text on the latter topic is Clodovis Boff, *Teología de lo político. Sus mediaciones* (Salamanca: Sígueme, 1980).

21. The technical resources of capitalist globalization can work to the advantage of groups in principle opposed to it by allowing them to network more rapidly and effectively.

22. In this particular community of faith, the principle of *sola Scriptura* is axiomatic and unquestioned.

ability to weave the ideas of the group together into some sort of cohesive whole. The role of the theologians in the group tends to be to contribute to these two latter tasks in particular.

Through this practice of discernment, the person of the Holy Spirit has taken on new life in the piety and imagination of the group. Discourse about the Spirit's character and action is being articulated in a way that is less modalistic and more perichoretic than the stereotypical formulations previously preferred. For instance, when concrete issues led the group to struggle with the problem of the relation between the spiritual and the material and the implicit anthropological dualism many had long held, the group came to the following conclusion: The conception of the Eternal Son was by the Spirit; the incarnation took place in the Spirit; the resurrection was in the power of the Spirit. When we speak of "spirituality" or "spiritual" aspects, our point of reference is this same Spirit. Therefore nothing material can be indifferent to Christian spirituality, if by "spirituality" we really mean something related to the Spirit of the Son and the Father.[23]

Admittedly, these formulations belong to one of the trained theologians in the group, but they do faithfully attempt to reflect the ideas proposed by the group in its discussions. The role of academic theology as represented by the theologians involved in the group has been to articulate and synthesize implicit and explicit ideas expressed by the group and then to hold them up to the group for further work. The theologians have also tried to ask pertinent, focused questions, rather than trying to come up with all the answers. The process of discernment as experienced by the group, then, requires analytical tools and the ability to weave the ideas of the group together into some sort of cohesive whole. The theologians in the group are expected to contribute to these two latter tasks in particular, but their formulations are in themselves up for discussion and debate and are not considered definitive by the group. This sort of give-and-take of

---

23. The necessary "spirituality of materiality" and "materiality of spirituality" inherent to the practices of the faith is reflected especially in the essays by Christine Pohl, Tammy Williams, and Gilbert Bond in this volume. The process of discernment at Betel has points of contact with some of the situations they have described, perhaps because they focus on the ecclesiality of people who tend to be at the periphery of socioeconomic power. The character of a practice of faith and the character of its relation to theology is marked strongly by the social location of the practitioners.

academic and practical theology within a concrete ecclesial community is very healthy for theology.[24]

It should be added that in many evangelical circles in Argentina today the word "discernment" evokes the idea of quasi-magical abilities by which certain people are able to tell "good spirits" or demons from the bad. In this use, the term has an anti-intellectual bias. By contrast, the exercise in discernment at Betel has not had an anti-intellectual bias but rather has integrated intellectual effort into the spiritual discipline of trying to understand as a group what to do and how to do it in a way that is coherent with the dynamic of the trinitarian God. The presence of academic theologians in the group has helped it to keep that balance.

Finally, in unexpected ways, the simple exercise of figuring out how to respond faithfully and concretely to human needs tends to radicalize the community. In this sense, looking for "little moves against destruction" is not a mere privatization of the wider dream of transformative praxis articulated by early liberation theology. What is needed is continued commitment and imagination on the part of discerners open to the Spirit's unleashing of enough imagination and creativity in their midst for them to envision new ways to transform structures effectively.

Popular Protestant Spirituality and Discernment

The specific context of pneumatology in the River Plate area today is worth further consideration. To speak of the Spirit in Argentina and perhaps in Latin America generally today means taking into account the centrality and ambiguity of popular spirituality. Particularly for a great many Protestants (understood broadly as non-Roman Catholic and non-Eastern Orthodox Christians), post-Pentecostal and neo-charismatic conceptions of the Spirit have become almost normative. In speaking of discernment and spirituality, many Protestants refer to the "magical" or "supernatural" practices reputedly carried out by post-Pentecostals and neo-charismatics.

---

24. In Latin America, especially within minority faith groups, there is less specialization and compartmentalization of theological tasks than in countries like the United States or Germany. Therefore the academic theologian is constantly confronted and challenged by many different groups and situations outside the university or seminary and is required to develop a certain flexibility and malleability that I consider salutary.

Adherents to these groups are often perceived by themselves and by others as somehow more "spiritual" and thus more able to "discern spiritually" than other Protestants — even by those Protestants who are suspicious of their theology or consider them gullible.

Latin American religiosity, Christian and non-Christian, is highly complex. Sociologists are presently struggling to find a proper nomenclature to describe the various non-Roman-Catholic Christian faith groups that are gaining influence in the River Plate area, particularly within the poorest sectors of society. Recent studies[25] illustrate the extent to which Roman Catholicism has lost its monopoly of symbolic goods — though not its hegemony — and the high growth rate of Protestantism and Afro-Brazilian religions, such as *umbanda,* among the poor. Most of the "Protestants" reflected in such studies belong to groups many sociologists refer to as "neo-Pentecostal," meaning a series of autonomous groups, born of classical Pentecostalism but theologically and ethically quite different from it and institutionally separate from it. The sociological profile of these neo-Pentecostal churches includes leadership by charismatic pastors and a system of practices that stress divine healing, personal and family prosperity, ecstatic trances with speaking in tongues, laughing and fainting, war against spiritual powers, and liberation from spiritual ties that cause sickness and disgrace.[26] As a result of conversation with Norberto Saracco, a Pentecostal theologian who prefers to speak of "post-Pentecostalism," I have come to adopt his term for these groups, because I think it better re-

25. For instance, Juan Esquivel, Fabián García, María Eva Hadida, and Víctor Houdin, "Creencias y prácticas religiosas en el Gran Buenos Aires. El caso de Quilmes" (unpublished monograph). Their study, conducted from the perspective of sociology of religion, concentrates on the inhabitants of Quilmes, a region in the Greater Buenos Aires area with about half a million people. It seems to provide yet another indication that phenomenologically speaking, the "option of the poorest" does not seem to be the Roman Catholic "option for the poor."

26. See Hilario Wynarzcyk, "The Transformation of Christianity: Evangelicals and Pentecostals in Latin America" (unpublished lecture), p. 13; cf. also Cecilia Mariz, "El debate en torno del pentecostalismo autónomo en Brasil," in *Sociedad y Religión,* March 1995. Heinrich Schäfer, for instance in "'¡Oh Señor de los cielos, danos poder en la tierra!' El fundamentalismo y los carismas. La reconquista del campo de acción en América Latina," *Revista Latinoamericana de Teología* 15 (1998): 61-78, defines his terms somewhat differently. He provides a valuable analysis of how theological fundamentalism works as a social strategy to create symbolic meaning in certain groups in Central America.

flects the fact that they depart sharply from classical Pentecostalism; for instance, the traditional Pentecostal sense of eschatological urgency is missing, and with it the strict apodictic set of moral rules — mostly prohibitions — characteristic of classical Pentecostalism in Latin America. Within both Pentecostalism and post-Pentecostalism, one finds a wide variety of theological orientations.[27] As a general rule of thumb, the highly visible post-Pentecostal groups that meet in large refurbished cinemas in urban areas tend toward an individualistic prosperity gospel and are not very critical of structural injustice, whereas small autonomous and autochthonous congregations more closely linked to classical Pentecostal theology often function in more critical and alternative ways, for instance within *villas,* developing most of their leadership and methods from within the community. Whereas the former groups often seem like masters in self-deception and the deception of others, these latter Pentecostal congregations often have a great deal to teach other Christians about the practice of discernment and about how to make small moves against destructiveness.

It is particularly important to take gender into account when thinking

---

27. Pentecostals and post-Pentecostals are further to be differentiated from what I call "neo-charismatics": Baptists, Brethren (Hermanos Libres), Mennonites, Presbyterians, and others, who adopt many of the forms of post-Pentecostalism, thus radically departing from the traditional ecclesiology and doctrine of their traditions, without leaving their denominational structures. They share with the cinema-variety of post-Pentecostals a weak hamartiology (theology of sin) and a shamanistic understanding of leadership; their membership tends to be drawn from the middle or formerly middle socio-economic sectors. Significantly, both in neo-charismatic and in post-Pentecostal groups, "discernment" tends to be understood as a gift given to few, rather than as a practice accessible to all. One of their most common catch phrases is "Only the [male] pastor has the vision for the church." Sociological studies show that adherents to this sort of Protestantism emphasize the necessity for pastors to be mediators between God and the people more than nominal and even more than practicing Roman Catholics. See Esquivel et al. (note 25 above), who add: "Moreover, among Protestant pastors, personal charisma predominates over the functional charisma, although the latter is also present because they are pastors. The former, which leans on rites and ceremonies such as healings, anointings, and exorcisms, allows the faithful to follow the pastor independently from any territorial boundaries and to consider him an indispensable mediator before God." On this topic see Nancy Bedford, "Las 'iglesias libres' en América Latina. Una vision teológica de su dinámica en la Iglesia universal," *Iglesia y Misión* 19 (2000): 10-16.

about discernment in this context. This was brought home to me by a Pentecostal woman living in a *villa miseria* (literally, "misery village" or "misery neighborhood"). The dynamic equivalent to this term would be the Brazilian *favela,* or in American English a "slum," although living conditions in the *villa* tend to be more precarious than in similar communities in economically developed countries. In large Argentine cities such as Buenos Aires or Córdoba, the *villas* are where many of the poor and indigent live. Some have particular ethnic characteristics and are made up mainly of migrants from a particular province in Argentina or of immigrants from neighboring countries. Drug dealing, gang violence, widespread alcoholism, and poor nutrition are widespread. They also increasingly include people formerly belonging to the middle socio-economic classes. I think the *villas* are an important testing ground for theology; what is irrelevant or incommunicable there may well not be worth pursuing.

I spoke about the Sermon on the Mount, forgiveness, and its application to family life to a group of women at *Villa 20* in Buenos Aires. Afterwards, we shared tea, and a shy woman in her late fifties, sitting in a wheelchair, hands and legs twisted from rheumatoid arthritis, said something chilling to me in the mildest of tones: "You know, I wonder how to do what you were talking about: this business of treating others as we would like to be treated. I try to and pray about it, but my husband is an alcoholic who drinks and beats me, and at the same time I depend on him for everything. I can't even get from the bed to the wheelchair without his help. I never know whether he'll say 'Aren't you going to church?' or 'You're not going to that damned church again, are you?' and hit me." Trying in vain to peer into her eyes, which were hidden by dark glasses, I couldn't help but wonder whether my theology, in the form of a lifestyle I was describing as a "consolation from God," might be contributing to her doom rather than to her liberation.[28]

Her situation illustrates two important points. First of all, it reflects the extent to which theology, discernment, and (pastoral) praxis need to

---

28. Hadewijch of Brabant, in her poem "On Discernment," speaks of the ambiguity and possible self-deception inherent to the process of discernment: "People think that they are led by the Spirit/When mostly it is their own will that leads them,/And they regard as consolation from God/What leads them to their doom." Fiona Bowie, ed., *Beguine Spirituality: An Anthology,* trans. Oliver Davies (London: SPCK, 1989), p. 100.

intersect. It would seem one can best discern fallacies and problems inherent to a given theological discourse by means of a pastoral mediation that tries to work out the theopraxis proper to that theology. This in turn leads to the reformulation of the theology, fueled by the hermeneutics of suspicion and retrieval proper to the practice of discernment. In one sense, this is simply another form of the theological or hermeneutical circle described by Paul Tillich or Juan Luis Segundo. Secondly, however, her insightful reaction, marked by pain and sincerity, sheds light on how discernment can be sharpened by a perspective of gender. By speaking the truth in love, she showed me how shallow my understanding of the *Sitz-im-Leben* of women in the *villa* was — specifically how little my theology was taking realities such as domestic violence into account. She wondered aloud whether leaving her husband would make her unworthy of salvation, which in turn allowed me to speak (thereby adjusting my theological discourse in consonance with pastoral practice) both of God's unconditional grace and of an understanding of love in which boundaries can be marked as well as overcome.[29] We also spoke of our hope in the resurrection of the body. She told me she often dreamed of being able to get up and do things as she once did, such as cooking; the implication was also that in dreams she was able to defend herself bodily. Her dreams[30] opened up a space for the development of a practical counterpart of the theology I'd been trying to transmit: an embodiment of hope in the resurrection and the faculty to serve others in a love born of dignity and self-respect.

29. The idea of the necessary boundaries to practices has appeared several times in the discussions of our group, particularly in the preliminary contributions written by women, as in the exercise of women putting on boxing gloves at a church (Serene Jones), learning how to say "no" (Amy Plantinga Pauw), and understanding the limits of hospitality (Christine Pohl).

30. The theology in the content of dreams has begun to intrigue me for two main reasons. First, in speaking to women, especially those who practice a Protestantism marked by Pentecostalism, I have noticed that they often refer to dreams, which they sometimes understand as prophetic visions. Second, the discourse of psychoanalysis, which permeates the educated classes in Argentina, tends to center on the interpretation of dreams, leading me to wonder about how to incorporate its insights into theology.

The Practice of Discernment and Opening Up
Horizons in Latin American Theology

Christian discernment is a trinitarian practice: the Spirit/Wisdom who guides practitioners of discernment is not the spirit of naked power and ambition, but the Spirit of the incarnate Son/Word, who has shown concretely in history how to resist evil and pursue justice. Effective Christian discernment necessarily involves a trinitarian vision of the world, in which the three divine Persons, who are one, invite all of creation to discover creative ways in which to participate in their dynamic of love and equality. The interaction between the practice of theology and the practice of discernment on the one hand leads to a deepening of theology's sense of its own provisional character and on the other hand prods theologians to become involved in a praxis of concrete "moves" against destructiveness. Such moves promise to open up new possibilities in the midst of apparently closed horizons. They also serve to put theological discourse to the test. A theology shaped by the practice of discernment will rediscover its own finitude, its need for prayer, its dependence on the Spirit of God, and its profound resonance with the beliefs and practices that guide the community of faith on its pilgrimage.

Early liberation theology conceived of itself as second-order reflection on a first-order *praxis* capable of transforming the world. In consequence, when that structural and liberating transformation fell through, theologians were rightly disconcerted. Reflection on and involvement in transformative *practices*, such as the practice of discernment described here, allow theologians and their theology to move out of a defensive, disconcerted mode into a constructive mode oriented to the community of faith and its calling in the wider kingdom of God. In other words, for Latin American theology today, the small moves against destructiveness that are allowed by the practices of the Christian faith open up glimpses of new horizons of hope in a time of apparently closed horizons. From the perspective of the social sciences, García Canclini points to the need in Latin American thought for narrating stories, for integrating a sense of the intercultural in our understanding of what is happening in the world, and for imagining new possibilities, rather than believing that the future holds only the two options of McDonald's or Macondo.[31] This is an important

31. Canclini, *La globalización imaginada*, p. 52. "Macondo" is the town described

challenge for the future of theology as well: Latin American theology needs to develop a dynamic capable of thinking and acting dialectically between micro and macro dimensions of reality. This means being able to develop the flexibility necessary to understand the world in multifaceted new ways and to go beyond the rigidity of thought structures that are no longer helpful. It means thinking and living in terms of *practices* and *praxis* in imaginative, playful, and constructive ways through which David can hope to discern and even triumph over Goliath. A Latin American theology aware of and in dialogue with the *practices* of the Christian faith opens up new doors — but it also implies an invitation to cross over new thresholds, out toward wider horizons of hope.

---

in Gabriel García Márquez's novel *Cien años de soledad (One Hundred Years of Solitude)*. In Latin America it is a symbol of subtropical backwardness.

181

PRACTICING THEOLOGY,
BECOMING THEOLOGIANS

Beliefs, Desires, Practices,
and the Ends of Theological Education

L. GREGORY JONES

For nearly a century, the preparation of men and women for ordained Christian ministry in most North American denominations has relied on a presumed division of labor. Churches, according to this presumption, are responsible for initiating future ministers into Christian beliefs and practices. Subsequently, seminaries are supposed to teach them the critical thinking and leadership skills that equip them for their professional roles. If each party fulfills its part of the task, so the thinking goes, the churches will have leaders who are well equipped for faithful and effective ministry.

This "relay race" understanding of education for Christian leadership has dominated the churches' vision of ministerial preparation and the curriculum and the self-understanding of theological educators throughout most of the twentieth century. Imagine the student as a baton. During the first leg of the race, the future leader is held by the church, which forms him or her in particular beliefs and practices through congregational life and a whole array of other church-supported activities, such as church camps, mission projects, and church-related colleges or campus ministries. Then the church passes the baton to a seminary. Seminaries, which prize forms of scholarship that challenge the inevitably incomplete and distorted formation students will have received thus far, then subject the institutions and ideas of the first leg of the relay race to critical scrutiny, while also providing the student with the specialized skills ordained leaders need, such as preaching and administration. Upon graduation, the seminary passes the baton once again, handing the student off to the larger church, and especially to the series of congregations he or she will be expected to shepherd.

Alas, there is an increasingly widespread sense that various partners in the relay have not been running their share of the race very well. Within theological schools, this sense has given rise to searching conversations about how better to prepare women and men for ministry. Sometimes these conversations focus on the failures of the churches — the runners seminary professors presume should have done a better job during the first leg of the relay race. "How is it that our students do not know the basics of Christian belief and worship?" they ask one another with chagrin at professional conferences. However, concerned theological educators have shown themselves capable of self-criticism as well, finding fault not only with the churches but also with their own curricula and assumptions.[1] Beginning in 1983, when the theologian Edward Farley published *Theologia: The Fragmentation and Unity of Theological Education,* seminary faculties have been rethinking the aims and purposes of their task and pondering (and sometimes enacting) a variety of proposals for reform. Books by such notable theologians as Charles Wood, Joseph Hough and John Cobb, Rebecca Chopp, and David Kelsey have stirred this conversation,[2] usually by proposing reforms that forge more explicit and integral relationships between the disciplined study that takes place in the seminary and the embodied life of Christian faith in church and world beyond the seminary.

A similar conversation is taking place in the churches. Occasionally, it takes the form of harsh criticism of seminaries, whom local congregations may blame for a perceived decline in the quality of ministers or for the

---

1. During the 1990s, a self-critical set of conversations emerged within Christian higher education. Diverse works such as George Marsden, *The Soul of the American University* (New York: Oxford University Press, 1994); Mark Schwehn, *Exiles from Eden* (New York: Oxford University Press, 1993); and James Tunstead Burtchaell, *The Dying of the Light* (Grand Rapids: Eerdmans, 1998) have sought to address a perceived "secularization" of higher education and a diminished role for religious belief among academic practitioners.

2. Charles Wood, *Vision and Discernment: An Orientation in Theological Study* (Decatur: Scholars Press, 1985); Joseph Hough and John Cobb, *Christian Identity and Theological Education* (Atlanta: Scholars Press, 1985); Rebecca Chopp, *Saving Work: Feminist Practices of Theological Education* (Louisville: Westminster/John Knox, 1995); and David Kelsey, *To Understand God Truly* (Louisville: Westminster/John Knox, 1992).

emergence of disturbing theological positions, which in their judgment "kill the faith" of the clergy. But thoughtful church leaders are also engaged in some searching self-criticism about the inadequacy of their own efforts in Christian education and formation. At the end of the twentieth century, a series of high-profile books, written from a wide variety of methodological and religious perspectives, confirmed anecdotal evidence that Christian practices and Christian understanding within both congregations and the broader culture are diminishing. The sociologist Robert Wuthnow, the legal scholar Stephen Carter, the historian Mark Noll, and the Christian ethicist Stanley Hauerwas, as well as many others, have drawn attention to the widespread lack of biblical knowledge and theological orientation among Americans, churched or not.[3] For example, few today would be able to understand Lincoln's Second Inaugural or Martin Luther King Jr.'s "I Have a Dream" speech. Both speeches contain biblical references and allusions that Lincoln and King trusted most Americans would understand, but which would today be missed even by many Christians, who have often received minimal instruction in the texts, practices, and beliefs of the faith. Such a populace produces few students who arrive at seminary well grounded in Christian basics.

Unfortunately, neither the self-criticism of each of these partners in the process of ministerial preparation nor the criticism they have directed at one another has adequately grappled with the deepest aims and the most pressing difficulties of providing faithful education and formation for Christian leadership. Conversations so far have tended to isolate one of the partners as the problem, rather than recognizing that each of the partners requires the effectiveness of the other and that each suffers from the other's ineffectiveness. Even if everyone were to agree that both partners need improvement, thinking of each as running a solitary leg in a relay race would ignore the fact that both operate in overlapping contexts of Christian life.

What if the relay race model is itself part of the problem? What if the development of an ordained Christian leader is not a matter of following a predetermined, linear path toward a single, dominant endpoint? What if,

---

3. Robert Wuthnow, *Christianity in the Twenty-First Century* (New York: Oxford University Press, 1993); Stephen Carter, *The Culture of Disbelief* (New York: Basic Books, 1993); Mark Noll, *The Scandal of the Evangelical Mind* (Grand Rapids: Eerdmans, 1995); and Stanley Hauerwas, *Unleashing the Scriptures* (Nashville: Abingdon, 1993).

instead, we conceive of this development as a pilgrimage that wends its way through a complex constellation of communities where practices, beliefs, and desires are formed and educated in a variety of ways? What if we think of the aim of this process not as graduation to pastoral responsibility but as membership in an ever-widening chorus that draws pastors, church members, seminary professors, and everyone else involved into the doxological praise of God?

This alternative way of thinking about how the church's future ordained leaders might be educated and formed does not require us to abandon the idea that there is a cumulative and progressive character to the process. The image of the race, after all, comes from the Apostle Paul, who described the Christian life in these terms in his letter to the Philippians. At the dawn of the twenty-first century, however, it is clear that the path this race follows does not usually resemble the smooth, straight track on which a relay race might be run. Instead, it more often takes shape as a pilgrimage through a less regular, yet still potentially rich, constellation of communal settings, all of which belong to and point toward the chorus of praise to God that is the inclusive end of humankind.

I shall argue in this essay that three distinct but overlapping sorts of communal settings are of special importance to Christian education and formation conceived in this way: congregational life, formal education, and situations of social engagement. Pilgrimage to faithful church leadership necessarily includes the variety of elements in which these communal settings might be said to specialize: catechesis, critical reflection, and faithful living in the world. Today, however, these are not necessarily encountered in sequence; individual pilgrims come to each at various stages and by diverse routes. Ultimately, however, the special strengths of each setting are needed if Christian leaders are to develop as persons whose beliefs, desires, and practices have Christian integrity.[4]

Education and Formation: The Parts and the Whole

Why do Christians — and more specifically, ordained Christian leaders — need the ongoing integration of practices, beliefs, and desires through com-

---

4. Amy Plantinga Pauw's chapter includes desires (in addition to beliefs and practices) as a crucial element in addressing the concerns of this volume.

munal settings that emphasize catechesis, critical reflection, and faithful living in the world? Answering this question is at least partly a matter of recognizing how thoroughly our lives are shaped by the complex interrelations between what we do, what we think, and what we passionately want. These are often difficult for us to disentangle in trying to make sense of our lives. For example, St. Paul wonders in Romans 7 why it is that he so often fails to do that which he thinks he ought to do. He attributes the problem to the bondage of sin. Sin's bondage is shaped by corrupt habits of activity, confused and even wrong convictions, and distorted desires. It is also shaped by the ways in which these factors mutually reinforce each other in spirals that degenerate downward into further destructiveness and frustration. By contrast, embracing an authentically Christian way of life involves us in redirecting our desires toward God; unlearning wrongly held convictions in order to learn and discern the truth about God, the world, and our own lives; and reshaping our activities to enable faithful living in the world.

To be sure, doing any one of these things almost inevitably means that we will be engaged in the others as well; such are the interrelations of desires, beliefs, and practices. For example, in order for me to redirect my desires toward God, I need help in challenging wrong beliefs about the importance of money and the problem of greed. I also need to begin to live in ways that separate me from practices that reinforce consumerist impulses and convictions grounded in greed.

More generally, we need broader pedagogical movements that shape beliefs, practices, and desires within communal contexts to form and educate persons for faithful Christian leadership. This was particularly apparent in the social engagement of resisting apartheid in South Africa. Regrettably, many Christian congregations in South Africa catechized people in ways that supported the ideology of apartheid. Similarly, seminaries and other institutions of formal learning developed curricula to reinforce that ideology. People sought to buttress this with patterns of social life that would maintain the structures of apartheid.

Yet there were also people whose faithful living in the world challenged the presumptions of apartheid and offered resistance to a racist, oppressive regime. Several seminaries raised crucial challenges to apartheid's intellectual and theological rationale and supported congregations and individuals in their resistance. Similarly, some congregations offered catechesis — often through Bible study and prayer — that shaped and formed people to challenge the broader patterns of social life that oppressed the majority of South African citizens based on the color of their skin. Their faithful living in the world then enabled them to understand the tasks of both catechesis and seminary education in deeper and more transformative ways.

These mutually reinforcing pedagogical movements of catechesis, formal learning, and faithful living in the world were crucial in the leadership of such key figures as Archbishop Desmond Tutu, Bishop Peter Storey, and the Reverend Beyers Naude. But they were equally significant in shaping the faithful witness of countless other pastoral leaders and lay people. Indeed, as he received the World Methodist Peace Award in 2000, former President Nelson Mandela indicated that were it not for the Methodist churches and their educational institutions, people such as him would never have developed their leadership capacities beyond their neighborhoods. Mandela's own embrace of a spirit of forgiveness and reconciliation during his release from prison and ascendance to the presidency of a free and democratic South Africa bear powerful testimony to the importance of nurturing mutually sustaining beliefs, practices, and desires through Christian education and formation.

To be sure, the new South Africa now faces many of the problems that beset us in North America. The churches in South Africa face the task of reconstructing their congregational life, their educational institutions, and their witness in the world in the midst of an increasingly secular, modern society where people's desires are often more shaped by consumer culture than by the grace of God, where convictions are often more shaped by state power than by the cross, and where activities are often shaped by habits of division and violence rather than reconciliation.

Within North America, we are less obviously confronted than are South Africans by the tasks of reconstructing the churches, the schools, and the structures for faithful living in the world. In many ways, it would appear that we in North America could keep muddling along with our current structures and practices. Yet the task facing us in North America is no less urgent than the task facing South African Christians. It is just more difficult to discern.

Our task is urgent because the fabric of our churches is rending, often because neither the laity nor the clergy are adequately formed as Christians. Too few know how to embrace a faithful way of life in its fullness or even how to have an articulate theological conversation about our disagreements regarding what such a way of life would involve. Acknowledging that beliefs, practices, and desires are integrally related to one another and recognizing the ways in which contemporary institutions of Christian formation separate them will be an important step as we begin to take up our task.

Dis-Integration in Contemporary
Christian Education and Formation

Unfortunately, the relay race model and other pressures have led these necessary and integrally related elements of Christian formation to become far more estranged from one another than they should be — an estrangement with implications for congregations, seminaries, and the life settings where Christian faith engages society. It is obvious that each of these sites of education and formation depends upon the health of the other two; the desires, beliefs, and practices that Christians fail to develop within any one of these will diminish their capacity for full involvement in the others. For a variety of reasons, indeed, each one has been limited in making its own distinctive contribution to the building up of leaders, thereby limiting the other two as well. Taken together, the effects of these limitations multiply.

Catechesis, the initial learning of beliefs, practices, and desires that allows individuals to participate in the life of the Christian community, has been weak among many American Christians in recent decades. Efforts flagged at least partly because many mainline Protestants took it for granted that people would become Christian simply as part of the process of growing up as Americans. Their assumption contrasts with that of many minority Christian groups in the United States — for example, ethnic groups such as African-Americans and Hispanics, as well as traditions such as Catholics and Anabaptists — which have long had a stronger awareness that Christian living must be nurtured as a clear alternative over against dominant American self-understanding. Mainline Protestants today seem to be increasingly aware of the need for more extensive catechesis as the dominant culture has become less overtly supportive of religious beliefs, desires, and practices. Even so, most congregations have failed either to sustain the structures that once nurtured Christian faith (such as camp meetings, Sunday schools, magazines and other literature, catechism classes, and summer camps) or to develop rich alternative methods of Christian initiation. They often fail even to address such basic questions as the one asked by the disciples: "Lord, teach us to pray." Few people who seek to join contemporary mainline Protestant churches are asked to change much about their way of life — their beliefs and habits of thought, their desires, their actual daily practices — nor are they given the resources to do so.

It is notable that formal academies — which, for mainline Protestants, have typically included primarily colleges, universities, and seminaries — have done a poor job of educating and forming leaders to understand the catechetical processes needed in local congregations. They have also often overlooked the catechetical and social engagement dimensions of their own mission. Enlightenment images of the self-sufficiency of reason, failures of church-related undergraduate education, and the hold of academic guilds on seminary curricula have conspired to promote critical reflection to the near-exclusion of other aspects of student development. Although seminaries and church-related colleges and universities were well-positioned to play key roles in shaping faithful patterns of belief and inquiry while also nurturing key desires and practices, they generally drew back from these tasks during the twentieth century. Unfortunately, the spread of relatively uncritical uses of technology in coming years may only increase this trend by heightening an *in*formational understanding of the purposes of education, rather than an understanding that aims at formation in Christ. Such informational understandings encourage the transmission of discarnate beliefs and unreflective techniques — a particularly dangerous combination for Christian life and thought.

Parallel problems of disconnection have arisen with regard to the engagement of Christians in the social life of the world. Although congregations are places where Christians are formed in and for such engagement, many North American Christians would have a difficult time making any connections between what happens in worship and their everyday lives; very few could reflect critically and theologically on the nature of faithful worship and righteous living (Amos 5:21-24). Church-related colleges and universities also miss opportunities to prepare people for Christian social engagement through study that links theology and congregational life to the concerns and structures they will encounter as citizens and in the workplace. While many encourage students to do good, particularly through community service, they rarely link such activity to critical reflection about that service or tie it to the content of courses.

However, once we begin to recognize how crucial are the interactions of beliefs, desires, and practices in Christian faith and life, and to understand how each is shaped in and through participation in congregations, academies, and social engagements, we take a first step toward cultivating more faithful education and formation.[5] Ideally, each context can provide a formative setting that both presupposes and enables formation in the other areas. To be sure, we ought not conflate the distinct aims of each context: an academy is not a congregation, nor is a congregation a law firm or a business. At the same time, neither should we so divide them as to suggest that their legitimately distinct aims are wholly separate.

Before exploring the implications of such a vision for today, we would do well to consider the example of baptismal catechesis, an ancient Christian approach to education and formation that embodies an exceptionally rich understanding of the interplay between beliefs, desires, and practices. The twenty-first-century social and cultural context differs in many ways from the context within which this approach to Christian formation arose and flourished, to be sure. Even so, baptismal catechesis, which we shall examine in the form it took under Augustine of Hippo during the waning years of the Roman Empire, remains an instructive example of a deliberate, theologically grounded approach to Christian formation that overcomes the divisions that so often cripple present-day methods.

Perhaps for this reason, baptismal catechesis is being widely retrieved at the dawn of the twenty-first century, through the Roman Catholic Rite of Christian Initiation for Adults and the several Protestant programs of Christian formation that emulate RCIA. Baptismal catechesis, its advocates report, is a powerful formative process for new Christians that concomitantly becomes a reformative process for the "old" Christians who welcome them into the faith — perhaps because it combines so aptly the dimensions of belief, desire, and practice. I draw attention to it here for that reason, and also because this approach incorporates in a profound way the recognition that the Christian life involves an ongoing reorientation of life in relation to God.

---

5. Obviously, I have not given sufficient attention to what I mean specifically by beliefs, desires, and practices in this paper. That has been intentional, as I have sought to leave it open both to a descriptive rendering — namely, what particular Christians as a matter of daily life actually believe, desire, and practice — and a normative rendering of what Christians ought to learn to believe, desire, and practice. In my judgment, congregations, academies, and situations of social engagement ought to be contexts in which descriptive realities are evaluated within struggles for normativity.

An Ancient Example of Formational Integrity

Implicit in the ancient understanding of catechesis was the conviction that Christian initiation involves entry into a complex way of life that encompasses the beliefs, desires, and practices of the initiate. This conviction itself challenges our modern tendency to see beliefs as disembodied convictions, desires as uncontrollable feelings, and practices as meaningless actions. Rather, ancient catechesis was predicated on the understanding that our convictions are embodied in material practices and desires, that our desires are always already being educated and formed in one way or another through our convictions and activities, and that our practices are the carriers of beliefs and desires.

The recognition that the Christian life involves an ongoing journey of conversion, a process of embracing a Christian way of life by turning from one way of living to another, was intrinsic to the catechesis of the third and fourth centuries. The process offered specific beliefs to be learned even while other beliefs were discarded; specific practices to be enjoined while others were avoided; specific desires to be cultivated while others were cast off.[6]

Those interested in exploring this way entered this process by presenting themselves to the church as seekers who wished to receive basic instruction in Christian faith. Those whose interest increased during an initial period of instruction and personal struggle were then received into the catechumenate through a process of inquiry that concluded with the marking of the sign of the cross on the forehead, exorcism, and the imposition of hands. Being designated as catechumens meant that they could be present at worship for scriptural readings and homilies; they were dismissed prior to the Eucharist in order to reserve the mysteries of the sacrament for those already baptized.

---

6. Thomas Finn, *Early Christian Baptism and the Catechumenate*, 2 vols. (Collegeville, MN: The Liturgical Press, 1992), vol. 1, p. 3. My exposition will focus particularly on the patterns in Augustine's North Africa, though similar patterns existed in other areas at other times during the third and fourth centuries. I have learned a great deal about these issues from Finn's work and from William Harmless, *Augustine and the Catechumenate* (Collegeville, MN: The Liturgical Press, 1995). I provide a more complete description and analysis in a currently unpublished essay, "A Dramatic Journey Into God's Dazzling Light: Baptismal Catechesis and the Shaping of Christian Practical Wisdom."

In fourth-century North Africa, the catechumenate normally lasted for two years. Augustine explained this requirement succinctly: "What is all that time for, during which they hold the name and place of catechumens, except to hear what the faith and pattern of Christian life should be?"[7] Beliefs were nurtured through Scripture study and homilies. Desires for the fullness of Christian faith were encouraged, for example through the patterns of inclusion and exclusion that catechumens encountered as they were successively invited into Christian worship and dismissed from it. Simultaneously, catechumens were guided into Christian living by mentors, through whom, as Augustine proclaimed in one of his sermons, "Christ is announced through Christian friends."[8] As the apprenticeship continued, it was presumed that the catechumens' patterns of life would exhibit — albeit often slowly and painfully — transformations of thinking, feeling, and living. For example, catechumens would realize that they could not enjoy both the saving scriptural "spectacles" of mystery and miracle and the withering far-from-scriptural spectacles of theatre, racetrack, and the fights — a matter on which Augustine's near-contemporary Quodvultdeus chided both catechumens and those who had long been Christians.[9]

When, after months or years, catechumens appeared ready for baptism, they were encouraged to submit their names at the beginning of Lent. Those who did so began the second pivotal stage in their journey.[10] The focus of this second period was on prayer, further instruction in Scripture, exorcism, and a strict observance of Lent: no wine, no meat, no baths, no public entertainment, and no sex even within marriage.[11] Dur-

---

7. Augustine, *De fide et operibus* 6.9, cited in Harmless, *Augustine and the Catechumenate*, p. 156.

8. Augustine, cited in Harmless, *Augustine and the Catechumenate*, p. 152.

9. See Finn, "It Happened One Saturday Night: Ritual and Conversion in Augustine's North Africa," *Journal of the American Academy of Religion* 58/4 (Winter 1990): 591.

10. As the number of people affiliated with Christianity increased, a problem appeared: many catechumens would delay baptism for extensive periods. This was a status of "nominal" Christianity, neither pagan nor subject to the full expectations of being Christian. In the East, John Chrysostom and Gregory of Nazianzus used both scathing criticism and enticing rhetoric to discourage delays in baptism and to encourage becoming formally enrolled.

11. See the discussion in Finn, "It Happened One Saturday Night," p. 591, with references.

ing this time the homilies in worship focused particularly on moral formation. As Augustine put it in a sermon to catechumens, "We teach with words, you make progress with your deeds."[12] These Lenten homilies, we should note, became a means by which baptismal catechesis not only initiated new persons into God's reign but also renewed the faith and life of the larger congregation; both were encouraged to embrace inward renunciation and efforts on behalf of the poor.[13] Dramatic rites of exorcism, renunciation of sin, and physical and spiritual scrutiny by church leaders also took place within the Lenten period of preparation for baptism.

As Lent moved toward Holy Week, the catechumens received instruction in the Creed, including memorization of the actual words (typically guided by mentors) and instruction concerning its meaning. Memorization was important because it helped preserve the secrecy of the mystery, but Augustine also treasured it because he thought that memorizing the Creed helped new Christians to *internalize* the truth of God and God's ways.[14] Characteristically, he linked this emphasis on doctrinal clarity to the crucial context of Christian living. "May this belief imbue your hearts and guide you in professing it. On hearing this, believe so that you may understand, so that by putting into practice what you believe you may be able to understand it."[15] Here belief, desire, and practice are one.

During the final week before baptism, instruction emphasized the Lord's Prayer. Augustine's instructions most frequently focused on the petition concerning forgiveness. Its prominence in Matthew's text (Matt.

12. Augustine, Sermon 226.1; translation mine (with thanks for assistance to Angela Russell Christman).

13. Note Augustine's description that in his sermons he presented a "cross-weave" of doctrine and of moral admonition and that "both were given to catechumens, both to the faithful"; in this way, the "catechumens were instructed," while the "faithful were roused from forgetfulness." *De fide et operibus* 7.11, cited in Harmless, *Augustine and the Catechumenate*, p. 156.

14. See Augustine's account of his own recitation of the Creed at his baptism in Book VII of the *Confessions*.

15. Augustine, Sermon 214.10, cited in Harmless, *Augustine and the Catechumenate*, p. 277. Augustine's formulation here has broader implications in his work concerning the importance of authority in relation to reason, an issue particularly pertinent to his arguments with the Manicheans. It also suggests the importance of "submitting" to participation in disciplined practices as a necessary part of learning to understand what it means to be a Christian.

6:14-15) may have been part of the reason for this focus; but another reason was his awareness that the failure to forgive was a local vice and that this petition seemed "especially applicable" to Christians in Hippo, newcomers and longtime believers alike. Augustine stressed that the Lord's Prayer offers a "daily baptism" for forgiveness, noting that he too was a sinner who needed the cleansing of forgiveness: "You might ask, 'And you, too?' I [must] answer back: 'Yes, me too!' 'You, reverend bishop — you, a debtor?' 'Yes, I am a debtor as you are.'"[16] Augustine also linked prayer to Christian living as he had linked belief, encouraging his hearers to love their neighbor by sharing their material resources.

On Easter morning, the third stage of the journey occurred. After "baptismal water was consecrated, the candidates processed to the font while chanting the now familiar Psalm 42. They removed their garments (the coarse leather penitential tunic), responded to a final inquiry into their faith and firm will as they stood waist-deep in the water, and were immersed three times in the name of the Father, and of the Son, and of the Holy Spirit." The historian Thomas Finn describes the drama of this event:

> When they emerged the bishop imposed his hand on them, anointed their heads with chrism, and traced the sign of the cross on their foreheads, probably also with chrism. The newly-baptized then dressed in white, including a linen head cover. They then received a baptismal candle and the embrace of the congregation.[17]

After the baptisms were completed, the newly baptized received a cup of milk and honey at their first Eucharist. They would return later on Easter morning for a second Eucharist, and perhaps that afternoon for a third. In Augustine's sermons to the whole congregation on Easter mornings, he would point to the newly baptized, noting that they themselves had become the first day of a new creation; they who "were once darkness" were now "light in the Lord" (Eph. 5:8).[18] He called them to live always in this light.

With the celebration of both Easter Eucharists, the newly baptized had

---

16. Augustine, Sermon 56.11, cited in Harmless, *Augustine and the Catechumenate*, p. 293.

17. Finn, "It Happened One Saturday Night," p. 594.

18. See Augustine, Sermons 225 and 226; see also the discussion in Harmless, *Augustine and the Catechumenate*, pp. 313-14.

moved into the fourth stage of their journeys of conversion. As a part of their "homecoming," the newly baptized received a new name to signify their new life in Christ. Further, their homecoming typically included liturgies and continuing instruction over a period of eight days. For those eight days, they continued to wear white robes and to come each day for a celebration of the Eucharist, including a homily. The newly baptized were given pride of place in these liturgies, as their white garments testified to the completion of this phase of their journey into the dazzling light of God's reign. They served as living icons of God's new creation.

The primary concern of Augustine and other teachers at this point was whether these new Christians would continue to walk in the ways of light after the catechetical journey into baptism had been completed.[19] As Augustine saw it, the problem was to keep unstained the inner renovation symbolized by their robes, which they would wear for the last time on the octave day of their baptism. Would they also put away what had been accomplished in baptism?[20] Augustine reminded the congregation that the neophytes would continue to need mentoring as they ventured forth into the world:

> You see: today, the *infantes* mix with the faithful — as if flying out of the nest. It is necessary then that we birth-laborers address them. As you know, brothers and sisters, when young swallows . . . begin to fly out of the nest, their mothers flap around them noisily and, with dutiful chirpings, testify to dangers their children face.

It is evident that he was more worried about the baneful influence of unfaithful Christians than about the effects of pagan society. In the same sermon, he noted: "We know that many who are called 'faithful' live badly and that their mores do not square with the grace they have received; that they praise God with the tongue and blaspheme him with their lives."[21]

---

19. It is important to remember, however, that their journey of conversion would never be fully complete; it would continue as an ongoing process throughout Christian living, as Augustine's reference to the Lord's Prayer as a "daily baptism" signifies.

20. This is the focus of Augustine's sermons 259 and 260. I am indebted to Finn, "It Happened One Saturday Night," p. 594, for this way of phrasing Augustine's concern.

21. Augustine, Sermon 376A.2, cited in Harmless, *Augustine and the Catechumenate,* p. 332. Note also the following passage from John Chrysostom in the Christian

Even amid dangers, many of the newly baptized continued along the journey toward full communion with God. By the time the catechumens had passed through the various stages of baptismal catechesis, they not only desired new life in Christ, they had already begun to see transformations occurring in their lives — transformations accomplished by the Holy Spirit, yet not apart from the practices, beliefs, and desires into which the new believers had been initiated through the catechumenate. Of course, Augustine did not offer the newly baptized any illusions about life on the far side of baptism; drawing on the Exodus imagery so common in baptism, he reminded them that while they had crossed the Red Sea, they were not yet in the Promised Land, and desert wanderings still lay ahead of them. Yet Augustine also reminded the neophytes that they had been initiated into eschatological living. He pointed to the Octave, the eighth day, as a symbol for the new life in the Kingdom: "Today is a great sacrament, [a sign] for us of unending joy. Today itself will pass away, but the life it symbolizes will not pass away. . . . For this day, the Octave, symbolizes the new life at the world's end."[22] This eighth day, the day of Christ's resurrection, thus focused the neophytes' attention on the destiny — the *telos* — of human life: the unending joy of fellowship in communion with the Triune God. As he called them to keep their "concentration fixed on the eighth day," so he also reminded them of the power and the importance of eschatological living — particularly on behalf of the poor.

Overall, this dramatic journey of baptismal catechesis highlighted the centrality of initiation into the spectacular drama of God's creating, redeeming, and consummating work. Thomas Finn draws on Quodvultdeus's description of the "new spectacles" of Christian life to describe the process as follows: "Here in Roman Africa at the end of the fourth century and in the early fifth the ritual drama of baptism and its Lenten preparations were the *spectacula christiana* — the new theatre, the new racetrack,

---

East: "I see many after their baptism living more carelessly than the uninitiated, having nothing particular to distinguish them in their way of life. It is, you see, for this cause, that neither in the market nor in the Church is it possible to know quickly who is a believer and who an unbeliever; unless one be present at the time of the mystery, and see the one sort dismissed, the others remaining within — whereas they ought to be distinguished *not by their place, but by their way of life.*" In *s. Matthaei evangelium*, 4.14, cited in Harmless, p. 74.

22. Augustine, Sermon 259.1-2, cited in Harmless, *Augustine and the Catechumenate*, p. 334.

and the new boxing ring. It is difficult to overestimate the impact of this long-extended ritual drama on convert and community alike."[23] Through a combination of scriptural preaching and teaching, formal instruction, dramatic ritual, spiritual direction, and apprenticeship in the deeds of holy living, the practices of baptismal catechesis fostered a spectacular vision — and, more importantly, embodiment — of what it means to become part of a journey into the reign of God's dazzling light.

It is worth noting that some of the features of ancient catechesis are akin to the patterns of Christian formation described by Sarah Coakley elsewhere in this volume. Like the ascetical and mystical disciplines, this form of baptismal catechesis involved an extended journey of preparation whose true and ultimate end was participation with all the saints in the eternal praise of God. However, the earliest steps were simple ones that emphasized very specific "external" guidance and instruction. At first, instructions were almost mechanical, and mentors had enormous power to guide and teach. However, as the catechumens unlearned sin and began to develop habits of virtuous thinking, feeling, and living, they also moved closer to baptism and, with it, the responsibilities of membership in Christ. The period leading up to baptism intensified the focus on Christian life, and the period immediately consequent upon baptism was seen as a pivotal time for establishing the life patterns that would sustain ongoing habituation in Christian living, even amid the dangers that would be encountered when the newly baptized were no longer explicitly guided by mentors and teachers, and even when they would themselves become mentors to others in the faith. They needed to be able both to live as Christians and to articulate the implications of their living to others.

In keeping with traditions of ascetical and mystical theology — though speaking, usually, to those who would not be entering monastic life — Augustine warned the newly baptized of the need to continue in their journey toward sanctification, and to do so in a way that would continually open up and deepen their beliefs, passions, and practices. The extended catechetical process thereby came to incorporate critical reflection and social engagement. Through and within this process, patterns and habits of study, prayer, and holy living could give rise to a further intensifi-

---

23. Finn, "It Happened One Saturday Night," p. 595. For a firsthand description of the effect of the baptismal liturgy on a pilgrim visiting Jerusalem, see *Egeria's Travels*, trans. John Wilkinson (London: SPCK, 1971).

cation whereby beliefs, desires, and practices became "second nature." This process required perseverance, vigilance against demonic forces, and the cultivation of profound friendship with God. Such friendship was cultivated through prayer, to be sure (as Coakley's references to Evagrius and the Carmelites suggest), but it could also be cultivated through study (as with Thomas Aquinas) or through holy living (as, for example, with St. Francis).

It is also noteworthy, as we prepare to turn our attention back to theological education in twenty-first-century North America, that the rich interplay of belief, desire, and practice in catechetical instruction encouraged deeper theological reflection and more faithful social witness in other ways as well. Augustine's more formal theological reflection — enshrined in such classic texts as *De Trinitate, The City of God,* and *Confessions* — stands in fundamental continuity with the homilies he directed toward catechumens, and many of them arose in response to thoughtful questions asked by well-catechized Christians.[24] Similarly, this extensive catechesis sharpened Christians' awareness that powerful alternatives — the spectacles, the racetrack, the fights — were competing for their allegiance. In North America, might we need to reflect more seriously about the deleterious impact of such forces as entertainment, sports, and rampant consumerism in offering alternative loyalties to the worship of God?

Toward the Reform of Christian Formation

The contexts in which contemporary Christian education and formation are pursued today are more complex and fragmented than those available to a bishop in fourth-century North Africa. Without romanticizing the past or unduly despairing about the present, however, we can learn from the example of ancient catechesis how and why beliefs, desires, and practices inherently belong together in all the contexts of Christian education and formation. We certainly need a much richer conception of catechesis than we currently tend to deploy. But we also need to cultivate the special

24. This is a point that has been shown with persuasive clarity by John Cavadini, in an unpublished essay entitled "Simplifying Augustine." He shows the continuity in the method and substance of Augustine's reflection between his homilies and his more sophisticated theological work.

strengths that can be offered through the structures of churches, academies, and faithful living in the world. How, then, might we begin to envision the dynamic interrelations of practices, beliefs, and desires as we seek to educate and form Christian people in the midst of contemporary North American society?

Congregations ought to be settings for catechesis in which desires are shaped by faithful instruction and inquiry, prayer and worship, and other corporate practices that are constitutive of the church's life. Such catechesis will be informed by, and will in turn inform, the inquiries, understandings, and critiques developed by Christian theologians and intellectuals in the context of academies. Congregational catechesis will also be enriched by, and will in turn enrich, the lives of Christians as they negotiate individually and corporately the various challenges, opportunities, and resistances intrinsic to faithful social engagement. Congregations are particularly crucial in nurturing the faith along the journey toward mystical union in friendship with God.

Colleges, universities, and seminaries ought to be settings for formal education and inquiry in which people's beliefs are tested, nurtured, criticized, and revised by faithful doctrine, inquiry, and study. Such inquiry and study will be informed by, and will in turn inform, the catechetical process. They will also be enriched by, and will in turn enrich, the lives of Christians as they seek to understand and more faithfully witness to their faith in the midst of particular social and systemic engagements. Academies play a crucial role in clarifying and testing the faith to ensure a more reflective, and hopefully less distorted, transmission of Christian life and thought from generation to generation.

Faithful living in the world draws Christians into contexts in which the distorting and sinful desires, practices, and structures of our world ought to be challenged by the light of the gospel. Such witness will be informed by, and will in turn inform, the normative practices of Christian catechesis. It will also be enriched by, and will in turn enrich, the study of how beliefs, desires, and practices interrelate in an overall vision of God's inbreaking reign. Social engagements play a crucial role in forming our lives as doers of the Word, and not hearers only.

This is, admittedly, a truncated and highly schematized account of the interrelations that ought to exist among the diverse but overlapping contexts of congregations, academies, and social engagements. There is nothing intrinsically necessary about these particular institutional forms in themselves — Christians have developed a wide range of structures for education and formation over the centuries and may well develop new ones as we embark on a new millennium. As future structures emerge, however, we need to ask how the institutions we have can address the issues we have been considering.

Insofar as the diagnosis here set forth has merit, it suggests several significant implications for reshaping theological education as it is currently carried out in seminaries, which are the academies most responsible for the preparation of church leaders. How can seminaries themselves model the ongoing interplay of beliefs, desires, and practices? How can they hold church, academy, and social engagement together in complex interaction, in ways that prepare ministers to build up faithful ways of life beyond the seminary?

My overarching proposal is that seminaries ought to focus on cultivating a love of learning and a desire for God that becomes manifest in transformative service. Seminaries should not limit their focus to "understanding God truly" (in the words of David Kelsey) through attention to beliefs and doctrines. Rather, they should add to this concern ways of nurturing desire for God and for the well-being of others and ways of cultivating faithful Christian practices.

First, even within the classroom, seminaries need to attend to the process of *forming* students as much as, if not more than, the process of transmitting information to students. To be sure, seminaries are educational institutions, and a central component of their task is to cultivate a love of learning. However, this need not override formation when the intrinsic relationships among beliefs, practices, and desires are understood. As Augustine put it in one of his sermons, "the very desire with which you want to understand is itself a prayer to God." Or, as Chaim Potok rightly notes in his novel *In the Beginning*, "A shallow mind is a sin against God."[25] One result of such an understanding might lead seminaries to become more attentive to the character and quality of seminary-sponsored worship while also encouraging classroom study of Christian worship and prayer. A similar link could be made between courses that explicitly address the character of Christian social engagement and activities that engage students in it. With the love of learning and the desire for God more closely attuned to

---

25. Augustine, Sermon 152.1, cited in Cavadini, "Simplifying Augustine," typescript p. 1. I am indebted to Mary Boys for the reference from Potok.

one another, not only the seminaries but also the churches and the wider society would recognize that they have a significant stake in supporting substantive scholarship by both faculty and students. Through such scholarship, moreover, seminaries could better serve as intellectual centers for the churches and contributors to intellectual engagements with other disciplines and traditions.

Even as they emphasize the importance of formation to theological education, seminaries also need to develop a more expansive conception of the role of study in the process of formation — something that attention to interrelations among beliefs, desires, and practices will assist them in doing. This emphasis is particularly important in an era when too many seminaries have become uncritically interested in making seminary easier, either through lessened academic expectations or through the transmission of information over the Internet.

Second, seminaries currently face the daunting task of doing not only what they are most equipped to do — namely, providing education and formation to prepare people for faithful Christian ministry and leadership — but also of providing remediation in catechesis and social engagement if these have been lacking in students' lives prior to arrival at the seminary.[26] The character of formation for ministry requires seminaries to attend to this need by focusing on both education in the classroom and the shaping of desires and practices through such activities as prayer, worship, and faithful living in the world. Although seminaries ought to have been, and historically have been, involved in these matters in every age, attention to them is especially important today. Not only will such attention better prepare their students for ministry; it can also help seminaries to become resources as the church re-envisions lay catechesis and social witness in the contemporary world.

Third, those seminaries and divinity schools that offer the Ph.D. ought to attend more carefully to the challenges and opportunities involved in preparing the next generation of seminary teachers. Rather than simply

---

26. This is not meant to glorify theological education at the expense of other contexts, nor is it to place a peculiarly unfair burden on it. Similar points could be made both about the burdens that local churches, church-related higher education, and diverse social contexts of engagements all face. My point is simply that, in a situation where all three contexts are relatively weak, each of the contexts will have to attend in richer and more complex ways to tasks that — ideally — will be presupposed as healthier interactions develop.

replicating the disciplinary divisions of the modern university, perhaps we ought to cultivate patterns of scholarship that integrate attention to beliefs, desires, and practices, thereby offering future theological educators richer conceptions of their topics of study. Although this might disturb prevailing career planning and force graduate students to make earlier decisions about their future work, difficulties might be surmounted if the churches could be persuaded to invest financially on the grounds that such an approach would ultimately strengthen Christian education and formation in seminaries, congregations, and other settings.

Fourth, seminaries should consider expanding their offerings in continuing education to include academies of education and formation that could serve learners across the span of Christian life. Seminaries' contributions to lifelong learning would continue to include professional continuing education programs, but they would also include lay academies independent from formal degree programs. Such academies would more closely link congregations to seminaries and would also link both of them to the social engagements of the laity.

The proposals set forth so briefly here need to be more fully articulated and defended against potential objections. Even so, they suggest emerging patterns that may lend more coherence and theological integrity to the education and formation of church leaders. They offer alternatives to the "relay race" image of ministerial preparation and its negative impact on relations between congregations and seminaries. They provide glimpses of how congregations, academies, and social engagements might assist one another as overlapping, rather than competing, contexts of Christian faith and life. I hope that these proposals will help both the church and seminaries to begin to envision theological education less as a process leading up to each minister's graduation and more as an academic setting whose purpose is to support, through lifelong formation and education, many ongoing journeys of Christian life and thought toward friendship with God. Although the formation of Christian leaders is the special focus of theological education, its ability to achieve even this special purpose can only be strengthened when theological education is itself understood as one movement within the faithful formation and education of the entire church for the doxological praise of God.

Hospitality and Truth:
The Disclosure of Practices
in Worship and Doctrine

REINHARD HÜTTER

Hospitality and honoring the truth are practices held in high regard by many people. Indeed, one might claim that they are — if not universally practiced — at least widely acknowledged as central to human life.[1] Yet we hardly

1. Cf. Dorothy C. Bass, ed., *Practicing Our Faith: A Way of Life for a Searching People* (San Francisco: Jossey-Bass, 1997). Here I can only gesture toward the kind of theological taxonomy of practices that I presuppose in my essay. Fundamental to this taxonomy is the distinction (*not* dichotomy) between God's economy of creation and God's economy of salvation. Those fundamental practices that we encounter as central to the sustenance and enhancement of human life across a variety of cultures and throughout time and that we therefore tend to call "universal" are theologically to be identified as belonging to God's economy of creation — due to their very "point," namely the sustenance and enhancement of human life. Practices belonging to God's economy of salvation, on the other hand, are those through which God's salvific activity is communicated and mediated and which are crucial embodiments of this communication and mediation. It is, I argue, the Christian faith that uncovers the inherent interconnectedness of all of these practices. To be precise: practices are not legitimated by the Christian faith, but the very fact that they cannot stand alone but depend decisively on other practices makes sense in light of the Christian faith. This is true of both "universal" practices and "distinctly Christian" practices that bear witness to God's salvific activity — and of practices that fall in both categories, such as forgiveness. I suggest that what makes these practices possible in the first place, as well as what represents their final fulfillment, is revealed through their particular Christian equivalent as

think about these practices as somehow connected. Indeed, it can seem that they are opposed to one another: to be concerned for truth is to be inhospitable, and to be hospitable means being "mushy" on matters of truth. It is the task of the present chapter to show that, as a matter of fact, they are deeply interrelated — to the point of being mutually dependent. I will also argue that Christian beliefs disclose reality to be such that practicing hospitality and honoring the truth in their integral relation turn out most appropriately to correspond to the way things are. That this is so is the result of God's own practice of hospitality, in the course of which we receive the truth that is the triune God as the communion of the Father with the Son in the Holy Spirit, and thus also are called to share in the triune God's hospitality and truth.[2]

How does this happen? My argument is that this happens through two modes of reception: *worship* and *doctrine*. *In worship we continuously receive the very hospitality of God's truth, and in doctrine the very truth of God's hospitality.* Worship thus relates in a fundamental yet complex way to the practice of hospitality, and doctrine in an equally fundamental yet complex way to honoring the truth. Making my case would, of course, require far more than the space one chapter allows; thus I will only sketch the contours of such an argument in these pages. I will begin by retelling a theologically pregnant story.

Beginning with a Story: C. S. Lewis's *The Great Divorce*[3]

Stories often catch the hidden interrelationships that make up our world in subtler and quicker ways than our conscious, thoughtful reflection can.

---

this communicates and reflects God's own practice (let us say, of forgiveness). This is possible because the enactment of such practices is rooted in the church's core practices. This theological taxonomy also makes sufficiently clear that the use of the term "practice" for the church's core practices is an ultimately analogical use, since the Holy Spirit is the subject who works his mission through these practices.

2. For a rigorous and compelling account of how this theological claim needs to be thought through in light of the most recent advances in analytic philosophy of language, see Bruce D. Marshall, *Trinity and Truth* (Cambridge: Cambridge University Press, 2000), esp. pp. 242-82. On the logic of the epistemic primacy of Christian beliefs that is presupposed in the following, see Marshall's account, pp. 44-49, 115-26.

3. C. S. Lewis, *The Great Divorce* (New York: Macmillan, 1946). Page references from this edition are given parenthetically in the text.

C. S. Lewis's allegorical recasting of heaven and hell captures the counter-cultural commerce between practicing hospitality and honoring the truth in a surprisingly powerful way.

You may remember that the story begins in a gray and rainy place on a dusky late afternoon right before dark. "Time seemed to have paused on that dismal moment when only a few shops have lit up and it is not yet dark enough for their windows to look cheering" (p. 11). The otherwise unidentified narrator finds himself at a bus stop in some forlorn section of a sprawling metropolis. The place is more than a little reminiscent of London. Yet, as the description unfolds, this city — let us call it Twilight City for convenience's sake — differs from London in being surprisingly empty of people. As our protagonist eventually finds out from another bus passenger, the city is constantly expanding *ad infinitum* into the dusk. Later he will learn that this expansion is a form of negativity, a gradual thinning-out into nothingness. As it turns out, the increasing emptiness of Twilight City is caused by its inhabitants' becoming more and more isolated from themselves and from each other.

It is hardly surprising that the practices of hospitality and honoring the truth are glaringly absent in this place of impending nothingness. Yet it is interesting that their very lack seems to be connected with the city's endless growth. On the bus, our narrator gets this growth explained to him:

> As soon as anyone arrives he settles in some street. Before he's been there twenty-four hours he quarrels with his neighbour. Before the week is over he's quarrelled so badly that he decides to move. Very likely he finds the next street empty because all the people there have quarrelled with their neighbours — and moved. So he settles in. If by any chance the street is full, he goes further. But even if he stays, it makes no odds. He's sure to have another quarrel pretty soon and then he'll move on again. Finally he'll move right out to the edge of the town and build a new house. You see, it's easy here. You've only got to think a house and there it is. That's how the town keeps on growing (pp. 18-19).

It is clear that, instead of practicing hospitality, the people inhabiting Twilight City are remarkably *inhospitable* in their constant quarreling with each other. Yet it is less clear in what way the truth is not honored. The quarreling might give us a clue. Left to their emptiness and to the endless rewinding of their self-indulgent and therefore precisely self-deceptive memories,[4] the Twilighters cannot stand their own company. And because they cannot bear their own company, they are unable to bear the company of anyone else. Being able to bear and actually enjoy one's own company presupposes the ability to face and thus honor the truth of one's own life. As we will see, acknowledging, and therefore receiving, the truth of who and whose one is liberates one for genuine hospitality. Yet because the inhabitants of Twilight City lack this truth, they are intensely absorbed in themselves — the self-absorption of a void in search of a substance. They want to grasp and own what can only be received as a gift: the gift of a self transparent to the truth that it owes its existence not to itself, but rather to the Giver of Life. Honoring this truth in its constant reception is what makes the self open to the other, to genuine hospitality. Yet in their complete incurvature upon themselves, the inhabitants of Twilight City can neither offer themselves to others nor welcome them into their own lives — for there is nothing to offer and nowhere into which to invite.

As our protagonist quickly finds out, this place is not hospitable to the truth, either. Questions pertaining to the future (and thus, by implication, to the nature) of Twilight City are not to be raised. Answering these questions would make it necessary for its inhabitants to face the truth about this city's precarious predicament on the very brink of utter darkness. Having nevertheless raised this politically incorrect question, the narrator finds himself subjected to an "enlightening" discourse from one of Twilight City's many intellectuals:

> There is not a shred of evidence that this twilight is ever going to turn into a night. There has been a revolution of opinion on that in

---

4. Napoleon serves as the paradigmatic example. "'The nearest one of those old ones is Napoleon. We know that because two chaps made the journey to see him. . . . He'd built himself a huge house all in the Empire style — rows of windows flaming with light, though it only shows as a pin prick from where I live. . . . They went up and looked through one of the windows. Napoleon was there all right.' 'What was he doing?' 'Walking up and down — up and down all the time — left-right, left-right — never stopping for a moment. The two chaps watched him for about a year and he never rested. And muttering to himself all the time. "It was Soult's fault. It was Ney's fault. It was Josephine's fault. It was the fault of the Russians. It was the fault of the English." Like that all the time. Never stopped for a moment. A little, fat man and he looked kind of tired. But he didn't seem able to stop it'" (pp. 20-21).

educated circles. I am surprised that you haven't heard of it. All the nightmare fantasies of our ancestors are being swept away. What we now see in this subdued and delicate half-light is the promise of the dawn: the slow turning of a whole nation towards the light. Slow and imperceptible, of course. . . . A sublime thought (p. 24).

Interestingly, there still seem to exist loose intellectual circles where the possibilities of change, improvement, and transformation in Twilight City are discussed. Yet in their inherent instability and their abundant self-deception about the truth of the Twilighters' common predicament, these circles are only a lively witness to the degree to which the practices of hospitality and of honoring the truth are, indeed, absent from Twilight City. Interpreting the twilight as the beginning of a great "enlightenment" only works as a loan on the truth by allowing for a semblance of meaningful intellectual interaction: a discourse among shadows, the whole point of which is the endless deferral of the truth — that they are nothing but shadows.[5]

Conspicuously absent from Twilight City are both real, existing persons and real, existing relationships, both of which — as will become clear later — are the gift of the truth and can only be acknowledged by honoring the truth that makes it possible to be hospitable to the presence of other persons. Instead of being the rich ground of endless occasions of hospitality fueled by the acknowledgment of the truth, both space and time become endless wastelands of negativity, dramatically pictured by Lewis as imploding into nothingness.[6]

And yet, in a completely random spot somewhere in this vast desert of gray inhospitality and self-deception covered by dusk and drizzling rain — or to be precise: "thousands of miles from the Civic Centre where all the newcomers arrive from earth" (p. 19) — there is a bus stop. From there,

---

5. Lewis offers in these lines a wonderful Augustinian satire of the hopes and pretensions of modern philosophical discourse in the form of their postmodern demise.

6. "'Do you mean then that Hell — all that infinite empty town — is down in some little crack like this?' 'Yes. All Hell is smaller than one pebble of your earthly world: but it is smaller than one atom of *this* world, the Real World. . . .' 'It seems big enough when you are in it, Sir.' 'And yet all loneliness, angers, hatreds, envies and itchings that it contains, if rolled into one single experience and put into the scale against the least moment of the joy that is felt by the least in Heaven, would have no weight that could be registered at all'" (pp. 122-23).

once a week, a bus takes anyone who wants (which is to say, anyone who is able for long enough to stand all the other people waiting in line) up to Heaven for free — in and of itself already an overabundant act of hospitality. After watching a significant number of people leave the line because of quarrelling, our protagonist and a few others manage to get onto the bus. And after a quite "enlightening" flight — an ever-intensifying heavenly light increasingly revealing the passengers' true ghostlike condition — the bus lands on a level grassy area under a penetrating blue sky.

In profound contrast to Twilight City, life on the light-bathed green plain, the "beginning" of Heaven, is characterized by moving acts of hospitality and of honoring the truth. And as it quickly turns out, both hospitality and truth are inherently connected to the practice of forgiveness. On leaving the bus, the passengers from Twilight City are welcomed by delegates from Heaven and invited in. Hospitality to these lost souls, to these strangers to Heaven, is obviously essential to the character of Heaven.

But accepting Heaven's hospitality turns out to be a deeply painful affair. Hospitality — in a way fundamentally different from paternalism, even heavenly paternalism — presupposes real existing persons that are capable of personal relationships. Yet being a person and thus being capable of personal relationships depends on the gift of truth in and through which one's own personhood is received; this reception is actively acknowledged by honoring the truth. Heaven's hospitality turns out to be painful because it does not trade truth for hospitality — the former *in* its hospitality simply being Heaven's identity. Hospitality can only be truthful and thus truly hospitality if it does not betray the nature of the host and thus not undercut that truth that presupposes a personal relationship. Thus Heaven's light, true to its own nature, unavoidably reveals the truth of each passenger as he or she increasingly enters the abode of its hospitality. Precisely because of its nature, the light at first seems strikingly *in*hospitable.

> It was a cruel light. I shrank from the faces and forms by which I was surrounded. They were all fixed faces, full not of possibilities, but of impossibilities, some gaunt, some bloated, some glaring with idiotic ferocity, some drowned beyond recovery in dreams; but all, in one way or another, distorted and faded. One had a feeling that they might fall to pieces at any moment if the light grew much stronger (p. 25).

211

As it turns out, not just the light but the very solidity of the grass and everything else on the green plain makes it hard for the ghost-like passengers to stand. Heaven's hospitality hurts, because the passengers from Twilight City are not — yet — real enough to receive and fully participate in it. Thus even walking around is painful. And reality, as it turns out, is a matter of truth — the truth that makes one a person and thus real. Yet acknowledging this truth means encountering the sum of our deeds and sufferings, the innumerable ways we have failed others and others have failed us. Thus, receiving the truth about ourselves implies our asking for forgiveness as well as our granting forgiveness and thereby actively acknowledging and ultimately receiving our own personhood and that of those who have failed us and whom we have failed. The challenge each passenger faces is therefore to become hospitable to the truth and thus to be transformed by it into the person he or she is meant to be.[7]

What is of crucial importance is that Heaven's hospitality is practiced and sustained by a truth that fundamentally shapes both the hospitality of the welcomers and their own truth-telling. It is here that the "disclosure" of the practices of honoring the truth and of hospitality begins to emerge.

The persons who meet and extend Heaven's hospitality of forgiving truth to the passengers from Twilight City are not random characters. They play a key role in understanding the truth of the lives of the shadow-persons whom they are welcoming. As it turns out in the unfolding dialogues, accepting Heaven's hospitality is identical with being willing to receive the truth about one's own life — a truth that always includes the recognition of our need to be forgiven as well as our readiness to forgive, well illustrated in the following dialogue between a ghostly passenger from Twilight City and his heavenly greeter.[8] Particularly interesting in this exchange is that the ghostly passenger uses "rights" language, which, one could argue, is a way of asking for "truth." Yet here the very nature of "truth" is at stake in the manner of its sharing. Having a "right" to the truth establishes a claim of ownership that antecedently precludes reception of the truth — a reception that cannot be possessed but can only be acknowledged in honoring the truth. And thus also the hospitality that the

---

7. See the moving account of such a transformation, pp. 102-3.

8. I have found the nuanced and penetrating analysis of the Christian practice of forgiveness by L. Gregory Jones to be profoundly instructive: *Embodying Forgiveness: A Theological Analysis* (Grand Rapids: Eerdmans, 1995).

truth makes possible cannot be claimed as a "right," but can only be asked for as "Bleeding Charity."

> "Only be happy and come with me." — "What do you keep on arguing for? I'm only telling you the sort of chap I am. I only want my rights. I'm not asking for anybody's bleeding charity." — "Then do. At once. Ask for the Bleeding Charity. Everything is here for the asking and nothing can be bought." — "That may be very well for you, I daresay. . . . I don't want charity. I'm a decent man and if I had my rights I'd have been here long ago and you tell them I said so." The other shook his head. "You can never do it like that," he said. "Your feet will never grow hard enough to walk on our grass that way. You'd be tired before we got to the mountains. And it isn't exactly true, you know" (p. 34).

Yet since Heaven *is* truth, accepting Heaven's hospitality also means accepting Heaven's truth — which is first of all nothing other than the truth about oneself and one's need to receive and grant forgiveness. Unforgiving spirits simply cannot bear the sheer brightness of Heaven's penetrating reality — a reality that is constituted by real existing persons and their perfect intersubjectivity — and thus eventually flee back to the bus in order to be embraced again by the implosive void.

> "I'd rather be damned than go along with you. I came here to get my rights, see? Not to go snivelling along on charity tied onto your apron-strings. If they are too fine to have me without you, I'll go home. . . . I didn't come here to be treated like a dog. I'll go home. That's what I'll do. Damn and blast the whole pack of you. . . ." In the end, still grumbling, but whimpering also a little as it picked its way over the sharp grasses, it made off (p. 36).

The unforgiving spirit shuts itself up against the truth that can only be received as a gift, not claimed as a right. In consequence, both the hospitality that is the host's very identity and the painful transformation from shadow to person that it implies seem simply unbearable.

The Countercultural Commerce between Hospitality and Truth:
Lessons from *The Great Divorce*

In his allegory of heaven and hell, Lewis offers a narrative account of the deep theological reason why practicing hospitality and honoring the truth mutually depend on each other. He achieves this insight by approaching them from a perspective that allows him to perceive them first of all as God's practices. In the course of this "disclosure," he shows that our very capacity to honor the truth and to practice hospitality presupposes that we first receive the hospitality of God's truth — which at the above-quoted point in the story is called "Bleeding Charity" — and, in turn, that we be transformed by it so as to live in the truth of God's hospitality. Thus *The Great Divorce* ever so gently prepares us for the crucial insight that the triune God is both truth and host in one. In his self-giving in Christ, God offers abundant, costly, and holy hospitality to a humanity hopelessly entangled in practices and habits of sin. God's own distinct and radical hospitality culminates in opening Israel "for the many" — through Christ's eucharistic self-giving (Mark 10:45, 14:24) — and thus in welcoming the Gentiles into God's own household in the body of the crucified and risen Christ (Eph. 2:11-22). If this is indeed true about the Gospel, then we should rightly expect that the Gospel — precisely in its particularity — should disclose the very web of creation, should offer us particular insights into the way things are. Thus we will be guided by God's saving work in the life, death, and resurrection of Jesus Christ in now asking how two particular practices that are known among virtually all of humanity fundamentally depend on each other.

Why and How the Interplay between
Honoring the Truth and Hospitality Is Crucial

Lewis's allegorical account helps us to begin discerning the hidden but profound forces that militate in and among ourselves against the practices of hospitality and honoring the truth. Let us first consider two fundamental obstacles and then the various subtle and not-so-subtle distortions that they elicit in both practices.

Probably the most significant obstacle to honoring the truth is *self-*

deception.[9] This is the self-protective reaction to our conscience's convicting us when we are forced to face the truth without the gift of forgiveness. Self-deception shields us from this prospective final conviction through strategies of tacit self-justification, strategies too covert to rise to the level of consciousness, strategies that make it effectively impossible to receive the forgiving truth that would allow us to fully honor the truth in the first place. Yet one whose self cannot accept the truth about herself has no way to share herself with others, no way to give himself away in genuine personhood; in short, no way to practice hospitality in any authentic sense.

Yet self-deception is never fully successful in muting our conscience. There always remains a disquieting difference between the account rendered by our conscience and our self-deceptive strategies. Like an open wound, this ongoing difference lies at the root of a common obstacle to real hospitality — our pervasive *need to please others in order to be liked in return.* (I am not talking about the acts and feelings of sympathy that characterize genuine friendship,[10] but about the specific need for affirmation that is supposed to bridge the difference between the convicting work of conscience and the justifying work of our self-deceptive strategies.) This deep-seated desire renders hospitality purely functional and undercuts honoring the truth. The convergence of entertainment (instead of hospitality) and complimentary lying (instead of honoring the truth) is the telling outcome of the urge to be liked and approved by others.

9. The life, self-interpretation, and self-justification of Albert Speer, Nazi architect and organizer of Hitler's armament program, offer a fascinating example of the power and intricacy of self-deception. See Stanley Hauerwas with David B. Burrell, "Self-Deception and Autobiography: Reflections on Albert Speer's *Inside the Third Reich*," in Hauerwas, *Truthfulness and Tragedy: Further Investigations in Christian Ethics* (Notre Dame: University of Notre Dame Press, 1977), pp. 82-98. Gitta Sereny dedicated a fascinating book-length account to the debate: *Albert Speer: His Battle with Truth* (New York: Knopf, 1995). See the perceptive review of the latter by L. Gregory Jones, "Becoming a Different Man: Inside Albert Speer," *Christian Century* 113 (1996): 516-19.

10. See Paul Wadell, *Friendship and the Moral Life* (Notre Dame: University of Notre Dame Press, 1989), for a substantive account of friendship as distinct from the exchange of nicety, that is, the patterns of pleasing others with acts of nicety in order to be liked in return — what Aristotle would call friendships of use and friendships of pleasure. While they might have their place, these kinds of friendships become detrimental when they start to dominate basic interactions in the Christian way of life and especially in the practice of theology.

Not so on the green plain. There hospitality is extended at the same time that the truth is honored in love because those who practice Heaven's hospitality by greeting the passengers from Twilight City know that all that they are, and all that those whom they welcome are, ultimately rests on God's forgiving grace. The hospitality of Heaven's truth requires and effects a transformation that amounts to nothing less than becoming "real," being filled with Heaven's truth and thus receiving a gloriously imperishable body — which is identical with receiving an irreversible personhood that is capable of self-giving in personal relations and thus also of extending true hospitality.[11] As a result of participating in this reality, Heaven's greeters can honor the truth without falling into self-righteousness and uncharitableness and are thus able to extend a hospitality that is genuine and substantive.

Besides these two fundamental impediments, we all know — from our own lives as well as from our experience with others — manifold ways in which the practice of honoring the truth can be belied. I will just point to the most common and obvious ones: avoiding, abstracting, and functionalizing the truth.

Avoiding the truth by avoiding oneself and others: As Lewis's story brings out so clearly, hospitality is the training ground for retrieving the practice of honoring the truth.[12] Only by letting ourselves be welcomed by the greeters of Heaven and by ultimately welcoming them, only by accepting Heaven's hospitality and by extending it, can the truth about one's own life and past be truthfully faced — and thus be forgiven. In welcoming others, especially strangers and needy persons, into our lives, we have to face the truth about distinct persons, the state of the world and society, and even ourselves in new and challenging ways. On the other hand, honoring the truth is about as challenging, demanding, stretching, and threatening as welcoming others into our lives in a genuine, open, and substantive way. Yet practicing true hospitality in successful ways and succeeding in honoring the truth cannot be taken up without developing at the same time a

---

11. See note 7. For a full account of the crucial relationship between embodiment and personhood, see Pope John Paul II, *The Theology of the Body* (Boston: Pauline Books and Media, 1997).

12. The theologian and ethicist who first taught me the fundamental link between hospitality and truth was Stanley Hauerwas. See his *The Peaceable Kingdom: A Primer in Christian Ethics* (Notre Dame: University of Notre Dame Press, 1983), pp. 142-46.

distinct set of virtues. Courage, patience, hope, humility, prudence (in the classical sense), self-restraint, and readiness not to be in control are among those that immediately come to mind.

Abstracting the truth from one's own calling into an isolated entity: Honoring the truth occurs always in distinct relationships of responsibility and accountability that are both concrete and relevant (distinguished from presumptuous talk and from gossiping, both of which can very well fulfill the formal criterion of "truth-telling").[13] Honoring the truth starts with the reception of the truth about ourselves. Yet it does not end there. One of the most pervasive temptations to flee the truth is by abstracting it from the relationships of commitment, duty, and office in which we always already find ourselves and where we have to honor the truth in very concrete ways. Abstracting the truth from these prior moral settings means to betray the truth.[14] It is the "hands-on" character of practicing hospitality that can become a schooling in precisely those virtues that we will need in order to face the challenge of honoring the truth in the midst of the commitments and duties that claim us.

Making the truth purely functional: This happens most blatantly when — due to particular interests — we willfully abandon the shared referentiality of terms, temporarily assigning our own meanings to words and statements to suit our own purposes, all the while accusing others of misunderstanding us. While the "truth" of internal consistency with a personal

13. See Dietrich Bonhoeffer, "What Is Meant by 'Telling the Truth'?" in *Ethics,* trans. N. H. Smith (New York: Simon & Schuster, 1995), pp. 358-67. Bonhoeffer's achievement was to show how distinct relationships of responsibility and accountability are crucial for a genuine honoring of the truth.

14. Telling a Gestapo officer the "truth" when he asks me about the whereabouts of my dissident friend does not mean honoring the truth but betraying a friendship. Here lies the fundamental difference between Kant's absolute prohibition of lying and Augustine's. While the former sees it as the result of a purely formal moral law, the categorical imperative, the latter rests it on what it means to be a Christian, namely living in the ongoing reception of the gift of God's truth. For Kant, see his *The Metaphysics of Morals,* trans. and ed. Mary Gregor (Cambridge: Cambridge University Press, 1996), pp. 182-84; and also his "Über ein vermeintliches Recht, aus Menschenliebe zu lügen," in *Werke in sechs Bänden,* vol. 4: *Schriften zur Ethik und Religionsphilosophie,* ed. Wilhelm Weischedel (Darmstadt: Wissenschaftliche Buchgesellschaft, 1968), pp. 637-43. For Augustine, see the excellent essay by Paul J. Griffiths, "The Gift and the Lie: Augustine on Lying," *Communio: International Catholic Review* 26 (Spring 1999): 3-30.

"language game" might thus be maintained,[15] the reality is that this kind of "truth" only serves our own self-justification. In employing such a tactic, we abandon the hospitality of sharing a common set of linguistic conventions.[16]

By contrast, Lewis's story teaches us that the practice of honoring the truth is itself a significant way of practicing hospitality. Since truth is not produced but acknowledged, honoring the truth cannot be anything else than inviting others into the same acknowledgement. This is the very life of the greeters of Heaven: only by first having been guests of the truth can they become its host, in the practice of honoring it and extending it to others in truthful speech.

The practice of hospitality can be distorted at least as easily as the practice of honoring the truth. For the sake of brevity, I will only mention the most common way that this happens: "entertaining" as a subtle form of lying. We present an appearance that is estranged from ourselves, that is, we do not give ourselves as persons. Rather, we use our appearance as a means for other ends and thereby betray both our own personhood and the personhood of those whom we use as instruments. Thereby our hospitality is turned from an end (reflective of the guest as an end) to a means serving other ends.[17] Again Lewis's story is ahead of our reflective insight. Truthful, undistorted hospitality is constantly in need of the practice of honoring the truth, because it is in the course of acknowledging the truth that our personhood is received. In the most fundamental way, the practice of hospitality is itself a significant way to honor the truth; we tell the truth by giving ourselves as persons to other persons and by receiving others as

15. Ultimately, this is of course either another form of self-deception (if unintentional) or a form of lying (if intentional). Linguistic meaning is inherently public and cannot be privately fixed. See Marshall, *Trinity and Truth*, pp. 197-98.

16. In recent times, the most widely recognized and devastating case of this form of applied nominalism was President Clinton's "clarification" of what he meant by "sex." The meaning of "sex" that he and his lawyers used was a clear betrayal of the tacit linguistic consensus that he shared with virtually all interlocutors (including both the U.S. Senate and the American public in general) and obviously only served the purpose of self-justification.

17. For more ways in which the practice of hospitality is distorted, see the fine account in Christine D. Pohl, *Making Room: Recovering Hospitality as a Christian Tradition* (Grand Rapids: Eerdmans, 1999). I am indebted to Pohl's account of hospitality for understanding the inherent link shown by the Christian faith between the practices of hospitality and honoring the truth.

persons. The practice of hospitality thus also points to the fact that truth is something in which we mutually participate as persons.

How the Christian Faith Discloses the Interplay between Practicing Hospitality and Honoring the Truth

As we have come to see, what emerges in the course of a deeper questioning of why these two practices need each other is the disclosing nature of Christian beliefs. Furthermore, as *The Great Divorce* so convincingly displays, it is in light of these Christian beliefs that both practices are eventually "disclosed" and thereby actually received in their fullness. Rather than simply being at the center of human life in general, they turn out to have a much deeper presupposition: they form the very center of God's own dealing with humanity and the world. If the latter is indeed the case, then these practices imply much more than they themselves are ever able to convey to us. They bring us into touch with the way things really are and thus beg for their very disclosure.

How would the Christian theological tradition have expressed this matter? Very likely in the following way: according to the Christian faith, truth does not rest on the dead abstractness of contingent correspondences;[18] rather, truth rests on the threefold identity and agency of the triune God as these unfold in creation, the election of Israel, the life, death, and resurrection of Jesus Christ, and the calling of the many into communion with the life of the triune God through the Holy Spirit.[19] This calling restores full and genuine humanity, yet has a superabundant end: humanity's everlasting participation in God's love.

The practice of hospitality is, therefore, both a reflection and an extension of God's own hospitality — God's sharing of the love of the triune life with those who are dust. At the very center of this hospitality stands both a death and a resurrection, the most fundamental enactment of truth from God's side and precisely therefore also the threshold of God's abundant hospitality.[20] The truth that needs to be said, and the reality that must be

18. See Marshall, *Trinity and Truth,* pp. 24-49, 242-82.

19. Robert W. Jenson, *Systematic Theology,* vol. 1: *The Triune God* (New York/Oxford: Oxford University Press, 1997), pp. 42-89.

20. For an extensive meditation on God's costly hospitality in Christ, see Hans Urs

concretely judged and concretely undone through its full bearing by one (and once) for all, is that humanity is radically estranged from God because of a fundamental betrayal of God's original truth-telling and hospitality.

The one who does not participate in this predicament but is the embodiment of God's truth is therefore able to restore God's hospitality. Yet this occurs through a judgment, a death-sentence, that we receive as our forgiveness. The truth and thereby the condition for re-entering God's hospitality can only be spoken through God's own embodiment and self-abandonment in Jesus' death on the cross. We receive this death ("given for you") as the gift of forgiveness, the one particular truth of God's abundant, costly, and holy hospitality on the ground of which we can welcome our company and that of others and can therefore overcome the urge for self-deception and the desire to please and to be liked, both of which decisively undercut the practices of hospitality and of honoring the truth. This is, in briefest terms, the voice of the Christian theological tradition on the nature of God's hospitable truth and truthful hospitality in Christ.

Worship: Receiving the Hospitality of God's Truth in Christ

By now we are ready to ask how we concretely receive the truth of God's hospitality. It is by no means accidental that the broad stream of the Christian tradition has pointed to "word and sacrament" for an answer. From its very beginning, the central elements of Christian worship have been gathering for table fellowship with the risen Christ, reading the Scriptures together in light of his cross and resurrection, praying the prayer that Jesus taught his disciples, and thereby receiving the Spirit that rested on Jesus.[21]

---

von Balthasar, *Mysterium Paschale: The Mystery of Easter,* trans. Aidan Nichols (Edinburgh: T&T Clark, 1999).

21. See Ferdinand Hahn, "Gottesdienst. III. Neues Testament," *Theologische Realenzyklopädie* 14 (Berlin and New York: de Gruyter, 1985), pp. 28-39, esp. pp. 33-35. Hahn counts the following among the elements of the earliest Christian worship: reading of Scripture (Old Testament), proclamation of the Gospel, prayer and praise, gifts of the Spirit, Lord's Supper, and baptism. According to Frank Senn, Justin Martyr, in his *First Apology* (c. 150), reports a unified morning service of word and meal, or *synaxis,* to Emperor Antonius Pius and the Senate of Rome. Senn points out that one can discern a "shape of the liturgy" in Justin's report that has virtually remained intact

It is nowhere else than in worship that the hospitality of God's truth in Christ is continuously received.

The German word for worship — *Gottesdienst,* "service of God" — conveys this in a striking way. In worship we receive God's service in Christ. Christ humbles and empties himself (Phil. 2:5-11) for our sake by becoming our servant. (Our service of God, in contrast, does not occur in worship but in what St. Paul calls "spiritual [or reasonable] worship," namely "to present your bodies as a living sacrifice, holy and acceptable to God" [Rom. 12:1].)[22] The two main poles of our reception of God's service in Christ are word and sacrament: Christ is the host who proclaims his self-giving in the word and enacts it in the Eucharist.

It is well known that the Reformation tradition has emphasized the sacramental character of the word and the word-conveying character of the sacrament, while the Roman Catholic tradition has emphasized the prophetic character of the word and the disclosing and representative character of the Eucharist. Yet underlying both emphases is the *setting in worship* in which the word is proclaimed and the Lord's Supper celebrated. The one is not reduced to the other. In the proclamation of the word, the truth of God's hospitality in Christ is announced and promised; in the celebration of the Supper, the hospitality of this truth is concretely remembered and tangibly received. God's own truth grants itself, enacts its own hospitality whenever the Gospel is proclaimed and the Lord's Supper celebrated. They point to each other. The one cannot exist without the other: the one announces and effectively promises God's hospitality in Christ, the other executes it; in both, Christ gives himself to and in faith. Yet neither is by any means to be isolated from the rest of worship.

Rather, we need to understand worship as a rich web of activities, among which some are so important that they, preeminently, constitute worship. I call these distinct activities "core practices."[23] At their center,

---

since that time: "It is: gathering, readings, preaching, intercessory prayers, kiss of peace, presentation of bread and wine, great thanksgiving, distribution and reception of eucharistic gifts, extended distribution to the absent" (*Christian Liturgy: Catholic and Evangelical* [Minneapolis: Fortress Press, 1997], p. 76).

22. See Ernst Käsemann, "Worship in Everyday Life: A Note on Romans 12," in *New Testament Questions of Today,* trans. W. J. Montague (London: SCM Press, 1969), pp. 188-95.

23. This is somewhat at variance with the dominant usage of "practice" in this volume. Yet for a number of reasons, I think it is crucial to use the term "practice" in an

undoubtedly, we find the proclamation of the Gospel and the celebration of the Eucharist. Yet of great importance also are baptism, confession of sin and absolution, and binding and loosing (church discipline).[24] For some traditions, the practice of foot washing belongs to this list; for others, confirmation, Christian marriage, priestly ordination, and the last unction.[25] While for a long time this was an open list in the Christian tradition, it has become a hotly contested issue only since the Reformation and Counter-Reformation in the sixteenth century.

The truth of God's hospitality in Christ is actively received and announced in word and witness in and through these core practices. Only on the basis of this reception does the fundamental connection between our practicing hospitality and our honoring the truth become clear. That is, only in retrospect do we come to understand how much we indeed depend on the hidden and revealed ways of God's hospitality and truth-honoring simply by being the truth. Yet once we have received it explicitly, there is no alternative but to recognize our prior and full dependence on the truth of God's hospitality. As the Gospel of John puts it: "You have already been cleansed by the word that I have spoken to you. Abide in me as I abide in you. Just as the branch cannot bear fruit by itself unless it abides in the vine, neither can you unless you abide in me. I am the vine, you are the branches. Those who abide in me and I in them bear much fruit, because apart from me you can do nothing" (John 15:3-5). Worship is where the grapes receive their strength from the vine, where they continuously become part of the vine. Worship is, therefore, the fundamental setting in which we receive, again and again, the hospitality of God's truth — and

---

analogical way in order to capture the particular theological character of these kinds of activities. For a more detailed argument see my *Suffering Divine Things: Theology as Church Practice* (Grand Rapids: Eerdmans, 2000), pp. 128-33.

24. My own understanding of these matters is drawn primarily from Martin Luther's account as developed especially in his treatise "On the Councils and the Church" (1539) in *Luther's Works,* vol. 41, *Church and Ministry III,* ed. E. W. Gritsch (Philadelphia: Fortress Press, 1966).

25. For the practices that emerged in the radical wing of the Reformation and their contemporary relevance and interpretation, see John H. Yoder, *Body Politics: Five Practices of the Christian Community Before the Watching World* (Nashville: Discipleship Resources, 1992); and for a nuanced brief account of the seven sacraments in Post-Tridentine Roman Catholicism, see *Catechism of the Catholic Church* (New York: Doubleday, 1994), ##1066-1658.

thereby the "reasons for hope" that enable Christian living to make its way into a future that otherwise appears profoundly uncertain.[26]

Doctrine: Receiving and Honoring
the Truth of God's Hospitality in Christ

A question less often asked, yet equally pressing, concerns how we receive and continue to hold on to, and thereby honor, the truth of God's hospitality in Christ. This is what is at stake in a claim of St. Paul that is quite disturbing to modern sensibilities: "If you confess with your lips that Jesus is Lord and believe in your heart that God raised him from the dead, you will be saved" (Rom. 10:9). What must we profess and teach under all circumstances and in every context in order to receive and continue to hold on to the truth of God's hospitality in Christ? This is what is at stake in "doctrine" — and, if ecumenically ratified, in "dogma."

Yet approaching doctrine and especially dogma in these days of late modernity is far from easy. The reservations against it are too deep-seated, the resentments too pervasive. Is not doctrine exactly contradictory to whatever we might associate with hospitality and truth? Is not dogma the very enemy of hospitality and truth? Under the powerful influence of the Enlightenment, Christianity in many of its Protestant strands became non-dogmatic and even anti-dogmatic. Dogma was seen as an ossified, reified set of propositions functioning only to oppress the free and critical thinking of individuals in search of the living truth as it emerged in the context of an unencumbered inquiry into the world. Dogma thus came to stand for everything backward, outmoded, and inimical to new critical insights. In other words, dogma was — and still is, pervasively — seen as the

---

26. In 1 Pet. 3:15 we find the following exhortation: "Always be ready to make your defense to anyone who demands from you an accounting for the hope that is in you." In no other setting than worship do we become ready, again and again, to offer this account of our hope, because it is in worship that we tangibly receive, again and again, the reason for hope; it is in worship that we find, again and again, "that the Lord is good" (1 Pet. 2:3). On this profound connection between worship — especially the Lord's Supper — and hope, see Peter Brunner, *Worship in the Name of Jesus* (St. Louis: Concordia, 1968); Geoffrey Wainwright, *Eucharist and Eschatology*, 2d edition (London: Epworth Press, 1978); and, most recently, Gerhard Sauter, *What Dare We Hope? Reconsidering Eschatology* (Harrisburg: Trinity Press International, 1999), esp. pp. 202-8.

enemy of truth. Furthermore, as a result of the Inquisition and the religious wars, doctrine and dogma carry connotations of intolerance, exclusion, and worse, persecution. In short, dogma was — and still is, pervasively — feared as the enemy of hospitality.

As alleged enemies of truth and hospitality, doctrine and especially dogma seem to be nothing less than opponents of true humanity itself. So the stakes are high for those who continue to oppose "doctrine" and "dogma" for these reasons, and the prospects dim for those who think their rehabilitation long overdue. Yet if we agree at all that in Jesus Christ's life, death, and resurrection the truth of God's hospitality is at stake, nothing next to worship matters more than doctrine and dogma. Why?

The answer is that the very point of doctrine is to receive and to hold on to the truth of the Gospel's hospitality. But why not, instead of the Gospel's hospitality, the hospitality of a "love" or "tolerance" that only excludes the excluders? What is at stake in receiving and holding on to the Gospel's specific hospitality? As I have argued earlier, only the latter assures us in no uncertain terms that reality is of such a kind that practicing hospitality and honoring the truth in their integral relation correspond most appropriately to the way things are. The truth of the Gospel's hospitality thus carries with itself a reality claim that simply has no equivalent in a hospitality that is based on anthropological principles such as "tolerance" or sentiments such as "love." What is at stake in the truth of the Gospel's hospitality — and what, consequently, doctrine both receives and holds on to — is a comprehensive claim about "the ends of God and the end of the world," about God's love and humanity's calling.

And how do worship and doctrine relate? In worship the Gospel addresses and claims us in tangible, specific ways. Yet the Gospel proclaimed and taught does not exist without its normative specification. More strongly put: without its normative specification, the Gospel could neither be proclaimed nor taught. Precisely because the Gospel is a specific proclamation and teaching, it is open to manifold concrete misrepresentations and distortions. And in order to remain faithful and hold on to the Gospel's proclamation and teaching, it becomes necessary to specify in a normative way what the Gospel proclaims and teaches — by offering definite formulations that concretely clarify particular misrepresentations and distortions.[27]

27. For an account of this concept of doctrine, see my *Suffering Divine Things*, pp. 134-45. In developing this account I have learned a great deal from Luther via Eeva

The formation of the biblical canon and the emergence of the rule of faith[28] reflected the necessity that the Gospel's proclamation and teaching require its own normative specification. This is the task of doctrine or dogma — with the biblical canon and the rule of faith as their earliest instantiations. The development of the trinitarian, christological, and pneumatological doctrines, but also the development of the doctrines of *creatio ex nihilo*, of grace, and eventually, of justification by faith alone, as well as of Christ's real presence in the Eucharist, need to be understood in this light. Far from being an estrangement from the Gospel, doctrine enables and secures the Gospel's proclamation and teaching.[29] While doctrine always presupposes the Gospel and continuously depends on it, there is simply no Gospel without the doctrine of the Gospel.

It is, of course, crucial to distinguish between the Gospel and doctrine — yet without playing them off against each other. The Gospel is, at its core, nothing else than Christ's own presence in the promise. Received in faith, Christ thus becomes faith's "form."[30] Traditionally put, in Christ as the "form of faith," both faith's content *(fides quae creditur)* and the act of faith *(fides qua creditur)* are inseparably one. It is rather obvious that faith's form cannot be isolated from the locus of its ongoing reception — worship. It is less obvious but equally true that it cannot be isolated from the distinct subject matter of its reception, either. And precisely this subject matter, the truth of God's hospitality in Christ, is what is at stake in doctrine. Doctrine is our continuous reception, holding, and honoring of the truth of God's hospitality in Christ, in the form of specifying what must be

---

Martikainen's important study, *Doctrina: Studien zu Luthers Begriff der Lehre* (Helsinki: Luther-Agricola-Gesellschaft, 1992).

28. See Karlmann Beyschlag, *Grundriß der Dogmengeschichte*, vol. 1: *Gott und Welt* (Darmstadt: Wissenschaftliche Buchgesellschaft, 1982), pp. 149-72. See also the very instructive essay on the "rule of faith" for theological statements by Bengt Hägglund, "Die Bedeutung der 'regula fidei' als Grundlage theologischer Aussagen," *Studia theologica* 12 (1958): 1-44.

29. For a discussion of the relationship between doctrine and core practices, see my *Suffering Divine Things*, pp. 137-38.

30. Here I draw upon the Finnish Luther research of Tuomo Mannerma's school. For a fine introduction to this significant movement of re-reading Luther's theology in light of the Lutheran dialogue with Eastern Orthodox theology, see Carl E. Braaten and Robert W. Jenson, eds., *Union with Christ: The New Finnish Interpretation of Luther* (Grand Rapids: Eerdmans, 1998).

maintained under all circumstances in light of those alternatives that misrepresent and distort — and thereby miss — that reception.

Yet in order to be able properly to fulfill this task, doctrine needs to be constantly re-appropriated, re-interpreted, and re-communicated, lest it become a reified quasi-knowledge of God substituting for the Gospel itself. It is the specific task of theology to help avoid or overcome this danger.[31]

Instead of a Conclusion

It is the task of this chapter to suggest the ways in which honoring the truth and practicing hospitality are deeply interrelated — to the point of mutual dependence. But it is an even more important task to argue that their integral relation is disclosed by nothing less than the core of the Christian faith, inasmuch as that core shows that practicing hospitality and honoring the truth, properly related, most appropriately correspond to the way things are. The Christian faith is capable of doing this because it is itself the result of God's own practice of hospitality, through which we receive the truth of the triune God as the communion of the Father with the Son in the Holy Spirit, and by which we are called to share in the triune God's hospitality and truth.

We are connected to and drawn into the Christian faith's disclosure of the triune God's hospitality and truth through two modes of reception: worship and doctrine. In worship we continuously receive the very hospitality of God's truth, and in doctrine the very truth of God's hospitality. Ultimately it is this "disclosure" of hospitality and truth as enacted in worship and doctrine that displays the necessity and the significance of prac-

---

31. Both worship and doctrine nourish and inform the practice of theology, which in faithfulness to its specific task will turn out to be nothing less than "dogmatics" — the art of discerning and judging theologically. It is beyond the scope of this chapter to unfold the practice of theology in relationship to worship and doctrine. It will clearly need to be a practice that is shaped by worship, lest it fail to practice the hospitality of God's truth in its own discourse, and accountable to doctrine, lest it fail to honor the truth of God's hospitality in its own work. On this particular dynamic of theology as church practice, see my *Suffering Divine Things*, pp. 147-93, and my chapter "The Church. The Knowledge of the Triune God: Practices, Doctrine, Theology," in *Knowing the Triune God: The Work of the Spirit in the Practices of the Church*, ed. James J. Buckley and David Yeago (Grand Rapids: Eerdmans, 2001), pp. 23-46.

ticing hospitality truthfully and of honoring and thus being hospitable to the truth.

With these reflections I have obviously not answered why it is that many Christians both past and present (and I mean here those who have regularly participated in worship and held on to doctrine) have failed and still fail to practice hospitality and to honor the truth — and why at the same time we find many practitioners of hospitality and of honoring the truth who do not share the Christian confession of Christ as Lord. While crucial, these questions must invite further theological exploration beyond this essay. Yet I can at least suggest that they teach us three things: first, that there is a knowledge of created goods dispersed among all humanity; second, that worship and doctrine obviously do not "function" *ex opere operato*, that is, what has been received does not transpose itself machine-like into a way of life; and third and most importantly, how utterly serious a matter it is and how deeply the reality claims of the Gospel are called into question when Christians fail to practice hospitality and to honor the truth.[32]

32. I have benefited from suggestions offered and criticisms raised by the authors of the other essays in the course of debating the key issues that drive this volume. In addition, I am indebted to Stanley Hauerwas, Kendall Soulen, and Nancy Heitzenrater Hütter for important suggestions on a much longer earlier draft of this chapter, and to Miroslav Volf for his editorial advice on how to cut that draft in half.

Theological Reflection and Christian Practices

KATHRYN TANNER

To see the importance of theology for everyday Christian life, one must understand how theological inquiry is forced by the vagaries of Christian practices themselves and is, consequently, a necessary part of their ordinary functioning. Theological reflection does not merely come to Christian practices from the outside — either before the fact, as a means of educating people into Christian practices, or after the fact, as an external aid and supplement at best or an irrelevant distraction at worst, to practices that might run well without it. Theological reflection instead arises within the ordinary workings of Christian lives to meet pressing practical needs. It figures importantly in Christian life not just because Christian beliefs are an essential ingredient of activities with a meaning for their participants, theology in that case holding out the option of giving a reflective depth and breadth to one's understanding of what one does. More than this, I suggest, theological deliberation is a critical tool to meet problems that Christian practices, being what they are, inevitably generate.

Social-scientific (especially neo-Marxist) accounts of the prerequisites for large-scale, ongoing forms of coordinated social action aid in understanding the features of Christian practices that generate theological reflection.[1] These accounts can help overcome the unrealistic assumptions about

---

1. See, for example, A. P. Cohen, *The Symbolic Construction of Community* (London and New York: Tavistock Publications, 1985); Pierre Bourdieu, *Outline of a Theory of Practice* (Cambridge: Cambridge University Press, 1977); and James Clifford, *The Predicament of Culture* (Cambridge, MA.: Harvard University Press, 1988). My use of

Christian practices to which academic theologians are inclined by the intellectual investments of their own enterprises. To see Christian practices for what they are, one must not (ironically) be misled by the way theologians commonly portray Christian commitments; one must not read into the ordinary functioning of Christian practices what theologians say about them.

Theologians, especially academically trained ones, are adept at making fully explicit and developing the sense of Christian commitments. They often try to establish commonalities in Christian values and beliefs in an effort to sum up what Christianity (or a particular Christian community) is all about or try to construct norms for general Christian subscription. In helping to make sense of what Christians do and say, theologians tend to fix and strictly delimit Christian practices — for example, by offering rules or codes by which they abide. Theologians construct systems of ideas and draw systematic connections between Christian actions and beliefs. Thus, beliefs about God and the world seamlessly suggest the propriety of certain courses of Christian action, and these actions supply the social circumstances that make those beliefs seem natural. In the abstract light of theological reflection, what Christians do often takes on a kind of self-contained or isolated sense. Christians do this or that sort of thing because, as Christians, they believe this or that.

While theological reflection can make helpful contributions to Christian practice when difficulties develop, the characteristics that such reflection strives for and prizes in its own constructions are rarely found displayed in everyday Christian life. In order to maintain themselves as ongoing forms of coordinated social action, Christian practices do not in fact require (1) much explicit understanding of beliefs that inform and explain their performance, (2) agreement on such matters among the participants, (3) strict delimitation of codes for action, (4) systematic consistency among beliefs and actions, or (5) attention to their significance that isolates them from a whole host of non-Christian commitments. More often than not, Christian practices are instead quite open-ended, in the sense

---

the term "Christian practice" in this essay agrees with that of Dorothy Bass and Craig Dykstra in this volume in every respect except perhaps emphasis (mine being on the effort-filled and always only temporarily successful struggles to make Christian practices a whole way of life). I merely use tools from the social sciences to talk about the characteristics that Christian practices (on their understanding) exhibit insofar as they are ongoing forms of large-scale coordinated social activity.

of being rather undefined in their exact ideational dimensions and in the sense of being always in the process of re-formation in response to new circumstances. Apart from deliberate efforts to make them so, Christian practices, and many of the beliefs and values that inform them, do not hang together all that well. Rather than reward sharp and focused attention precisely to them, Christian practices seem to be constituted in great part by a slippery give-and-take with non-Christian practices; indeed, they are mostly non-Christian practices — eating, meeting, greeting — done differently, born again, to unpredictable effect.

Christian practices tend to be like this because practices generally are. In general, practices, especially when they involve ongoing forms of coordinated social action on a large scale, simply do not require a great deal of reflective depth for their common functioning. Indeed, the more diverse the social group organized around such practices is (especially a community, such as the church, oriented around the ideal of universal membership), the greater is the pressure to keep the belief and value commitments involved in such practices undeveloped, ambiguous, or many-sided. In that way, the actions of participants remain coordinated — the practice of offering and accepting the Lord's Supper, for example, runs smoothly — despite the fact that the participants do not precisely agree on what they are doing, or why. Rather than having a rigidly fixed structure, practices in general are fluid and processional in nature, working through improvisation and ad hoc response to changing circumstances. Exemplifying this general fact, Christian practices would be essentially improvisational in the way the practice of making someone feel welcome in one's home is — in that case, adjusting one's responses to the special needs of one's guests, disguising the degree to which one is being inconvenienced without encouraging guests to make one's life miserable, balancing other responsibilities against the requirements of hospitality, determining on an ongoing basis one's treatment of guests, in part at least, by whether they prove to be "good" guests, and so forth. Practices that are constructed piecemeal over the course of the messy realities of social relations rarely achieve, moreover, much in the way of consistency. Certain Christian practices sit uneasily with others in the same way that in the wider society personal relations in the family sit uneasily next to the impersonal contractual relations of economic life, or political democracy sits uneasily next to hierarchical structures of labor management. Beliefs embedded in one set of practices often hang loosely at best with those of another, like the way in which beliefs about individual freedom hang loosely, and always in potential conflict, with demands for equality in American life. Finally, rather than having some self-contained sense, Christian practices cannot be understood in abstraction from their tension-filled relations with the practices of the wider society in which Christians live. Like those of most subcultures, Christian practices are bifocal in nature, involving constant processes of negotiation with, and critical revision of, the practices of the wider society. One might say the Christian practice of celebrating a crucifixion does to ordinary festivities (in most times and places) what punk style, for example, does to good taste.

Particular practices of course vary in the degree to which they conform to these trends towards ambiguity, inconsistency, and open-endedness. A lot depends on their scale and inclusiveness (for example, the aspects of life they impact). Thus practices of tight-knit nuclear families on the one hand or specialized pursuits (such as chess playing) on the other might buck such trends. While the mere fact of coordinated social action does not require consensus in beliefs and values or rule-bound behaviors, particular practices might. For example, practices of classical musicianship do, while jazz improvisation does not.

I do not believe, however, that there are good theological reasons to expect or demand that Christian practices be different from the description offered above. The concrete shape of Christian beliefs and practices may be quite unusual — indeed, to the extent Christianity represents a redeemed way of life, we should insist on its distinctiveness over against other ways of living — but Christian practices need not be an exception to the general, very formal features of any wide-ranging, socially inclusive practice, as I have described them. God works to shape human lives together in and through the ineradicably human character of their ordinary lives. God's direction of us through the institution of Christian practices no more has to evacuate those practices of their typically ambiguous, conflict-filled, fully historical character than God's being a human being had to mean exempting Jesus from the vicissitudes and struggles of everyday life. God can very well shape our lives in and through the still, small voices, as we make our way through disagreement and ambiguity.

To refuse in principle to admit as much — by, say, insisting that Christian practices are much more prescriptively rule-bound than other comparably complex practices — is to be less than fully cognizant of human fallibility before a finally unapproachable Truth that is God's alone. Trying to enforce a fully explicit, deep agreement in beliefs and values among all participants in Christian practices presumptuously anticipates a peace that will arrive, if at all, only through the ordinary, awful processes of give-and-take among people who do not in fact presently agree with one another "all the way down" about the character of their Christian commitments in and out of church. Or it may involve restricting the scope and inclusiveness of Christian practices, narrowing them down to manners of proceeding that hold only for much more specialized pursuits (like scientific experiments under a unified research program) or to ones that prove feasible only in small-scale interactions among intimates — a conflict, to my mind, with a Christian commitment to the church universal.

To the extent Christian practices constitute a whole way of life with the capacity to address fundamental needs of the human condition and are not specialized practices like chess playing, the ambiguities, inconsistencies, and open-endedness of real life practices are in fact functional. Such features of Christian practices help sustain a Christian way of life in a complex, conflictual, and unpredictable world. They are what enable Christianity to be an abiding force in human life whatever the circumstances. While theological reflection makes an essential contribution to Christian practices so understood, if those practices existed simply as theologians tend to describe them, they would be unworkable — inflexible, unresponsive, and impossibly constricting.

The ambiguities, inconsistencies, and open-endedness of Christian practice are, however, the very things that establish an essential place for theological reflection in everyday Christian lives. This is the essential point of this chapter: because Christian practices are like this, they will not work without critical theological engagement. No fully thought out, perfectly consistent, or neatly circumscribed Christian practice precedes the needs of the moment to guide the exercise of that practice into the future. In order to figure out how to go on, one must, with some measure of reflective exertion, figure out the meaning of what one has been doing, why one does it, and what it implies — in particular, how it hangs together (or fails to hang together) with the rest of what one believes and does. Because of their ambiguities, inconsistencies, and open-endedness, practices, in short, do not run by automatic or mechanical routine but through at least quasi-reflective or deliberative efforts to figure out what to do next, how to proceed.[2]

2. Therefore the practice of discernment is an ingredient of every other Christian

Through engagement with Christian practices in this critical, reflective fashion, we are called to be active witnesses to what God has done for us in Christ and active disciples of the way of living that Christ himself struggled against the forces of sin and death to bring into existence. Being witnesses and disciples means establishing through effort-filled deliberative processes what Christianity stands for in our own lives for our own time and circumstance. Doing so is not a matter of passive reception, of simple immersion in established practices — it cannot be, given the messy facts of our existence. Doing so requires ever-renewed personal and church-specific decisions, aided by the whole church universal, about how to deepen the insights that come by way of Christian practices, how to make into a coherent whole the various things we think it right to believe and do as Christians, how to extend those practices to the unforeseen in interaction with the wider, changing world, how to fight our way through tendencies to self-righteousness and self-deception in honest intellectual conflict with those, in and out of church, with whom we do not agree. Being witnesses to and disciples of Christ does not allow us to escape the ambiguous world but puts us, at least ideally, more responsibly within it.

Situational forces, moreover, make the ambiguities, inconsistencies, and processional character of communal practices explicit; they thereby turn these very features of Christian practice into problems requiring explicit, reflective solution. For example, hard cases make a church attend to what it means by what it is doing; a merely apparent consensus in action thereby breaks down into overt disagreement and will threaten church unity if left unresolved. Similarly, the day's headlines — say, about genetic dispositions to forms of action Christians consider sinful — can force into awareness conflicts between what Christians believe about the world and their sense of sin and salvation, conflicts that cannot be shunted aside, once raised, without threatening a basic Christian belief that one God both saves the world and created it good.

By all these avenues, because of the ambiguous and inconsistent character of Christian practices, theological reflection becomes a necessary moment in the regular functioning of Christian practices in ordinary life. A church body must reflect on its practices if they are to be set back into the well-running, working order they had before the members of the

---

practice. For more on the practice of discernment, see Nancy Bedford's essay in this volume.

church started to think harder about them. Called to the difficult work of being a disciple and witness of Christ in a way appropriate to one's own time and circumstance, one comes, by way of theological investigation into Christian practices, to understand more fully what one is doing and why, and to have a sense for how all that one believes and does as a Christian holds together. Working toward these ends, theological reflection deepens engagement in Christian practices — for example, by developing the religious values and ideas that inform them and uncovering the awareness of spiritual realities that participation in them conveys. Through such deepened engagement, one gains the critical distance from customary forms of action and belief necessary for thoughtful reconsideration and reconstruction of them. Academic theology in particular — the sort of theological inquiry one is trained to do in divinity schools and seminaries — aids the flexible extension of Christian practices by exploring, through historical and global studies, how such practices have provided a Christian sense and direction to life in quite varied historical and cultural circumstances. In short, sustained and explicit theological reflection helps establish Christian practices as a whole way of life by sharpening commitments; by guiding performance of Christian practices in the face of the ambiguities, disagreements, and shifting circumstances of everyday life; by contributing to the excellence of such practices by making them more meaningful and meaning-giving; and by imbuing them with a historical, contextual, and theological richness that might otherwise be lost from view at any one place and time, and thereby enhancing their resourcefulness to meet the challenges of that place and time.[3]

The Practice of Welcome

A general understanding of how theological reflection arises in everyday Christian life can be made more concrete by looking at a particular Christian practice. How might theological inquiry be prompted, for example, by the practice of welcome as that takes shape in most Christian worship services? Once we have this more concrete understanding in hand, we will re-

3. See Craig Dykstra, "Reconceiving Practices," in *Shifting Boundaries,* ed. Barbara Wheeler and Edward Farley (Louisville, KY: Westminster/John Knox Press, 1991), pp. 50-56, for a helpful discussion of many of these points.

turn in the concluding section to the question of how the sort of theological reflection that goes on in divinity schools and seminaries might aid processes of theological deliberation in everyday Christian life.

Many Christian churches welcome all comers — the doors are open on Sunday mornings, newcomers are greeted warmly by the ushers, little yellow cards are placed in the pews so they can announce their presence, their prayer concerns may be addressed in the service, members of the church go out of their way to pass them the peace of Christ, they are specifically invited to the Lord's table, the minister may "personalize" the gifts of bread and wine by asking their names, they may be invited to a shared meal after the service and have their hands shaken by the minister as they leave for home. Such a complex practice of welcome often runs well without much attention, without the connections between it and other Christian or non-Christian practices being spelled out, without any full, shared apprehension of why it is done and what it means. And that is probably all to the good, in that efforts to straighten any of this out might be highly contentious and therefore disruptive of the practice, even divisive. When the meanings and connections are specified, some people might decide that they cannot in good conscience continue to engage in the practice.

Nonetheless, circumstances often arise that require reflection on the practice in an effort to figure out how and whether the practice should be continued or applied. Ambiguous, open-ended practices are just the sort to require this kind of deliberation if they are to go forward. Should the welcome of a person not of one's own faith include an invitation to the Lord's table? Should people whose mental or physical capacities prove distracting to others be welcomed? Should people served by outreach to the homeless be encouraged to come to church? Should special efforts be made to draw into the church people outside its usual socio-economic, racial, or ethnic make-up? Should gay people be welcomed? Should those of moral ill repute be welcomed in the same way as others?

Often what prompts questions about particular cases of welcome is the sense of their possible tension with Christian beliefs, or with other Christian or non-Christian practices. How can I welcome a gay couple into my church if I believe they are unrepentant sinners? Does welcoming them to church conflict with my church's refusal to bless their union? How is my tending to the needs of the homeless in my church's soup kitchen compatible with my unwillingness to share the cup with them at the Lord's table? If I cannot accept with joy my son's being gay, how can I go along with my church's policy of being open and affirming? If I welcome them to church, must I object to my company's policy of denying benefits to same-sex partners? Recognition of such tensions is what threatens to derail the practice of welcome in particular cases; it usually halts the practice temporarily, at least as an instance of organized group effort. The practice of reflection together as Christians concerned about doing the right thing must intervene if the practice is to be set back on track.

In order to be answered in a way that will put the practice of welcome back into working order, circumstantially posed questions such as these require explicit attention to the underlying reasons for the practice and to its interconnections with the rest of what Christians say and do. Such questions reveal the degree to which participants have thought through what they are doing and are a demand for further reflection. Such questions bring into the open muffled differences of settled theological opinion among people who otherwise perform together a practice of Christian welcome without much thought. The group effort to answer them requires argument together concerning differences of opinion about what is at issue in the practice of welcome — why and whether there is a Christian mandate for its performance, what its importance might be, and how centrally it figures in the church's sense of mission.

These differences of opinion about what is at issue can take many different forms, depending on the particular congregational context in which they arise, but the following one is, I think, typical.[4] Is the practice of welcome primarily a means to increase church membership and therefore a way of sustaining the church in troubled times? If so, it would make little sense to welcome into church the very people (the homeless, the mentally ill, gay people, those of radically different ethnic or racial classification from present members) who would prompt current members to leave. The same outcome would not be especially problematic where the practice of welcome is thought to be part of the church's mission to reflect Jesus' own concern for the outsider even at the severest cost to himself.

Once raised, a difference of opinion like this requires explicit resolution for the sake of action together in future. The relative importance of,

---

4. Based on my own experience and Mary Fulkerson, "'We Don't See Color Here': A Case Study in Ecclesial-Cultural Invention," in *Converging on Culture: Theology and Cultural Analysis and Criticism,* ed. Sheila Davaney, Delwin Brown, and Kathryn Tanner (New York: Oxford University Press, forthcoming).

and warrants for, these background beliefs about the church — beliefs that may appear to be grounds for disagreement over who should be welcomed — must be assessed. How important is it for the church to survive if it doesn't stand for anything? Or, to the contrary, isn't the survival of the church the prerequisite for anything good coming of it — even if that good is submerged in the present effort simply to keep it afloat? What is more important — to witness to Jesus while declining to follow his way of concern for the outcast, or to follow that way to the decline of such witness, at least to the extent it is assessed by numbers and a strong group front? Or does an alternative like that make any Christian sense? What is the relationship between witness and discipleship anyway? Might not discipleship be the only genuine witness, or at least a necessary prerequisite for it? Even more fundamentally, can one question whether Jesus' way primarily means care for the outcast? How important is that sort of practice to Jesus' significance for Christian lives?

A strategy for answering these questions about background beliefs can be found by returning to what we said earlier was often an underlying worry in problematic cases: the sense that extending the practice of welcome in these ways would conflict with other Christian and non-Christian practices or with the beliefs and values ingredient in them. To address this worry, one must figure out how well a particular way of extending the Christian practice of welcome fits together with the rest of one's commitments — whether there really is such a lack of fit, and, if so, how it should be resolved (say, by eliminating the practice or reassessing what it conflicts with). To determine what fits with those prior commitments, one must first, however, give them some coherent shape (something with which they don't, as we've said, come already equipped). That effort requires in turn processes of selection and elucidation: because of the messiness of real-life practices, it is unlikely that *all* of them can be put together coherently (even leaving the disputed extension of the Christian practice of welcome out of the picture). Some of them might have to be dropped. And without further elucidation of the meaning of those commitments, it won't be evident what they do or do not conflict with. In short, one tries to figure out whether one's commitments would cohere better with or without the disputed practice of welcome, recognizing that its inclusion might mean a new elucidation of prior commitments and a different winnowing down of practices for the sake of greater coherence.

Similar judgments about fit establish the relative importance of, and warrants for, the different background beliefs that determine one's judgment on a disputed practice of welcome. Do Christian practices, along with the beliefs and values they instantiate, hang together better — that is, more elegantly, with less loss, and fewer cases of forced interpretation — when one or the other set of concerns about the church is pushed to the front? What would be highlighted about church practices if a point were made of welcoming outsiders to church, and would that make better sense, prove to be more illuminating, of the whole of one's commitments than turning away from such a practice of welcome?

Theological Schooling

While most Christians have probably already formed implicit judgments like these — about, say, the priorities of the church that best fit with their understanding of their denomination, their experiences of worship, and their reading of the Bible — such judgments of fit are obviously quite complex and therefore difficult to make explicit and argue for convincingly. The kind of theological reflection for which people are trained in divinity schools and seminaries can be of help here.

Indeed, almost any course taught in today's divinity schools and seminaries, falling under the usual area divisions of Bible, history, and systematic and practical theology, could be of help, especially were such courses to make the study of Christian practices their explicit object of concern — something they might easily do.[5] Such courses might explore the theological arguments by which comparable quagmires of Christian practice were resolved at other times and places, with course instructors offering and encouraging students to make their own normative assessments of those arguments in theological terms. Academic theologians in their teaching and research could also help church people make decisions by modeling arguments in favor of different points of view on the very matters currently at issue in Christian life. Thus, although the limitations of this essay's format do not permit me to make such an argument now, I would be inclined to argue in favor of a church practice of welcoming discomforting outsiders,

---

5. See Dykstra, "Reconceiving Practices," for this suggestion that little curricular reform is needed — just a shift in the content and direction of courses divided among the usual areas.

using my knowledge of the history of Christianity — concerning, for example, the historical importance to Christian life and thought of the claims that support such a practice and the way analogous cases of disputed practices of welcome have been resolved earlier and elsewhere by Christians. Arguments like this would have the same basic shape as those that disputed cases of Christian practice force any committed Christian to pursue. They would simply be more sustained or thorough versions of such arguments — since academic theologians, by virtue of their employment, are able to devote a great deal of time to their construction — and better informed ones, at least in the sense of being constructed from an unusually wide purview (though perhaps less informed on the matter of "real life" because of a tendency toward abstraction).

In their courses in biblical study and historical, systematic, and practical theology, students gain the general know-how to make comparably thorough and well-informed arguments on issues of Christian practice that presently concern them. For instance, the ability to elucidate the meaning of the values and beliefs that inform Christian practice — one prerequisite for making such arguments — is enhanced by knowledge of the diverse ways it has been done over the wide course of time and space in Christian lives. Historical theology, along with the creative ventures into systematic theology enjoined by faculty and student peers, expands students' imaginative horizons about the ways various Christian practices, and the beliefs and values informing them, can be made to cohere. Normative engagement with people of different views in a theological school context provides students with practice for what will face them in the course of their lives as Christians out of school.

One worry mentioned above that arises in Christian life — the concern about conflict between a Christian practice and practices in which Christians also engage by virtue of their other commitments — would, however, require curricular reform in most divinity schools and seminaries in order to be addressed. To be of help in this regard, courses would have to provide more than knowledge of Christian practices, and therefore theological education would need to move in the direction of the wider humanistic frame for the teaching of theology in university contexts: Christian practices would have to be set in relation to non-Christian ones, in all the wide arenas of human life — economic, political, and social — to show how tensions between them are resolved.

Tensions between Christian and non-Christian practices raise the whole question of the way Christian practices are formed vis-à-vis non-Christian ones. They raise the question of the distinctiveness of Christian practices in relation to what goes on outside church — the question of a church's identity in relation to the "world" — whether that distinctiveness is based primarily on the church's opposition to the world, or on its contributions to the improvement of civilization, or on a more complicated give-and-take that excludes neither the possibility of learning from the world nor correcting it in particular respects. Addressing tensions between Christian and non-Christian practices also requires the challenge of applying these sorts of general understandings of Christian identity to particulars. To use a presently hotly contested example, is welcoming gay people an example of moral relativism, the dilution of Christian moral rigor, through accommodation to the bad influences of the wider society? Or would the refusal to welcome them be just another example of the way denominations, as voluntary societies, have historically tended to replicate boundaries of importance to the wider society, such as economic, racial, and ethnic lines of division? If exclusion of gays and lesbians is thought to be a matter of drawing church lines along a boundary between sinners and the righteous, is that a properly Christian distinction or an instance of corruption by non-Christian principles of social organization? In what sense is the church properly a church for sinners? How might the welcoming of gays and lesbians involve not simple accommodation but transfiguration of the wider society's norms of simple tolerance? If welcoming gays and lesbians would be to go along with a trend of the wider society, should one oppose the world in this instance, or mirror it for Christian reasons, thereby allowing one's sense of a properly Christian practice of welcome to be corrected by it, to be brought back to Christian witness by being shamed by the wider world?

Knowledge of Christian thought and practice in diverse times and places and systematic expertise in drawing connections among Christian beliefs and practices are aids in answering questions like this. Systematic expertise helps clarify what judgments of either opposition or accommodation to the world tend to imply about the rest of one's Christian beliefs and practices — in the case of opposition, for example, sharp distinctions between creation and salvation, a strong sense of the sinfulness of the wider world, and practices that enforce high expectations about Christian morals.[6] Christian history, moreover, is replete with examples of such tensions

6. See, for example, the famous ideal types of church and sect developed by Ernst

and of the complex ways they have been resolved. Knowledge of Christian history reveals, for instance, that despite programmatic theological statements to the contrary, rejection (or accommodation) of practices of the wider society is rarely total. At any one time in the very same communities of Christian action, some practices of the wider society are opposed, some accepted almost unchanged, and some significantly transformed. This is so because of the complexity of Christian commitments themselves — Christians are never entirely in or out of participation in practices of the wider society — and also because of the complexity of the wider society — opposing it in one respect (e.g., its socially conservative element) is liable to mean agreeing with it in another (e.g., agreeing with its socially progressive elements). Programmatic theological judgments about the relationship between church and world are therefore rarely sufficient to decide particular cases; additional theological arguments have to be offered that concern the specifics of the matter at issue. Thus Christianity's stance against or for the world is not enough to decide the issue of welcoming gays and lesbians (assuming we could resolve the question of which rubric it falls under); more specific arguments have to be directed to the particulars of the case. What theological reasons can be given for homosexuality's immorality, and if those arguments are any good, in what ways is welcome predicated on the virtue of those to whom it is extended? Whether the decision is to welcome gays and lesbians or not, Christian practice thereby imitates practices of the wider society — either the wider society's discriminatory exclusions or its tendencies to openness and lack of judgment. Unless there are very good theological arguments to make exceptions of gays and lesbians, knowledge of similar cases of contested Christian practices of welcome in other times and places will suggest that Christians are just falling into the same old traps all over again.[7] In order for the welcome of gays to be more than a simple carryover of liberal lip-service to diversity as it is found in the wider society, Christians need good arguments for the specifically Christian sense it makes to be doing so. Where the practice of toleration in the wider society diverges from Christian mandates, the Christian practice of welcome should manifest that difference in action. For example, out of equal regard

---

Troeltsch in his *The Social Teaching of the Christian Churches* (New York: Macmillan, 1931).

7. For evidence of this, see H. Richard Niebuhr, *The Social Sources of Denominationalism* (New York: Meridian Books, 1957).

for all God's children, a Christian practice of welcome should contest the way that in the wider society power arrangements are often left as they are when room is made for diversity.

These sorts of tension-filled relationships between Christian practices and those of the wider society reveal how the meaning of Christian practices is not internal to them but established *in* these relationships, by what is done or not done in church about the practices of the wider society, by what Christian practices do or don't do *to* them. In other words, simply uncovering and developing the Christian beliefs and values that inform or are associated with a Christian practice of welcome will not establish its meaning. One needs to look, additionally, away from the Christian practice itself to its relations with similar practices in the wider society. How does a Christian practice of welcome differ from other practices of welcome current in the wider society? That, to a great extent, is the clue to its Christian point. On the basis of present church experience, confirmed by an academic's knowledge of the global history of Christianity, one might argue, for example, that the Christian practice of welcome is unusual in its disregard of prior acquaintance with those welcomed. One rarely, for example, welcomes into one's home people who are complete strangers, and strangers in those rare cases aren't welcomed without being "sized up" — "oh, this is a traveler in need of hospitality," or, "this is a neighbor on my block whom I've never met." The Christian practice of welcome is certainly exceptional in crossing usual barriers of social exclusion — Jew and Greek, rich and poor, slave and free, men and women. Without attention to the wider society in all its spheres — home life, economic transactions, and political arrangements and conflicts — none of this would be evident. In order to be of greater service to Christian practices, theological schools must therefore place Christian history in the context of world history and the study of contemporary Christianity alongside the study of a whole host of other fields not commonly found in today's divinity schools and seminaries.[8]

---

8. For more on this proposal for making divinity schools more like the interdisciplinary religious studies departments of universities — and for a defense of the place of theology in the humanities curricula of universities — see my "Theology and Cultural Contest in the University," in *Shifting Paradigms: Theology, Religious Studies, and the University*, ed. Linell Cady and Delwin Brown (Albany, NY: State University of New York Press, forthcoming).

PRACTICING THEOLOGY,
SERVING A WAY OF LIFE

Theology for a Way of Life

MIROSLAV VOLF

The Challenge of "Real" Life

"But what does that have to do with *real* life?" I have come to expect an occasional question like this in courses on systematic theology. I confess that I am often tempted to snap back, "If you would just abandon your vulgar notions of 'real' life and muster some intellectual curiosity you could spare us your question!" Usually, I overcome the temptation and give a little speech instead. If students complain that theology is too "theoretical," I invite them to consider Kant's argument that nothing is as practical as a good theory.[1] If they object that theologians entertain outdated and therefore irrelevant ideas, I offer them a Kierkegaardian observation that the right kind of non-contemporaneity may be more timely than today's newspaper. I conclude by explaining how ideas that seem detached from everyday concerns may in fact touch the very heart of those concerns.

And yet, when I am done with my disquisition, I have dealt with only half of the worry expressed in my student's skeptical question. We theologians sometimes do teach and write as if we have made a studied effort to avoid contact with the "impurities" of human lives. We do so partly by our choice of topics. The number of pages theologians have devoted to the question of transubstantiation — which does or does not take place dur-

---

1. Immanuel Kant, "On the Common Saying: 'This May be True in Theory, but It Does Not Apply in Practice,'" in "Kant: Political Writings," trans. H. B. Nisbet, ed. Hans Reiss, 2d edition (Cambridge/New York: Cambridge University Press, 1991), p. 61.

ing any given Sunday — would, I suspect, far exceed the number of pages we have devoted to the daily work that fills our lives Monday through Saturday. We also take flight from the concerns of the quotidian by how we treat great theological themes such as the Trinity, Christology, and soteriology. As thinkers we rightly focus on conceptual difficulties — "How can God be one and three persons at the same time?" "How can Christ be both God and man?" "How can we owe salvation to nothing but grace and yet be free?" — but in the process we sometimes lose the larger significance of these doctrines. Moreover, as academics we are caught in the movement toward increased specialization. On the one hand, specialization seems a necessary condition for fundamental research. On the other hand, it tends to make us lose sight of the overarching subject of theology. The scholarly interests of theologians then fail to match the realities of the people in the pew and on the street.[2]

There is yet another important reason for a perceived disconnect between theology and so-called "real" life. It lies in the distinction between the theoretical and the practical sciences that goes all the way back to Aristotle and his disciples. According to this distinction, the goal of the theoretical sciences is truth, and the goal of the practical sciences is action. Aristotle considered the theoretical sciences, in which knowledge is pursued for knowledge's sake, a higher wisdom than the practical sciences, which are pursued for their usefulness.[3] It has long been debated how theology fits into this Aristotelian scheme — Thomas Aquinas, for instance, weighed in on the side of theology being a theoretical science,[4] and Duns Scotus argued that it was a practical one.[5] Obviously, if theology is a theoretical science, then it only secondarily has something to do with practices; one has to make separate inquiry into practical implications of knowledge pursued for its own sake. But if theology is a practical science, then practices are from the start included within the purview of its concerns.

Often theologians have done theology as if it were a theoretical science; that, too, has contributed to a sense that theology is unrelated to

2. See Miroslav Volf, "Introduction: A Queen and a Beggar: Challenges and Prospects of Theology," *The Future of Theology: Essays in Honor of Jürgen Moltmann*, ed. Miroslav Volf et al. (Grand Rapids: Eerdmans, 1996), pp. ix-xviii.

3. See Aristotle, *Metaphysics*, 982a 14ff. and 993b 20-21.

4. Thomas Aquinas, *Summa Theologiae* I.1.4.

5. Duns Scotus, *Ordinatio*, prol. pars 5, qq. 1-2.

"real" life. In different ways, the essays in this volume all share the persuasion that theology is more properly described as a practical than as a theoretical science — "science" in the loose sense of critical and methodologically disciplined reflection.[6] In this concluding chapter, I will explore in more general terms how we should understand this claim. I will argue that theology is an (academic) enterprise whose object of study is God and God's relation to the world and whose purpose is not simply to deliver "knowledge," but to serve a way of life. Put slightly differently, my contention is that *at the heart of every good theology lies not simply a plausible intellectual vision but more importantly a compelling account of a way of life, and that theology is therefore best done from within the pursuit of this way of life.* I will begin with a story that revolves around a practice, and then reflect on its implications for the relation between beliefs and practices and therefore also for the relation between systematic theology (as a critical reflection on beliefs) and a way of life (as the sum of Christian practices).

Before I proceed, I should briefly indicate what I mean by "beliefs" and "practices." First, I am using the term "beliefs" in the sense of the "core Christian beliefs." In the life of individuals these are convictions implicit in the basic act of faith through which God constitutes human beings as Christians; they are the ideational side of the most basic act of faith.[7] In the life of Christian communities, core beliefs are convictions that a Christian community "must hold true in order to maintain its own identity."[8] "Beliefs," in my usage here, is equivalent to "authentic doctrines."

---

6. I am leaving aside here the question of whether or to what extent theology is a science in the same sense as other sciences. On this question, see Wolfhart Pannenberg, *Theology and the Philosophy of Science,* trans. F. McDonagh (Philadelphia: The Westminster Press, 1976), pp. 23-224; Philip Clayton, *Explanation from Physics to Theology: An Essay in Rationality and Religion* (New Haven: Yale University Press, 1989), pp. 154-67; Nancey Murphy, *Theology in the Age of Scientific Reasoning* (Ithaca: Cornell University Press, 1990), pp. 174-208; Wentzel van Huyssteen, *The Shaping of Rationality: Toward Interdisciplinarity in Theology and Science* (Grand Rapids: Eerdmans, 1999).

7. My "core beliefs" overlap in significant ways with the notion of "doctrine" that Reinhard Hütter employs in his chapter in this volume. See also Reinhard Hütter's notion of "doctrina evangelii" in *Suffering Divine Things: Theology as Church Practice,* trans. Doug Stott (Grand Rapids: Eerdmans, 2000), pp. 135-45.

8. Bruce D. Marshall, *Trinity and Truth* (Cambridge: Cambridge University Press, 2000), p. 19.

247

Second, I am using the term "practices" in the sense of cooperative and meaningful human endeavors that seek to satisfy fundamental human needs and conditions and that people do together and over time.[9] With this brief statement I could be done with describing my use of practices were it not that a relation between practices and sacraments features prominently in my text. Sacraments can be plausibly construed as practices, but I use "practices" in a narrower sense that does not include sacraments, for no other reason than to keep historically situated and cooperative activities that satisfy fundamental human needs ("practices") conceptually distinct from sacraments. The distinction is especially important to maintain in treatments of the relation between beliefs and practices, because beliefs — I am running a little ahead of myself here — relate to sacraments differently than they do to "practices." Core Christian beliefs are *by definition normatively inscribed in sacraments* but not in "practices." Hence sacraments ritually enact normative patterns for practices.

Strangers and Hosts

His name I have forgotten, but the image of him at our table is indelible. On the first Sunday of every month he would make his way from the back country to the city of Novi Sad in Yugoslavia, where my father was pastor of a small Pentecostal church. Our guest, the lone Pentecostal in his village, who was surrounded by a sea of hostile non-believers and Orthodox Christians, would come to our church for Holy Communion. After feasting at the Lord's table, he would join our family for the Sunday meal. A rough-hewn figure, both intriguing and slightly menacing, he would sit quietly, a bit hunched, at the table opposite me, a teenage boy. A moustache that put Nietzsche's to shame dominated his face.

I resented his coming, for when he entered our house my memory would always play back a sound from his previous visit. The sound was that of my mother's soup — delicious to the point that whatever preceded and followed it served only to frame its unsurpassable taste — leaping noisily across the gap between his spoon and his mouth through his moustache. And so the climax of the week's menu, as Mary Douglas calls the

---

9. See Craig Dykstra and Dorothy C. Bass's definition in this volume, p. 18.

Sunday lunch,[10] was ruined for me. Though my parents never said anything, I could sense their unease with our visitor's manners. Yet they not only thought it important to invite him repeatedly, but also admired the robustness of his commitment despite the great adversity he suffered on account of his faith.

One could apply a hermeneutic of suspicion to my parents' practice. They wanted to impress parishioners, atone for secret guilt, make payments into a heavenly investment portfolio. In their own minds, however, they were extending the invitation to this stranger because they did not think one should hold the table of the Lord at which my father presided in the morning apart from the table of our home at whose head he was sitting at noon. I am not sure how much they *knew* about the original unity of the Eucharistic celebration and the agape meal, but they clearly *practiced* their inseparability. Had I objected — "But must *we* invite him *every* time he comes!?" — they would have responded, "As the Lord gave his body and blood for us sinners, so we ought to be ready to share not only our belongings, but also something of our very selves, with strangers." The circle of our table was opened up by the wounds of Christ, and a stranger was let in. Had I continued to protest, they would have reminded me of that grand eschatological meal whose host will be the Triune God, a meal at which people of every tribe and tongue will be feasting. I had better be ready to sit next to him at *that* meal, they would have insisted.

The relation between the ecclesial and eschatological table and the many tables to which we do or do not invite guests is a case in point of the relation between beliefs — some of them ritually enacted — and practices. The sacrament of the Lord's Supper itself is very much a summary of the whole of Christian life, at whose heart lies the self-giving of God for sinful humanity,[11] and the eschatological Feast is the sum of Christian hopes for communion between the Triune God and God's glorified people. So how do some of the most basic and sacramentally enacted Christian convictions intersect with the practice of hospitality?

10. Mary Douglas, "Deciphering a Meal," in *Myth, Symbol, and Culture*, ed. Clifford Geertz (New York: W. W. Norton & Co., 1971), p. 67.

11. See the brief reflections on Eucharist as "ordering ritual" in Ingolf U. Dalferth, *Theology and Philosophy* (Oxford: Blackwell, 1988), pp. 222-23.

Belief-Shaped Practices

At one level, the answer to the question of how Christian beliefs and practices intersect seems plain enough — if my parents' practice offers a window on the way beliefs relate to practices. The celebration of the Lord's Supper, and a whole range of beliefs that are embedded in it and that explain why and how it is undertaken, shaped my parents' practice of hospitality. So Christian beliefs shape Christian practices. But how, more precisely? One can explore how beliefs shape practices from two angles — by examining the nature of Christian practices and the nature of Christian beliefs.

Let us look first at the issue from the angle of practices. Christian practices have what we may call an "as-so" structure (or correspondence structure): *as* God has received us in Christ, *so* we too are to receive our fellow human beings. True, the way in which Christ's life is exemplary has to be carefully specified. Above all, the important difference between Christ and other human beings should counter both the temptation to supplant Christ and the presumption that human beings can simply "repeat" Christ's work. But in an appropriately qualified way, in relation to the practice of hospitality as well as in relation to all other practices, we must say: "As Christ, so we."[12]

Beliefs about who Christ is and what Christ did, expressed in the form of narratives, ritual actions, or propositions, provide the norm for the Christian practice of hospitality. This practice is Christian only insofar as Christ serves as the model for its practitioners, and Christ is available as a model only through such beliefs. This is not to say that practices of non-Christians cannot be Christomorphic; they often are. But to be a Christian *is* to explicitly believe in Christ and commit oneself to follow his way of life. Thus the internal constitution of a *Christian* practice points to the story of Christ as its external norm. Hospitality as a Christian practice is suffused with particular Christian beliefs that shape it normatively. Put more generally, Christian practices are *by definition* normatively shaped by Christian beliefs.

Our guests have gone home. As we clean the dishes, we muse about whether we have been good hosts. We ask ourselves many different ques-

---

12. For an extended exemplification of the "as-so" structure of Christian practices, see Miroslav Volf, *Exclusion and Embrace: Theological Reflections on Identity, Otherness, and Reconciliation* (Nashville: Abingdon Press, 1996).

tions, but if we are engaged in Christian hospitality we will examine what we did in the light of the story of Christ, in the light of his words and deeds. We will, for instance, remember the following injunction from the third gospel:

> When you give a luncheon or a dinner, do not invite your friends or your brothers or your relatives or rich neighbors, in case they may invite you in return, and you would be repaid. But when you give a banquet, invite the poor, crippled, the lame, and the blind. And you will be blessed, because they cannot repay you, for you will be repaid at the resurrection of the righteous. (Luke 14:12-14)

From this we may conclude that hospitality at its best should not be part of the economy of exchange among equals or with superiors, but instead be part of an economy of donation to the destitute and weak. So to evaluate whether we were good hosts, we might ask ourselves whether we expected to get as much (or more) out of the invitation as we put in. If we did, we have missed the mark.

There is a second way in which Christian practices are unthinkable without Christian beliefs. The story of Christ, which informs the "as-so" pattern, is itself embedded in the larger story of God with Israel and the nations, and this larger story again is framed by the narratives of God's creation and final consummation. That nexus of stories draws a map of the normative space in which human beings exist as agents of Christian practices. As Charles Taylor has argued in *Sources of the Self,* such a space is essential for moral action because it is within it that "questions arise about what is good or bad, what is worth doing and what is not, what has meaning and importance for you and what is trivial and secondary."[13] Christian beliefs are indispensable for the creation of the Christian moral space in which alone engagement in Christian practices makes sense.

Practice-Shaping Beliefs

By attending to the character of Christian practices, we have observed an intimate link between beliefs and practices. We see a similar link when we

13. Charles Taylor, *Sources of the Self: The Making of the Modern Identity* (Cambridge: Harvard University Press, 1989), p. 28.

consider the nature of Christian beliefs. Shaping practices — shaping a way of life — is internal to the very nature of these beliefs.

To determine whether beliefs are essentially practice-shaping, it is particularly important to examine the nature of beliefs about God. These beliefs lie at the heart of the Christian faith, and the tradition has therefore rightly claimed that God and God's relation to the world constitute the proper "object" of theology.[14] Everything theology studies, is studied, as Wolfhart Pannenberg states in *Theology and the Philosophy of Science*, "from the point of view of its relation to God *(sub ratione Dei)*." "It is only this consideration *sub ratione Dei* which distinguishes the treatment of a wide range of topics in theology from their treatment in other disciplines which concern themselves with the same areas but from different points of view."[15] Because beliefs about God shape the whole of theology, the relation of these beliefs to practices is at the heart of the issue we are discussing.

Consider one important feature of beliefs about God. It emerges as soon as one remembers that God is not an object in the world to which human beings may or may not be related in significant ways. Rather, God is the creator, redeemer, and consummator of all that is. Human beings live in a relation of inescapable dependence on God — dependence which grounds human freedom along with all other human good and is in no way incompatible with it[16] — to which gratitude is the appropriate response. Moreover, the identity of human beings and the goal of their lives are bound up with the fact that God created them to image God and live in communion with God. The "as-so" structure, which we noted in how what Christ did for sinful humanity relates to our practices ("As Christ, so we"), applies more generally to the relation between who God is and who human beings are and therefore how they ought to behave ("As God, so we").

This claim is *already implied* in affirmation of God's existence —

<hr />

14. For different accounts of theological enterprise that are agreed on the basic idea that God is the subject of theology see, for instance, Pannenberg, *Theology and the Philosophy of Science*, and David Kelsey, *To Understand God Truly: What's Theological about a Theological School* (Louisville: Westminster/John Knox Press, 1992).

15. Pannenberg, *Theology and the Philosophy of Science*, p. 298.

16. See Karl Rahner, *Foundations of Christian Faith*, trans W. Dych (New York: Crossroad, 1978), p. 79; Kathryn Tanner, *Jesus, Humanity, and the Trinity: A Brief Systematic Theology* (Minneapolis: Fortress Press, 2001), pp. 2-4.

which is to say, in the affirmation that a relationship between God and human beings obtains such that human beings owe their existence to God and find their fulfillment in imaging God and living in communion with God. As a consequence, whenever we speak of God, we are always involved; the import of the claims about God for human beings does not need to be brought in subsequently but is already part and parcel of the talk about God. As Gerhard Ebeling puts it in commenting on the way Luther speaks of God, "what is said of God does not have to be applied later to man . . . what is said of God is addressed to man."[17]

What bearing does this claim about the nature of Christian beliefs have on the relation between beliefs and practices? Rightly to espouse the belief that God is "the God of peace" (Romans 15:33), for instance, *is*, among other things, to commit oneself to the pursuit of peace. Similarly, the obligation to ensure that one person does not "go hungry" while "another becomes drunk" is part and parcel of believing rightly about the Lord's Supper (1 Corinthians 11:21). No doubt one can believe and fail to act accordingly; one can believe and expressly intend not to act accordingly.[18] Indeed, as the Old Testament prophets' critique of religious devotion makes manifest, one can profess a belief precisely in order not to act accordingly.[19] But such situations are clearly at odds with the inner dynamics of beliefs themselves — otherwise one could not cover one's wrongdoing with a demonstrative profession of belief. Espousing a belief puts pressure upon the one who believes to act accordingly. Put more generally, basic Christian beliefs *as beliefs* entail practical commitments. These commitments may need to be explicated so as to become clear, or they may need to be connected to specific issues in concrete situations, but they don't need to be *added* to the beliefs; they inhere in the beliefs. Christian beliefs are not simply statements about what was, is, and will be the case; they are statements about what *should* be the case and what hu-

17. Gerhard Ebeling, *Luther: An Introduction to His Thought*, trans. R. A. Wilson (Philadelphia: Fortress Press, 1972), p. 248. See also Gerhard Ebeling, "Cognitio Dei et hominis," *Lutherstudien*, vol. 1 (Tübingen: Mohr, 1971), pp. 221-72.

18. For an analysis of disconnects between beliefs and practices see Amy Plantinga Pauw's chapter in this volume.

19. See Miroslav Volf, *Zukunft der Arbeit — Arbeit der Zukunft. Das Marxsche Arbeitsverstaendnis und seine theologische Wertung* (Munich: Kaiser, 1988), p. 106; Hans-Joachim Kraus, *Theologische Religionskritik* (Neukirchen-Vluyn: Neukirchener Verlag, 1982), p. 251.

man beings should do about that.[20] They provide a normative vision for practices.

To sum up my argument thus far: Christian practices are such that a Christian normative vision is part and parcel of what these practices are; and Christian beliefs are such that informing Christian practices is part and parcel of what these beliefs do. Practices are essentially belief-shaped, and beliefs are essentially practice-shaping.

Grace, Beliefs, Practices

The role of beliefs in relation to practices is not only providing a normative vision for practices; from a theological standpoint, this role of beliefs, though immensely important, is secondary. The whole Christian way of life, with all its practices, is supported and shaped by something outside that way of life — by what God has done, is doing, and will do. The Christian faith is not primarily about human doing; the gospel is not reducible to the barebones formal injunction, "Look at Christ and imitate a wholesome way of life," or "Understand God and act accordingly." The Christian faith is not primarily about human *doing* but about human *receiving*. The barebones formal injunction to which the gospel can be reduced is, "Receive yourself and your world as a new creation." More than just normatively guiding practices, Christian beliefs narrate the divine action by which human beings are constituted as agents of practices, by which they are placed into a determinate normative space, and by which they are inspired and charged to imitate God.[21]

Consider once again the Lord's Supper. Eating the bread and drinking the wine, we remember the body broken for God's enemies and the blood spilled to establish a "new covenant" with those who have broken the covenant. In that act of ritual commemoration we dramatize the central elements of a normative vision that should guide our practices. But if that were all we thought we were doing, we would be profoundly misunderstanding the Lord's Supper. Central to the celebration of the Lord's Sup-

20. See Jürgen Moltmann, *Theology of Hope: On the Ground and the Implications of a Christian Eschatology,* trans. J. W. Leitch (London: SCM Press, 1967).

21. On the constitution of the Christian subject see Karl Barth, *Church Dogmatics* IV/1, 749.

per is the truth that the body was broken and the blood spilled "for us" and for the "life of the world." The Lord's Supper is a sacramental representation of the gift of new life through Christ's death and resurrection — new life whose reality underlies every single properly Christian act and therefore all Christian practices. Understandings of how the gift of new life is re-presented in the Lord's Supper differ, but most agree about the primacy of the Eucharistic reference to the divine work for us, rather than our imitation of that work.

Of course, we would also be misunderstanding the Lord's Supper if we thought of it only as a sacrament of God's embrace, of which we are simply the fortunate beneficiaries. Inscribed in the very heart of God's grace is the rule that we can be its recipients only if we do not resist being made into its agents. In a precisely defined way that guards the distinction between God and human beings, human beings themselves are made participants in the divine activity and therefore are inspired, empowered, and obliged to imitate it. Which is where practices come in.[22] Christian practices may be construed as human "resonances,"[23] under a variety of circumstances, of the divine engagement with the world through which human beings are sustained and redeemed.

First Come Practices

My argument so far about the relation between beliefs and practices amounts to the claim that Christian beliefs do not express "pure knowledge" but are intended to guide Christian practices by situating the practitioner within the overarching narrative of God's dealings with humanity and by offering an account of his or her constitution as an agent. Seen from within that way of life, beliefs describe the constitution of agents of practices and offer normative direction for that way of life. So beliefs shape practices. But do practices contribute anything to beliefs?

One way to explore this issue is to ask the following question: Do we

---

22. In their essay for this volume, Dorothy Bass and Craig Dykstra have underscored that Christian practices are forms of participation in divine activity.

23. For a theological appropriation of the notion of "resonances," see Michael Welker, *God the Spirit*, trans. John F. Hoffmeyer (Minneapolis: Fortress Press, 1994), pp. 313ff.

first accept Christian beliefs and then engage in Christian practices, or the other way around? As attested by the accounts of those who have experienced conversion through reading the Bible without having had previous contact with Christians, one can accept Christian beliefs without previously engaging in Christian practices or even observing Christian practices. A person can start engaging in Christian practices because he or she has found Christian beliefs intellectually compelling. In such cases, Christian beliefs come first and Christian practices follow.

As a rule, however, this is not how things happen. People come to believe either because they find themselves already engaged in Christian practices (say, by being raised in a Christian home) or because they are attracted to them. In most cases, Christian practices come first and Christian beliefs follow — or rather, beliefs are already entailed in practices, so that their explicit espousing becomes a matter of bringing to consciousness what is implicit in the engagement in practices themselves.

Recall my parents' example. Notwithstanding my occasional grumbling at the liberality with which my parents practiced hospitality toward people around whom I felt uneasy, I arguably have embraced the Christian faith along with its core beliefs partly because I saw it embodied in their practices. Moreover, the way they engaged in the practice of hospitality profoundly shaped the way I came to understand basic Christian beliefs (just as the way my saintly nanny treated me as a young boy helped form my image of God). People make Christian beliefs their own and understand them in particular ways partly because of the practices to which they have been introduced — in which their souls and bodies have been trained[24] — in the course of their lives. Put differently, by being attracted to and habituated in a set of practices, they have embraced the set of beliefs that sustain these practices and that are inscribed in them.

The movement from practices to beliefs is, however, not as simple as my account so far suggests. It is not at all clear that I would have *rejected* the Christian faith had I seen a major discrepancy between my parents' beliefs and practices. What if I had overheard them say to each other the evening after we had entertained our guest, "What a brute! He will never step into our house again," and if from that day on we had invited to our table only those who "behaved"? It does not follow that I would have concluded

---

24. On the socially informed body, see Pierre Bourdieu, *Outline of a Theory of Practice,* trans. R. Nice (Cambridge: Cambridge University Press, 1977), p. 124.

either that the Lord's Supper was just a religious sham or that — my soul and body not having been trained in the practice of inviting strangers — the Lord's Supper does not contain an imperative to do so. Instead, I might simply have deemed my parents weak, inconsistent, or even hypocritical — and embraced the beliefs they espoused and ritually celebrated with a determination to live a more consistent life (much in the way a person might observe his or her parents' failed marriage and vow not to make a similar mistake).

On the other hand, even the excellence of my parents' Christian practices need not have led to my espousal of Christian beliefs. In fact, at one point in my life, the exact opposite happened. I rejected the faith precisely because my parents were such good practitioners and because their practices had had a claim upon my life. The dissonance between the practices of the peer group with which I identified and my parents' practices, and the clash between what I was taught at school (Marxist indoctrination!) and some basic Christian beliefs, were simply too great. In my teenage years, my parents seemed to me to be duped and dense people who were imposing on me an outdated way of life. When it comes to embracing or rejecting Christian beliefs, practices do influence beliefs, but they do so in complex and not always predictable ways.

The second way in which practices are crucial for beliefs concerns not so much the acceptance of beliefs but their *understanding*. What George Lindbeck says in *The Nature of Doctrine* about proclamation is true of all Christian beliefs: "[it] gains power and meaning insofar as it is embodied in the total gestalt of community life and action."[25] "Right (communal) doing" seems in some sense a precondition for right understanding. The obverse is also true: "wrong doing" — especially if deeply patterned and long lived — leads to twisted understanding. It would be, however, too much to claim that the wrongdoers *cannot* know rightly and that the "right-doers" *cannot* know wrongly. The connection between engaging practices and understanding beliefs is a loose one. Nonetheless, right practices well practiced *are likely to* open persons for insights into beliefs to which they would otherwise be closed.[26] Inversely, wrong practices can

---

25. George A. Lindbeck, *The Nature of Doctrine: Religion and Theology in a Postliberal Age* (Philadelphia: Westminster, 1984), p. 36.

26. See the chapter by Dykstra and Bass, p. 17, and the chapter by Sarah Coakley, p. 78.

"suppress the truth" (Romans 1:18) — that is, have an adverse impact on which beliefs are deemed true and how beliefs that are deemed true are understood.

For theology, the hermeneutical impact of practices is crucial for the simple reason that formulation of Christian beliefs is fundamentally a hermeneutical task. So far I have spoken only of "core beliefs" or "authentic doctrines." But we always hold these core beliefs in situationally rendered forms. Such rendering is done implicitly and explicitly simply as an integral part of living a Christian life,[27] and, whether it occurs in academic or non-academic settings, is an exercise in understanding. Which is where practices come in. Engagement in practices helps open our eyes to how core beliefs are to be understood and re-formulated as Christians live in ever-changing situations.

What Grounds What?

Here is a stripped-down sketch of my argument so far: Christian beliefs normatively shape Christian practices, and engaging in practices can lead to acceptance and deeper understanding of these beliefs. The crucial issue that remains to be addressed is this: Do beliefs ground practices, or do practices ultimately ground beliefs? In one sense, this is not quite the right way to put the question. Are not beliefs — core Christian beliefs — an integral part of Christian practices? I have argued that they are. And yet we still have to inquire about the *status* of beliefs precisely as components of practices.

Contemporary academic and popular culture tends to subordinate beliefs to practices to the point of completely functionalizing beliefs. Pierre Hadot's important book *Philosophy as a Way of Life* might serve as an example. In his account, as in a qualified sense in my own, "the choice of a form of life" comes first. Philosophical discourse "gives justifications and theoretical foundations" for that choice.[28] Hadot rightly sees discourse not as an end in itself but in service of a way of life. Notice, however, how he

27. See the chapter by Kathryn Tanner, pp. 228ff.
28. Pierre Hadot, *Philosophy as a Way of Life: Spiritual Exercises from Socrates to Foucault,* ed. Arnold I. Davidson trans. Michael Chase (Oxford: Blackwell, 1995), p. 281.

understands the service proper to discourse. The choice of the form of life is "justified *after the fact* by a given systematic construction." Choosing the good is not a consequence of holding a set of true beliefs, but the other way around.[29]

Would Hadot's account of the relation between "the choice of the good" and "philosophical discourse" work in theology as a model for the relation between Christian beliefs and Christian practices, between theology and a way of life? That depends on how one interprets Hadot. One could take him to mean that a set of beliefs will develop from a chronologically prior choice of the good. When such a set of beliefs does develop, it will be a *true* set of beliefs, capable of adequately grounding the choice of the good. The choice of the good would chronologically precede this set of beliefs, but this set of beliefs would logically ground the choice of the good.

Such reading of Hadot's ordering of "beliefs" and "practices" would be analogous to the way in which, according to John Zizioulas, the doctrine of the Trinity emerged: ecclesial communal practice led the church to claim that communion of three divine persons is ontologically ultimate. But what made possible the emergence of the church and its claims about the ontological ultimacy of communion was, of course, the reality of the divine communion, which can be expressed in the form of true Trinitarian beliefs.[30] Whether or not one agrees with Zizioulas's account of the emergence of the doctrine of the Trinity, the more general understanding of the relation between beliefs and practices which it instantiates is plausible.

---

29. Hadot, *Philosophy as a Way of Life*, pp. 282-83. Commenting on Stoicism and Epicureanism, Hadot notes as mistaken the view that from the theories of Chrysipus or Epicurus "would spring, as if by accident one could say, a morality. But the reverse is true. It is the abstract theories that are intended to justify the existential attitude. One could say, to express it otherwise, that every existential attitude implies a representation of the world that must necessarily be expressed in a discourse. But this discourse alone is not the philosophy, it is only an element of it, for the philosophy is first of all the existential attitude itself, accompanied by inner and outer discourses: the latter have as their role to express the representation of the world that is implied in such and such an existential attitude, and these discourses allow one at the same time to rationally justify the attitude and to communicate it to others" (quoted by Davidson in Hadot, *Philosophy as a Way of Life*, pp. 30-31).

30. John Zizioulas, *Being as Communion: Studies in Personhood and the Church* (Crestwood: St. Vladimir's Seminary Press, 1985).

It is unlikely, however, that giving chronological priority to a way of life and logical primacy to a set of beliefs would satisfy Hadot. He believes that the one and the same choice of the good can be "justified by extremely diverse philosophical discourses."[31] Depending on changing situations — depending on reigning plausibilities — the set of beliefs will vary, and will do so in order to be able to "justify" a given choice of the good.

Will this do as a model for the relation between Christian beliefs and practices? There are theologians who think so.[32] Whether they are right depends a great deal on how one understands theology's relation to its primary subject matter, God. Practices, I have argued earlier, are Christian insofar as they are "resonances" of God's engagement with the world. But how should we understand "God's engagement with the world"? Above all, does such talk purport to sketch — in human conceptualities and therefore in a broken way — what is truly the case and what is in accord with God's self-revelation in Christ as attested in the Scriptures?

I take it that theology is not simply reflection about how communities of faith use language about God — not "critical talk about talk about God." God, not just human talk about God, is the proper object of theology. If this is so, then Christian beliefs about God are not analogous to Hadot's philosophical discourse. No doubt, one's interest in God may be awakened and one's understanding of God will be deepened through engagement in practices. But we engage in practices for the sake of God; we don't construe a picture of God so as to justify engagement in a particular set of practices. As the highest good, God matters for God's own sake, not for the sake of a preferred way of life. Since we identify who God is through beliefs — primarily through the canonical witness to divine self-revelation — adequate beliefs about God cannot be ultimately grounded in a way of life; a way of life must be grounded in adequate beliefs about God.[33]

---

31. Hadot, *Philosophy as a Way of Life*, p. 212.

32. Consider, for instance, what Marianne Sawicki does with the creedal Christian claim that Jesus Christ is risen. She justifies it pragmatically: "The hungry little ones, always with the church, are the reason why the resurrection of Jesus must be affirmed as bodily, absolutely, for Christian faith." Sawicki, *Seeing the Lord: Resurrection and Early Christian Practices* (Minneapolis: Fortress Press, 1994), p. 275.

33. The way Hadot relates the choice of a way of life and philosophical discourse is analogous to the way in which some liberation theologians relate praxis of social engagement and theological reflection. In his recent book on theological methodology, at the end of a long chapter on his own fruitful and decade-long engagement with various

If Christian beliefs ultimately ground Christian practices, theology cannot limit itself to explicating the significance of "God" and of what "God has done" for a way of life, but must concern itself with the disputed truth claims about God — and *do so precisely also for the sake of a way of life.* It matters, for instance, a great deal for a way of life whether human beings are God's creatures or God a human creature, a projection of our greatest ideals or an imaginary rectifier of our own impotence. Ludwig Feuerbach, Karl Marx, and Friedrich Nietzsche rightly felt the need to offer alternative accounts of human history and of the cosmos to the one they inherited from the Christian tradition in the light of their persuasion that God is a human creation and not the other way around.

To be concerned with truth claims about God means also to be interested in how beliefs about God and God's relation to the world *fit* among themselves and with other beliefs human beings hold. The fit between Christian beliefs may be very tight (say, such that one can reduce all of them to a single complex belief) or rather loose (say, such that one can situate them in a narrative framework or a set of factually related but logically independent narrative frameworks),[34] but fit they must. If the truth of the Christian faith matters, then the way you understand the Lord's Supper must fit with your account of Christ's death, and this must fit with your doctrine of the Trinity, and all of this must fit with the way you understand the nature and predicament of human beings.

Moreover, since Christian beliefs coexist with a host of other beliefs about the world — from claims about the future of the universe to theories about the kind of work neurons do in human brains — the question of the relationship of Christian beliefs to all these other beliefs must also be posed. Theology must pursue the question of truth and must do so in conjunction with, and not in isolation from, other disciplines. In a word, because Christian beliefs relate to everyday practices as a fitted set of beliefs with a claim to express truth about God and God's relation to the world, theologians must be concerned with more than just how beliefs relate to

liberation theologies, Jürgen Moltmann asks the following critical question: "If praxis is the [ultimate] criterion of theory, what is the criterion of praxis?" *Experiences in Theology: Ways and Forms of Christian Theology,* trans. M. Kohl (Minneapolis: Fortress Press, 2000), p. 294.

34. In his forthcoming theological anthropology, David Kelsey argues powerfuly for reading the Scriptures as containing three factually intertwined but logically independent narratives.

everyday practices — and must be so concerned precisely *for the sake of* everyday practices.

The Apostle Paul, Theology, Practices

The Apostle Paul was arguably the first Christian theologian and certainly the most influential of the early Christian theologians. In conclusion it may be instructive to compare briefly the model I have developed above of theology's relation to a way of life with Paul's way of theologizing. True, contemporary theologians are in some important ways unlike Paul: the risen Lord has appeared to Paul, and his writings have a canonical status to us. This makes beliefs even more critical in our theologizing than they were in Paul's. This said, Paul's and our theological tasks are arguably analogous.

There is a long history of New Testament scholars' making what I think is on the whole a mistaken distinction in Paul's writings between the "indicative" and the "imperative" sections. In this distinction, the indicative sections come first; they are doctrinal (they explicate Christian beliefs) and foundational. The imperative sections come second; they are ethical (they admonish to Christian practices) and are of secondary importance because they are grounded in beliefs. Beliefs can and should be explicated in their own right, without relation to practices; practices can be understood only in relation to beliefs. According to this picture, Paul operated with something analogous to the accepted disciplinary distinctions between "systematic theology" on the one side and ethics and "practical theology" on the other, as well as with the corresponding clear demarcation between "self-standing" beliefs and "derived" practices.

Not everything is wrong with this picture. As the momentous "therefore" in Romans 12:1 attests ("I appeal to you therefore, brothers and sisters, by the mercies of God, to present your bodies as living sacrifice"), beliefs about God and what God has done do serve for Paul to justify ways in which Christians relate among themselves and with outsiders. And yet, to let the matter rest at this is to simplify things to the point of distortion. As Troels Engberg-Pedersen has shown in *Paul and the Stoics*, the parenetic sections in Paul do not simply follow the doctrinal sections; rather, "at the most fundamental level and from one end to the other" his letters are an "exercise in parenesis." "Parenesis has two components," a doctrinal and

262

ethical one, for it consists "in Paul's *reminding* his addressees of what *has* happened and his *appeal* to them to put it into *practice*."[35]

Significantly, the description of what has happened — what God has done and what God will do for Paul and his readers — is "tilted towards what we may call its anthropological side: towards what the 'objective' Christ event set going by God has meant to Paul and his addressees." The "tilting" is present because Paul offers what God has done "as a basis for his appeal to them [his addressees] to put it into practice." So in Paul beliefs *as beliefs* are practice-shaping. And yet, he does not consider beliefs to be justifications *after the fact* of a way of life. As Engberg-Pedersen puts it, "The 'objective' framework remains very solidly in place, of course. It is *God* who *has* done something in the Christ event and God and Christ who *will* do something in the future."[36]

Paul had a realistic perspective on what God has done for humanity, as Engberg-Pedersen recognizes. At the same time, he suggests that we, Paul's contemporary interpreters, reduce Paul's claims about God and God's relation to the world to "metaphysical 'constructions' whose function is to give ontological substance" to his ethical ideas.[37] Engberg-Pedersen's suggestion on how to appropriate the teaching of Paul is structurally similar to Hadot's recommendation on how to appropriate ancient spiritual exercises: he discards ancient justifying philosophical discourses and keeps the moral vision.

For Christian theology, this will not do. Such account of the status of beliefs would be deeply at odds with the nature of Christian practices themselves. For these are done precisely in response to what God has done for the life of the world, which is what Christian core beliefs seek to express. Like Paul, we should resolutely place theology in the service of practices and precisely for this reason concentrate our reflection on God, for whose sake we live a Christian way of life and therefore, as theologians, engage in explicating Christian beliefs.

Will theology so conceived have sufficiently to do with "real" life? Not nearly as much as the God for whose sake we are theologians, but more than enough, I believe, to satisfy the concerns of those who are justly troubled by theology's seeming irrelevance.

35. Troels Engberg-Pedersen, *Paul and the Stoics* (Louisville: Westminster/John Knox Press, 2000), p. 294.

36. Engberg-Pedersen, *Paul and the Stoics*, p. 295.

37. Engberg-Pedersen, *Paul and the Stoics*, p. 30.

List of Contributors

Dorothy C. Bass is Director of the Valparaiso Project on the Education and Formation of People in Faith, a Lilly Endowment project based at Valparaiso University.

Nancy E. Bedford is Profesora Titular de Teología Sistemática at ISEDET (Instituto Superior Evangélico de Estudios Teológicos)

Gilbert I. Bond is Assistant Professor of Theology at Yale Divinity School.

Sarah Coakley is the Edward Mallinckrodt Jr. Professor of Divinity at Harvard University.

Craig Dykstra is Vice President for Religion at Lilly Endowment Inc.

Reinhard Hütter is Associate Professor of Christian Theology at Duke University Divinity School.

L. Gregory Jones is Dean and Professor of Theology at Duke University Divinity School.

Serene Jones is Associate Professor of Theology at Yale Divinity School.

Amy Plantinga Pauw is the Henry P. Mobley Jr. Professor of Doctrinal Theology at Louisville Presbyterian Seminary.

Christine D. Pohl is Professor of Christian Social Ethics at Asbury Theological Seminary.

Kathryn Tanner is Professor of Theology at The University of Chicago Divinity School.

Miroslav Volf is the Henry B. Wright Professor of Systematic Theology at Yale University.

Tammy R. Williams is a Ph.D. candidate at Fuller Theological Seminary.